YOUTH WORKERS HANDBOOK

Third Edition, Revised

Steve Clapp and Jerry O. Cook

faithQuest

the trade imprint of Brethren Press
Elgin, Illinois

YOUTH WORKERS HANDBOOK
Third Edition, Revised

Steve Clapp and Jerry O. Cook

Copyright © 1990, 1992 by Mary Jo Clapp

First edition published 1981 by C-4 Resources

96 95 94 93 92   5 4 3 2 1

Printed in the United States of America

faithQuest
BRETHREN PRESS
1451 Dundee Avenue
Elgin, Illinois 60120

Biblical quotations, unless otherwise indicated, are from the New Revised Standard Version of the Bible. The descriptions of youth in the church (IABACs, IBSs, IDCAAs, IEPACs) appearing in the chapter "Understanding Young People" and exercises in the chapter "Looking at Your Group" originally appeared in *Arena* magazine in articles by Steve Clapp. They are reproduced here for your use with permission from the United Methodist Publishing House. Portions of the chapter on Worship originally appeared in the Summer 1980 issue of *Christian Studies for Late Teens*, and are reprinted by permission of the United Methodist Publishing House.

Library of Congress Cataloging-in-Publication Data

Clapp, Steve.
    Youth workers handbook / Steve Clapp and Jerry O. Cook.
  —3rd ed., revised.
      p. cm.
    Includes bibliographical references.
    ISBN 0-87178-979-5
    1. Church work with teenagers—Handbooks, manuals, etc. 2. Church group work with teenagers—Handbooks, manuals, etc. I. Cook, Jerry. II. Title.
BV4447.C5 1992
259' .23—dc20
                              91-47934
                                CIP

CONTENTS

INTRODUCTION

This book started years ago at O'Charley's Restaurant in Nashville. At that time, Jerry Cook was an editor at the United Methodist Publishing House in Nashville; and I was director of a large camping and youth program in Illinois. I was in Nashville for a routine conference with Jerry about some curriculum materials. We were both actively involved in conducting youth ministry workshops at the local church level, and we were frustrated by the problems that so many volunteer youth workers seemed to experience.

As we talked, we agreed that denominational agencies were not providing enough direct training and resourcing to local church youth workers. We also recognized that there are pragmatic limitations (primarily concerned with $$$$$) on how much direct resourcing of local churches can actually be done. A helpful alternative, we thought, would be a handbook which was clearly written and sufficiently complete to cover the basic concerns of most volunteer youth workers. Though we were both aware of some very fine youth ministry materials on the market, neither of us had discovered the kind of handbook which we thought was needed.

The conversation moved from O'Charley's to Jerry's office. Jerry smoked his pipe; I chewed Bazooka gum; and we brainstormed until 3 a.m. We produced a series of chapter titles and a general format for the book that evening. We then set up a schedule for the preparation of chapters.

We did not, however, make rapid progress from that point. When we got together on subsequent occasions over the years following our O'Charley's meeting, the first two hours of conversation were invariably spent sharing our excuses for having written so little on the handbook. The next hour, however, was spent sharing our experiences in working with local churches which intensified our conviction that the book should be written.

When I moved from a comfortable position in church bureaucracy into full- time religious research and writing, I gained the motivation to get the book written. I got my chapters finished and then had the time to nag at Jerry until he completed his work.

Response to the first edition both pleased and humbled us. The book sold beyond our best expectations and to people of over sixty denominations. The book proved basic, practical, and readable. The debt for those very real strengths was owed to volunteer local church youth workers, representing twenty different denominations, who served as our editorial board. They told us what was unclear, what would not work in large churches, what would not work in small churches, and what needed further explanation. We obeyed their commands and thoroughly revised the book under the *faithQuest* imprint.

While most of the fundamental principles of youth work had not changed, the years since the first edition have brought changes in the youth scene and in approaches to youth ministry which needed to be reflected. Major changes in the second edition included:

● Completely updated description of youth and their culture.

● A new chapter on "Theology and Youth Work." We made explicit what we hope was implicit in the first edition.

● Revisions in the "Media" and "Music! Music! Music!" chapters to reflect new technology, new performers, and new possibilities for ministry.

● A new chapter on "Video" gave specific suggestions on using this powerful technology in youth ministry. We also included discussion guides to 25 movies!

● Substantial additions to the "Recreation" chapter. We added 34 ideas for youth group programs.

● The addition of youth group trip guidelines and suggestions. The chapter titled "Lock-ins, Retreats, and Camps" is now called "Overnight and Longer."

No chapter was untouched. Many of the best changes were the result of helpful suggestions from readers who shared their questions and ideas with us. When all copies of the second edition sold out within 18 months, our instincts about the need for a book like this were confirmed. We have taken the opportunity to correct errors and make a few minor editorial changes and now present the third edition from *faithQuest*. We hope this improved book repays part of our debt to our dedicated readers and the original editorial board.

About the authors. You may (and then again you may not) want to know something more about the authors of this handbook. If you don't want to know anything more about us, quit reading on this page and skip to the first chapter, "Understanding Young People." There are some things wrong with both of us. Jerry is impatient in disposition and a chronic procrastinator where deadlines imposed by others are concerned. That grows out of Jerry's being an unreasonable perfectionist. The words never flow well enough; the chapter is never complete enough; the material has never been discussed enough. My major contribution to this book has not been writing or revising my own chapters. My major contribution has been getting finished copy out of Jerry. I have begged. I have threatened. I have (God forgive me!) even lied about my printing deadlines in order to get the copy out of

him. Jerry's other major failing is that he smokes. My pressure on him to get the first edition done probably made him smoke even more than usual.

Jerry's chapters, however, were worth the effort and the wait. Jerry is brilliant. I am not using the word lightly, and I am absolutely serious. Jerry is probably the most brilliant human being I know. He understands the English language and knows how to communicate. He edited my material for five years, and he invariably improved what I wrote. I would like to say that he was occasionally wrong when he modified my material—but he wasn't, not once. Jerry's major strength for this project, however, is in his deep understanding of young people and in his practical experience helping other adult youth workers.

Jerry is no armchair philosopher on youth ministry. He pastored in local churches before going to Nashville as a youth editor. While he was on the editorial staff, he conducted an amazing number of retreats for young people and workshops for adult youth workers. Young people love Jerry. He has an almost magical ability to make groups come to life, to help others feel at ease around him, and to give others confidence in themselves. Much of that ability comes through in the pages that follow.

Jerry is no longer in Nashville. His primary love has always been the local church, and he is now pastor of a large church in Massachusetts. He is actively involved in working with young people and adult youth workers every week. He has traveled across the country. He has worked with people from every conceivable denominational background, and he has worked with youth groups in churches of all sizes. He knows what he is doing, and he knows how to communicate it.

Media, music, and worship are particular loves of Jerry. That comes through in the chapters in this book. In fact, Jerry knows more about those topics than *anyone* else with whom I am acquainted. You will not find any other resource that gives you so much practical background on those topics as Jerry has provided in this handbook.

Enough about Jerry. Now you get to hear about me. I don't smoke (virtue!), but I do lie about printing deadlines (fault!). I have spent most of my professional ministry at the local church level and have been particularly concerned with finding ways to reach inactive and nonchurch youth through the institutional church. My success in that area (which was initially more dumb luck than knowledge!) was probably responsible for my being named to a position in church bureaucracy at a relatively young age. I spent five years in a position which included, among other things, the management of a large camping and retreat program. My responsibilities in that position also included working with local church and regional groups in the areas of Christian education and youth work. I had opportunity to work with a tremendously diverse range of churches, youth, and both professional and volunteer adult youth workers. I developed a spiritual life retreat model which proved very successful with young people and which was one of the factors that helped us experience tremendous growth in the camping and retreat programs for which I was responsible.

I've had the good fortune for several years to do full-time religious research and writing. That has permitted me to work with youth workers of many different denominations and to do extensive study of the needs and concerns of young people. I've continued, however, to learn the most from regular contact with the young people in the local churches which have been my "home" during my research and writing years. Nothing replaces working with the same young people week after week. The major qualification which Jerry and I share for this book is that we both love young people and the adults who work with them.

We have attempted to make each chapter reasonably self-contained. In working toward that goal, it has been impossible to avoid some duplication in chapter contents. Some of those purchasing this book will read it completely through in a couple of evenings. A great many others, however, will read first the chapters of greatest interest. Both groups will (hopefully) refer back to particular chapters from time to time. With that in mind, we did not want any one chapter to be overly dependent on another one. Where possible, we have tried to suggest other chapters in the handbook which can help you better understand a particular theme or issue.

No book can be exhaustive in coverage. We have tried to suggest good resources for further information both in the text itself and in the final chapter on "Resources." You will find many exercises in this book for use in your local church. You have our permission to reproduce the exercises for any local church class, group, retreat, or camp. It's also fine to reproduce them for workshops with other youth leaders in your community. For permission to reproduce the exercises for use beyond the local level, please write to: *faithQuest,* 1451 Dundee Avenue, Elgin, Illinois 60120.

Grace and peace,
Steve Clapp

Becky is seventeen years old, going on thirty-five. She is a teenager chronologically, but her appearance, intelligence, and maturity seem far beyond that. She is the kind of child for whom parents love to take credit, the kind of student that teachers adore, and the kind of church member that ministers want. She openly opposes premarital intercourse, homosexuality, and abortion. She is courteous and gracious to adults, and she tries to be a Christian presence to her peers.

Beth is also active in her local church. She has a fair amount of hostility toward her parents, teachers, and adults in general. She has just been treated for venereal disease and continues to have sexual intercourse with a seventeen-year-old fellow. She enjoys participating in her youth group, but she has no interest in "witnessing" to her friends.

Kathy is well-liked by other teenagers and adults. She's a beautiful girl and a cheerleader for her high school. Her grades are good though perhaps slightly below her potential. Kathy comes to a church school class but says very little. She hasn't responded to frequent invitations to attend the evening youth group. Something is tragically wrong in her life for she has attempted suicide three times in the last year.

Tom is an athlete. He is a junior in high school and extremely proud of his physical appearance. He is not very interested in the church but will come to some social and recreational activities. Many of the active youth resent his presence, since he never shares in fund raising or service projects but has a remarkable ability to appear just in time for parties, games, retreats, and trips.

Alan's family belongs to the church, but he has not yet made a public profession of his faith. He is a talented dancer and stars in school and summer theater productions. Some people make fun of his interest in dance and call him gay, queer, and homo. He doesn't display any homosexual leanings, but the school jokes have made it difficult for him to get dates. He is in his last year of high school and has been accepted by the drama department of a major university. He shares in a Bible study group which meets at 7 a.m. every Wednesday in the minister's office.

Sam is a very troubled junior high youth. He was recently hospitalized for thirty days because he repeatedly used crack. He has started coming back to his church group, but he's very sensitive. Others in the group are concerned about him but are also worried about "guilt by association" if they spend too much time with him. Thus, Sam is pushed to the periphery of the group precisely when he most needs the support of others.

Becky, Beth, Kathy, Tom, Alan, and Sam are young people whom I know, respect, and enjoy. I've changed the names for this chapter, but the descriptions are accurate. What are teenagers like? It depends on which teenagers we are talking about. Generalizations break down.

I didn't describe young people like Kathy and Sam in the first edition of this book. Of course teenagers attempted suicide and had drug problems when the first edition of this book appeared, but those problems were not as common as they've become. Most churches have young people like Kathy and Sam, or they should have young people like them involved. The church has a tremendous amount to offer troubled young people, and effective programs can prevent many other youth from having the same problems.

Effective youth programming must recognize the diverse needs that young people have. The church needs to share God's love with all young people, help them grow in the Christian faith, and help them develop a genuine sense of community with one another. In the 1990s, as well as in every previous decade, the church, empowered by Christ, has great potential to help young people; and young people have great potential to help the church.

Before thinking more about the youth of today, take a short trip back in time with me. Think about your own teenage years.

My junior high years rank among the more miserable of my life. I was a slow developer—physically uncoordinated, clumsy, a real "klutz." I was destined to lose a battle with acne until I graduated from college. When teams were chosen for baseball, basketball, football, tug-of-war, or anything else involving physical stamina, I was one of the last selected.

Some so-called authorities claim that junior high boys are not interested in junior high girls. I've always questioned the validity of that assumption. I was intensely interested in girls and so were most of my friends. But what quickly developing junior high girl takes seriously an undersized, awkward boy? I spent three years with an intense crush on a girl in my class. For awhile I sent her pathetic letters of admiration which she didn't take seriously enough to answer. I learned in time what I suspect many junior high fellows learn—if you can't have something, it's better to act as though you don't want it.

High school was better. I began to grow some, and I reached the magical age for a drivers license. Since I lived in a town of six hundred people, located twenty-five miles from the nearest movie theater or drive-in restaurant, that license opened up a whole new world. If you had a license and a car, you gained instant social acceptance. That created new problems—especially when I

ditched my father's brand new Pontiac—but they were, on the whole, less disagreeable problems.

What were your junior high and senior high years like? What were your happiest times? your times of greatest isolation? your greatest problems? your major dreams? Put the book aside for a few moments and reminisce. What was life really like for you as a young person? Whether that means thinking back five years or fifty years, do it RIGHT NOW.

In order to understand young people today, you need to get in touch with your own adolescence. As adults, we often fail to take seriously the hurts, anxieties, and dreams of the young. Remembering what those years were like for you can give a new sense of identity with young people of today. The times have changed, the temptations have changed, the opportunities have changed, but many of the hurts and dreams remain the same. If your immediate memories are primarily happy ones, do some more probing. Try to get in touch with the moments of loneliness, of panic, of frustration. Many of us romanticize our teen years, repressing the pimples that appeared on our faces and in our hearts.

Do not, of course, expect young people to live today as you did in your teen years. They will appreciate your identification with their hurts and dreams, but they will reject solutions to problems based on life ten, twenty, or thirty years ago.

The best way to understand what teenagers are like is to invest time and energy getting acquainted with teenagers rather than reading about them. A book like this one will only tell you a few generalizations. Visit them in their homes; share soft drinks with them; go to their school games and dances; seek all the

2

opportunities you can for direct contact with both individuals and groups of teens.

Many adult youth workers err at the point of having almost exclusive contact with teens only through the youth group or class with which they work at the church. That helps you get acquainted with a group rather than with individuals, and it may leave you with some misconceptions about youth who choose not to be active in the church. You need to take the time to visit with your active youth as individuals. You also need to seek opportunities to observe and get acquainted with some youth who are not connected with a local church. Your perspective will change, and your ability to communicate will be greatly enhanced.

Forces Influencing Teenagers

Several forces in society have significant impact on the development of young people. You need to be aware of the potential influence of the following factors.

1. **Far more teenagers are growing up in single-parent homes.** Some authorities estimate that four out of ten children born in the seventies will spend part of their childhood in a single-parent home. The divorce rate has continued to rise, and the number of unwed women who keep their babies has increased at a tremendous rate. Although there are growing numbers of exceptions, the single parent will still most frequently be the mother and not the father. The absence of a parent can have a profound effect on young people. When the divorce has been an unpleasant, angry experience, teenagers and younger children may feel that they have been responsible for the difficulty which their parents have had. Although some single parents cope with the situation extremely well, teenagers still

benefit from good role models of both men and women. Where possible, it is good if class and group adult leadership can be of a team nature with both a man and a woman (or both men and women).

2. **Television has had massive impact on the youth of today.** According to most estimates, the average teenager spends between twenty and twenty-five hours a week watching television. This affects not only the values and morals of teens but also the manner in which they are accustomed to thinking.

Although authorities differ in estimating the extent to which television values become internalized by youth, there is no question but that television programming presents attitudes about sexuality, violence, and human rights that few people would consider consistent with the Christian faith.

The brain has two sides or hemispheres. One side has primary control over visual and emotional experiences. The other side is more closely related to verbal and intellectual (problem solving) experiences. Youth who have spent many hours in front of the television may well have more development of the visual/emotional side of the brain. Thus, they may well perceive some situations and issues in a markedly different manner than do their parents (or youth group workers!).

Youth of today have not done as much reading as some past generations and will not respond well to religious instruction that demands a great deal of reading. On the other hand, they are very open to visual learning models and may also have considerable skill in working with electronic equipment, including computers and video recorders. Just as television has been part of their world, so too have other electronic marvels.

3

3. **Advertising influences the values and goals of teens.** Television programming is literally jammed with advertisements, and teens who watch television see those advertisements. Colognes, perfumes, after shaves, toothpastes, hair sprays, deodorants, and automobiles are merchandised as aids to sexual attractiveness or success. The selection of toilet paper, facial tissues, and canned soup becomes linked to one's love for family members. While we may laugh at individual advertisements, the overall impact works. We never have enough material possessions to be satisfied, and we delude ourselves into thinking that happiness lies in the right clothes, automobile, catsup, or soap.

4. **Music pervades the culture of the young.** It comes through stereos, tape players, compact disc players, radios, MTV, regular television, and live performances. It communicates love, hate, tragedy, celebration, concern for the poor, violence, sex, drugs, courage, and understanding. U2, Madonna, Guns N' Roses, Cher, and Sting help shape the values of teens. Some performers, like U2, though not always pleasant to the ears of parents, have concern about the values they communicate and a sense of social responsibility. In contrast Guns N' Roses, a group well-liked by teens, has this line in a popular song: "I used to love her but I had to kill her, I had to put her six feet under, and I can still hear her complain." The impact of music on youth is so great that this book devotes a chapter to "Music! Music! Music!"

5. **Today's youth have been raised in an extremely materialistic, money-conscious culture.** Adult society has done an excellent job teaching youth some very questionable values: that people who earn more money are better people than those who are poor; that the primary standard for evaluating success is in financial terms; that the purpose of getting an education is to be able to get a job to earn money; and that one's own financial needs come before the needs of other people. Those views are not consistent with the Christian faith as expressed in the Old and New Testaments, but those views are ingrained in our culture. Although some past generations of youth rejected the emphasis on materialism which characterized their parents, the present generation of young people seems to be accepting a materialistic view of life and of success.

6. **Birth control and abortion have been more readily available to today's youth than to past generations.** Though parental permission is often needed, birth control pills and devices are far more readily available to youth today than a few years ago. Growing numbers of parents would rather see their young people using birth control than becoming pregnant.

7. **Part-time and summer jobs are available to many young people.** A growing number of high schools have programs which permit their students to receive academic credit or school release time to work as store clerks, garage mechanics, or fast food employees. The probability of a young person finding part-time or summer employment is much greater than for some earlier generations. This means that youth have the opportunity to make money at a relatively early age and to cultivate good work habits. It also means that homework, church activities, social life, and family life may have to take second, third, fourth, or fifth place to the requirements of a job. Some busy youth have very little "dreaming time."

8. **Youth are strongly influenced by their peers.** The older youth become, the less they are influenced by parents, teachers, church youth workers, and other adults. They are, however, strongly influenced by the values and expectations of others their own age, their peers. This influence can be a positive one and can work to the benefit of church programming when youth find adequate peer contact with the active members of the youth group. It can also result in a greater tendency to cheat, to consume illicit substances (alcohol, marijuana, etc.), and to engage in heavy sexual activity.

9. **Many youth grow up in conditions of extreme poverty.** They are especially likely to do so if they are members of a nonwhite race. Black youth are four times as likely as white youth to grow up in families with incomes below the poverty level. Native American youth are twice again as likely to be in poverty situations. Local churches, for the most part, have not been effective in reaching large numbers of low-income youth (or adults, for that matter!).

10. **Financial pressures on schools have resulted in larger classes and in fewer music, art, and drama opportunities.** Tight budgets characterize elementary and secondary schools all across the United States. School districts that cannot generate more funds must increase class size and eliminate "nonessential" programming. "Nonessential" programming more frequently includes music, art, and drama than football, basketball, or baseball.

11. **Instances of reported child abuse and incest have increased significantly.** It is difficult to say whether one is dealing with increased instances or merely with increased reports of abuse and incest. In either event, certainly the general public is more aware of these flagrant violations of the rights of children and youth. Many youth need help in dealing with what they have personally experienced or in reaching out to their friends who have gone through negative home experiences.

12. **Illicit drugs are more readily available to teens today than to earlier generations.** In spite of the government's so-called "war on drugs," marijuana, crack, cocaine, and other illicit drugs are far more readily available to teens every year. Actual drug use by teens seems to have declined slightly in spite of the continuing availability, which does provide some evidence that education works where law enforcement does not. Alcohol also continues to be widely available to teens, widely used, and still causes a wide range of problems.

Drug and alcohol use are closely tied to other teen problems. The Carnegie Corporation recently reported that one-fourth of junior high students are involved in some combination of smoking, drinking, drug use, and unprotected sex. That statistic is sufficient to cause nightmares for parents, teachers, ministers, and youth workers!

Characteristics of Youth

Some of the following observations are significant, and others are in the "So what?" category. We still thought you might like to know that:

1. **Girls are getting taller.** Boys on the average are still taller than girls, but each decade brings about an inch less difference between average heights for males and for females.

2. **The percentage of white teens in the United States is decreasing.** An increasing percentage of teenagers are African American, Hispanic, Native Americans, or Asian in racial background. Since the Vietnam War, many Asians have immigrated to our country. Many Hispanics have also come from Mexico and Central America. Birth rates among nonwhite populations are slightly higher than in the white population. Yet mainline church programming continues to assume that most youth (and adults and children) are white.

Increases in the number of Hispanic teens have been especially striking over the last ten years. The National Council of La Raza in Washington D.C., reports that 10.5 percent of public school children and youth are now Hispanic. If your church is in a community with a significant Hispanic population, you could benefit from a youth worker who speaks fluent Spanish. Many Hispanic teens are very fluent in English, but that is not always the case.

African Americans, Hispanics, and Native Americans still do not have the same opportunities as white Americans. They are less likely to graduate from high school or enter college. They are more likely to live in low income households and, sadly, also more likely to have problems with the law. These realities provide important challenges for the church's ministry.

3. **Cheating has become increasingly common among youth.** In confidential polls conducted by the Gallup organization and others, almost two-thirds of American teenagers admit they have cheated in school. A third acknowledge cheating a great deal. Church-active teens are slightly less likely to cheat, but the difference is not as large as it should be.

4. **Illiteracy is a major problem among school-age children.** This is especially a problem among African American, Hispanic, and Native American teens; but many white teens also have low reading levels. Public school programs to improve literacy have made some advances but still fall short. As psychologist Sol Gordon has pointed out: "The plain fact is that it's excruciatingly boring to learn how to read at the age of 13, 14, or 15, though it's fun and exciting in the first and second grade." Young people with low self-esteem have trouble learning to read. Church programming needs to recognize the literacy problem and avoid putting youth in embarrassing situations. Church programming should also work at building self-esteem which in turn makes it easier to face problems, including a low reading level.

Many teens who are quite literate still read with considerably less proficiency than they should and have lower verbal SAT scores than teens had in the 1960s.

5. **Today's youth seem to have less historical consciousness or current events consciousness than earlier generations.** Polls and quizzes on knowledge of historical or current events show an alarming lack of knowledge on the part of today's youth.

One must also remember that today's youth have not been aware of a major war such as World War I, World War II, Korea, or Vietnam. They have also not experienced the high civil rights activism of the sixties.

The current generation is more inwardly turned and now-centered. They've been taught well by the media and by adults that getting ahead financially is more important than standing up for what's right. Yet they hunger for spiritual experiences and can become excited about service to others.

6

6. **Youth do believe in a wide variety of things.** The hunger for spiritual experiences leads many youth into a search for a sense of mystery, for that which transcends life as they experience it in their immediate environment. A 1988 poll shows that significant numbers of American teenagers believe in ESP (73 percent); angels (67 percent); UFOs (62 percent); witchcraft (36 percent); Sasquatch (35 percent); the Loch Ness monster (34 percent); clairvoyance (28 percent); and ghosts (24 percent). Compared to a similar survey in 1978, the percentages of belief were up for everything except Sasquatch! Apparently some movies of the eighties about Sasquatch had less impact than one might have expected.

7. **Alcoholism remains the major teenage drug problem.** So many studies have been done on drug problems in the eighties that the results are just plain confusing! Use of illicit drugs other than alcohol (marijuana, cocaine, crack, and others) increased dramatically in the eighties and has now begun to decline slightly in some parts of the country. Drugs unquestionably are a major concern in junior high as well as high school and in rural areas as well as urban areas.

Many teens included in startling statistics have simply experimented with marijuana or cocaine a couple of times and rejected it. A study by Newcomb and Bentler found that teens who use marijuana or alcohol once a month or less at social gatherings probably do not suffer major negative effects and cannot be distinguished later from teens who abstained from drugs. Use of crack is a significant exception because of its highly addictive qualities.

Drug use has gone down slightly among many groups of teens but not among those living in inner-city poverty conditions. Suburban, white, young people still have many serious drug problems and will continue to in the nineties.

But all that is background to say that alcohol remains the major teenage drug problem. That shouldn't be a surprise. There are 28 million children growing up in homes with alcoholic parents. The average person takes his or her first drink *by the age of twelve.* According to the National Institute on Alcohol Abuse and Alcoholism, 79 percent of teenage males and 70 percent of teenage females drink at least some; 40 percent drink once a week; and 35 percent drink alone. Those figures have remained almost constant over the last decade except for slight increases in drinking once a week and alone.

Church programming must intentionally address the issues of drug and alcohol abuse. The focus, however, must not only be on education about harmful effects but on helping youth build positive self-images. "Just say no" has not proven an effective strategy. Youth need understanding of drugs and alcohol, but they also need sufficient self-esteem to avoid relying on drugs and alcohol as artificial antidotes for depression and loneliness. Young people with positive self-images and a firm faith are not likely to have drug and alcohol problems. Many young people both inside and outside the church have low self-images and weak faith. The church has much to offer in these areas.

8. **Teens are very active sexually.** Fear of pregnancy, herpes, and AIDS has done relatively little to curb very high levels of teenage sexual activity. Research done with church-active teens shows that between the ages of sixteen and eighteen . . .

● almost 60 percent of males and over 40 percent of females have sexual intercourse.

7

• around 80 percent of males and females have been involved in heavy petting.

• two-thirds of males and over half of females have been completely nude with a member of the opposite sex.

These percentages decreased slightly from the early eighties, but the drop is too small to indicate any trend. Sexual activity for younger teens seems to be increasing. It's particularly disturbing that church-active teens seem just as likely as secular teens to be involved in early sexual activity. Much of the reason for that, of course, is that most churches do an inadequate job helping teens deal with sexual issues. The same study of church-active teens also showed that two-thirds of older teens (sixteen through eighteen years of age) feel that the church does a poor job preparing them for dating, sexual decisions, and marriage.

Masturbation is very common among teenagers with 90 percent of males and 75 percent of females practicing it at least some of the time. Most secular authorities continue to feel that masturbation is a healthy release of sexual tension. While many religious leaders agree with that position, some churches still doctrinally oppose the practice.

Around 10 percent of teenagers have some significant homosexual orientation. The percentage is slightly higher for males than females, but that gap seems to be narrowing.

9. **Teens commit a surprisingly high number of crimes.** The phrase "wilding" became popular following the brutal beating and rape of a 28-year-old investment banker in 1989 in New York City's Central Park. One of her teenage attackers said: "It was fun." Such incidents are not limited to urban centers. In 1988 three rural Mississippi teens

killed a friend out of curiosity. They wanted to know what it would be like to kill someone and concluded "it's fun."

Such incidents are far removed from the lives of most teens in our churches. Vandalism and shoplifting, however, remain common. Church-active teens can also be among the victims of crime. In fact, one study shows that 81 percent of the victims of violent crime are preteens and teenagers. While such incidents are far more likely to occur in some urban areas, the problem is nevertheless national in scope.

Church-active teens are definitely less likely to be involved in criminal activity than other teens, but they need help understanding our violent world. Teen slasher films, violent videos, and the news media carry disturbing messages. Teens need to recognize that aggression (forcing one's will on others) and assertiveness (standing up for one's rights) are not the same thing.

Our churches also need to think of creative ways to minister to teens involved in criminal activity. The low self-esteem that feeds violence can be overcome by the love of Christ. Sadly, many teens never have that love modeled for them or communicated to them.

10. **Car accidents and suicide are leading causes of death for teens.** Car accidents involving teens are very likely to be drug or alcohol related. Suicide, which grows out of low self-worth and the inability to cope with the pressures of life, is a major problem for youth. Most of our churches have yet to make a significant response to that problem.

11. **Youth want to deepen their self-esteem and are very interested in religious concerns.** The healthy self-esteem which comes through a close relationship with Christ provides a buffer against drugs,

8

alcohol, early sexual activity, crime, and suicide among teenagers. Teens may believe in ESP and UFOs, but those phenomena do not represent the focus of their beliefs. Studies continue to show that teens want to grow closer to God and will seek experiences that bring closeness. Gallup polls have shown that almost 50 percent of teenage boys and 60 percent of teenage girls would respond positively if invited to participate in a spiritual life retreat. Our churches need to provide adequate spiritual nurture and challenge to teens.

12. **All teens seek improvement in their lives, but most teens are relatively happy.** Awareness of teenage drug use, crime, and suicide can distort our perception of the teens with whom we work. Studies continue to show that most teens are basically happy with their lives. Like adults, teens don't feel their lives are perfect and certainly want change, but most teenagers aren't floundering in misery. When asked what they want to change about their lives, teens are most likely to identify:

- Changing something about their physical appearance
- Gaining more friends
- Liking themselves better
- Growing closer to God
- Improving self-control
- Improving family relationships
- Improving educational accomplishments

Some teens, of course, do live in misery, and our ministries to them are especially important. But we must not forget that most are relatively happy.

13. **Most teens like their families!** In spite of broken homes, conflict with parents, and other problems, the majority of teenagers do like their families. They like their parents even if their parents are separated. They like their brothers and sisters and can be fiercely protective of them. They like their grandparents. Family members are a source of pain, frustration, and aggravation to teens; but those realities don't change the basically positive feelings teens have about those closest to them.

14. **Youth are interested in diet, exercise, overall physical condition, and physical appearance.** Youth are concerned about their physical appearance and their health. Some young people, in fact, are downright obsessed with improving their looks! One recent study of junior high girls found that 45 percent wanted to lose weight and 44 percent wanted to alter their appearance in some way. Only 13 percent of the same group were dissatisfied with their intelligence!

Many teens are on diets to lose weight and are in vigorous exercise programs. The physical fitness enthusiasm benefits youth in many ways, but there can also be problems. Some teens diet in potentially dangerous ways. Others may base their self-worth too much on physical appearance. Youth with physical handicaps or obvious deformities are in danger of feeling completely excluded from their appearance-conscious and sometimes judgmental peers.

15. **Male and female roles are changing for youth as for the rest of society.** Signs of changing male and female roles are all around us:

● Publications increasingly use nonsexist language. It's no longer considered correct to use "man" to refer to both men and women.

● Though true equality in financial compensation has not yet been achieved, women are more likely than in the past to receive equal pay for equal work.

● More women now work as doctors, lawyers, accountants, and ministers than ever before. More women are also being promoted into the top ranks of business and industry.

● Men play a more active role in the care of children; and we even see a few men functioning as "house husbands," making the home their primary responsibility in a way that only women did in the past.

● Women are somewhat more likely to take the initiative in dating relationships and also more likely to share dating expenses. They are less likely to see the male entitled to any sexual privileges because of his paying for a date.

These changes are increasingly pervasive in our society and will be even more so in the days ahead. Most of these changes are positive. Women are receiving more opportunities and rights which they should always have had. Men are gaining the pleasure of more direct involvement with children. Women are showing more strength, and men are realizing that gentleness is not a sign of weakness.

But it's also a confusing time for teens. Forming identity as males and females and learning how to relate to the opposite sex are major tasks of the teenage years. The church can help with this task not only through discussion and study about male and female roles but also by comfortable, informal activities shared by male and female teens.

16. **Teenage expressions and language change too rapidly for adults to ever be fully current!** This means that trying to talk like teenagers inevitably dooms adults to failure! At the time of this writing, here are some teen expressions you can find commonly used in parts of the Midwest:

● A *Dorkmeier* is an unpleasant, unattractive person. Example: "I wouldn't go out with a Dorkmeier like him."

● A *slim* is a girlfriend. Example: "Annie's been my slim all month."

● *Rewind it* is a request to share what happened. Example: "You and your slim spent your night in a tent! Rewind it for me."

● A *mint* is an attractive fellow. Example: "She dropped that Dorkmeier and has a real mint now."

Don't try using these terms with your youth group! They will have been replaced by the time the first printing of this book reaches the bookstores. You may find it enjoyable to talk with young people about their favorite expressions, but remember that they are concerned that you care about them—not that you talk like them!

Church-active Youth

Now let's focus our concern. We've talked about societal forces which influence youth and about characteristics of today's youth. What about those youth with whom you are most likely to work in a local Roman Catholic, Baptist, Church of the Brethren, Methodist, Presbyterian, Lutheran,

Nazarene, Mennonite, Christian, or (fill in the blank) _____ church? As do persons of all ages, teenagers have diverse opinions about the church and various degrees of commitment to its ministry. Though categorizing persons can be misleading, you should be aware of the following general types of church youth. Of course, most young people will not fit neatly into one category, but these descriptions may help you better understand the youth group with which you work.

IABACs. "I've Always Been a Christian." These young people have grown up in Christian homes and have been exposed to prayer, the Bible, and discussions about God. They have attended church school and congregational worship with their parents on a regular basis. One would expect almost all young people with this background to be deeply committed to Christ and heavily involved in the church. Many IABACs are. Others, however, may have been exposed to their parents' faith without internalizing that faith and without developing their own relationship with Christ.

If these IABACs begin to rebel against their parents and to assert their independence, they may express their rebellion by refusing to attend church or by refusing to participate fully in youth activities. These people need help developing their own relationships with Christ. They need to understand that they are just as much a part of the church as their parents are.

IBSs. "I've Been Saved." These young people have had an intensely personal religious experience with Christ that has changed how they feel about themselves, about other people, and about the church. If their personal experience with Christ came through the church, they are deeply committed to the church's work. If their commitment was reached through the influence of a school friend or another religious group, IBSs may feel that their own church doesn't have a proper understanding of the Christian faith. They may avoid participation in activities of the church or may work at sharing their "correct" understanding of Christ with (in their opinion) the misguided people in the church. IBSs need help recognizing that people have differing experiences and understandings of the one Christ. The function of the church, as the body of Christ, is to unite its diverse members in common worship and service.

IDCAAs. "I Don't Care About Anything." Many young people seem eternally tired and are not concerned about anything except their own pleasure. Not only are they indifferent to the needs of starving children and to racial injustice, they may not even care about cleaning up the youth room or paying attention during group or class discussions. IDCAAs often feel disgusted with themselves and are unable to see and to respond to the needs of others. This same kind of apathy is present in many adults. IDCAAs need affirmation of their own worth and help in understanding how much the church needs the involvement of each member.

IEPACs. "I Enjoy People and the Church." These young people are deeply committed to Christ and to the church. They enjoy being with other people, and they responsibly complete important tasks. Though this group of young people may not be as large as an adult leader would like, they are extremely valuable to any group or class. They sometimes may be resented by

11

others in the group who feel intimidated by them, but they usually can be helped to understand the resentment. Pray for all the young people with whom you work, but don't forget to give thanks for the IEPACs.

Members of all four categories need help in several areas, including:

1. **Clarifying and deepening their own faith.** They need a clear understanding of how they have become church members or participants. If they have become Christians by uncritically accepting or observing the beliefs of their parents or friends, they need to evaluate those beliefs and to affirm them as their own. If they have had a recent conversion experience, they need help understanding that God speaks to people in different ways. They should share their faith with others, but they also should recognize that they can learn from the experiences of other young people.

2. **Feeling a part of the church.** All Christians need a sense of belonging to and taking responsibility for a local church. One cannot long remain a Christian in isolation from other Christian people. The help of each person is needed if the church is to be a strong and living witness in the community.

3. **Helping the church change.** Often young people see inconsistencies between what adults profess to believe and what they actually do. While such young people should be helped to recognize similar inconsistencies between what they themselves say and do, their insights into the failures of the church often are valid. They need help recognizing that they are a part of the church and, as such, can work for needed change.

Youth Are Part of the Church

Most churches do not provide separate categories for youth and adult members. Teenagers who have been confirmed are members of the church as fully as adults who have been confirmed. Since the trustees of a church may make some decisions of legal importance, all members of that group must generally be of legal age (as determined by the law in that community, county, or state). Teenagers can and should serve on most other local church boards and committees.

The church does not belong to adults. For that matter, the church does not belong to any person or group of people. The church is the body of Christ and is composed of all those having faith in Christ who are united in loving service. Differences among people in the church are not causes for regret but for rejoicing. Our differences mean that we have different skills and insights that can enable us to help one another and to further the work of the church.

This concept finds many expressions in the Scriptures, but one of the most familiar and eloquent is in 1 Corinthians 12. Here Paul compares the church as the body of Christ to the human body: If all were a single organ, where would the body be? As it is, there are many parts, yet one body. The eye cannot say to the hand, "I have no need of you," nor again the head to the feet, "I have no need of you" (vv. 19-21). Teenagers need to recognize that they are important members of the body of Christ, and they need to be aware of the responsibilities that membership involves.

In our culture teenagers are considered to be relatively young. Teenagers have not *always* been considered youngsters, however. In Jesus' time girls were married and began having children at the age of fourteen,

12

fifteen, or sixteen. The cultural context was different; life expectancy was shorter; and a lengthy formal education was less important. It is clear that young people are capable of assuming significant responsibilities. When God called Jeremiah as a prophet, Jeremiah resisted because of his young age: "Ah, Lord GOD! Truly, I do not know how to speak, for I am only a boy" (Jer. 1:6). God, however, had confidence in Jeremiah and gave him the help he needed. Some potential Jeremiahs may be members of your youth group or class.

I am personally convinced that our churches have far too often erred in the direction of expecting too little from the youth who are part of our congregations. We work too hard to entertain rather than to challenge. We allow ourselves to be caught in competition with secular society rather than providing opportunities for spiritual reflection, for meaningful service to humanity, and for Christian community and mutual support which cannot be found outside the church.

Many of today's youth seem selfish, materialistic, and inwardly turned because they have not been shown alternative and more meaningful lifestyles. Start with your young people wherever they are in their spiritual development. Understand them. Accept and love them just as they are, for that is the way in which God loves us. But nurture them, challenge them, and help them to grow. They are not simply the church of tomorrow; they are the church of today.

Responding to the Needs of Youth

A church youth program that accepts young people as they are, that wishes to respond to their developmental needs and help them change and grow in the faith, will endeavor to provide them with opportunities to:

● GROW in their relationships with Christ.

● DEVELOP greater self-worth and feel better about themselves.

● SHOW concern for the needs of others.

● SERVE those who are less fortunate.

● DEVELOP values and morals which they own (rather than ones that they have uncritically accepted from others).

● SHARE their deepest concerns and hurts with others who will protect their confidence and show them concern.

● FORM close friendships and trust relationships with other young people and with adult teachers and workers.

● RECOGNIZE the impact of advertisements, television, music, and peers on their values.

● DEVELOP a private devotional life.

● SHARE in congregational worship.

● LEARN what it means to lead a Christ-centered life.

● BECOME fully a part of the body of Christ as manifested in the local church.

Public schools, scouting groups, and many other worthy organizations offer continuing programs for the benefit of young people. While those of us in the Christian community want to work cooperatively with other organizations, we also need to remember that our approach to youth should be unique. We are not simply one organization among the many competing for the time and interest of teenagers.

There's an understandable tendency for the church to feel it must in some sense compete with school activities, youth employment, dating, motion pictures, and television for youth involvement. While we recognize that youth do have limited time, we must also keep ourselves, young people, parents, and the church aware that no other activities offer youth what the Christian community does. When we try to be as entertaining as motion pictures or television, we inevitably put ourselves in a losing position. When we offer genuine Christian community, young people find in the church what they desperately need and cannot find elsewhere.

Of course, we may use resources such as popular movies, music, and television in our work with youth. This book shares practical strategies for doing that. But we should never forget the factors that make the church's mission to youth and with youth unique.

People from twenty different denominations helped in the development of this book's first edition. In the years since then, people from over sixty denominations have used the book and shared helpful feedback. We've tried hard in this resource to avoid controversial doctrinal issues because we wanted the book to be useful to as many people as possible. The love of Christ binds us all together more than doctrinal matters and ecclesiastical polity pull

us apart. In our effort to avoid doctrinal controversy, however, we failed in the first edition to say enough about the importance of looking at youth work from the perspective of Scripture and theology. We think solid theology and Scripture undergird the whole book, but we want in this chapter to make that theology explicit.

As you read the following pages, reflect on your own faith in Christ and understanding of Scripture. We hope the following guidelines will further your own thinking and prayer.

1. **We should always seek to bring youth closer to Christ and to help them share their faith with others.** In the Great Commission, Jesus told his followers to "go therefore and make disciples of all nations, baptizing them in the name of the Father and of the Son and of the Holy Spirit" (Matt. 28:19). As discussed in the chapter "Understanding Young People," youth are at a variety of places in their spiritual life. Many already describe themselves as born again and have a deep faith in Christ. Others aren't certain what they believe. Some who attend church activities out of parental pressure or desire for companionship may not yet be certain about God's existence. All teens, like all adults, have a continuing need to grow closer to Christ.

Sharing the faith with others is also basic to the Christian life. While church-active teens often want to share their faith, they sometimes feel very inadequate about doing so. The chapter on "Evangelism" in this book offers some practical strategies to help youth share their faith in positive ways.

As we seek to share our own faith with youth, we should remember that what we do and how we live may have as great an influence as the words that we speak. Adult leaders can feel just as inadequate as teens about sharing their faith. The suggestions in "Evangelism" and in "Guidelines for Working with Youth" should be helpful to you. Teens who grow close to you will pay more attention to the overall manner in which you conduct your life and relate to them than to any particular words you say.

2. **Our work with youth should be grounded in Scripture and should help them better understand the Bible.** This doesn't mean you have to be a biblical scholar to work with youth or that you have to walk around quoting Scripture. In fact, we would recommend that you avoid quoting Scripture because that can be a turn-off to some youth. It does mean seeking guidance from Scripture as you work with youth and

helping them experience the pleasure and meaning that comes from exploring the Bible. Many excellent materials (see "Resources") are available to help youth study the Bible. The best of those materials provide the background you need to give leadership to youth. As you grow more comfortable working with the Scriptures, you'll often find yourself going directly to the Bible for more information or perspective on a particular topic.

Many young people who are active in the church remain almost biblically illiterate. Try the following quiz on the young people with whom you work. You'll find the answers provided immediately after the quiz along with relevant Scripture references and a few discussion questions.

WHAT DO YOU REMEMBER ABOUT THE BIBLE?

1. In what language was most of the Old Testament originally written?
2. In what language was most of the New Testament originally written?
3. What is the first book in the Bible?
4. What is the last book in the Bible?
5. What does the word *gospel* mean?
6. Name the four Gospels in the Bible.
7. Who met God at a burning bush?
8. What biblical character had a conversion on the Damascus Road?
9. What sign did God give Noah that the world would never again be destroyed by water?
10. What child of David and Bathsheba became perhaps the wisest ruler ever?
11. What biblical leader sent a good friend into battle to be killed so that he could have that friend's wife?
12. What biblical book gives us a history of Paul's ministry and of the early church?

13. Where did the wedding take place at which Christ turned water into wine?
14. What parable did Jesus tell to explain who our neighbors are?
15. What parable did Jesus tell that reminds us that we can always "come home" to God, our loving parent, no matter how much we have sinned or failed?
16. What short letter did Paul write about a runaway slave?
17. What New Testament letter contains a popular poem or song about love and describes the gifts of the Spirit?
18. What Old Testament prophet spoke to a valley of bones?
19. What Old Testament book is much like a hymnal?
20. What do we commonly call the speech in which Jesus shared the Beatitudes?

Answers to WHAT DO YOU REMEMBER ABOUT THE BIBLE?

1. Hebrew
2. Greek
3. Genesis
4. Revelation
5. Good news
6. Matthew, Mark, Luke, John
7. Moses, Exodus 3:1-12. What makes a place sacred?
8. Paul (or Saul), Acts 9:1-9.
9. Rainbow, Genesis 9:8-17.
10. Solomon, 2 Samuel 12:24-25 and 1 Kings 3:5-14. What would you ask for if given Solomon's opportunity?
11. David, 2 Samuel 11:2-5, 14-17. How can great good and great harm come from the same person? How are we like David?
12. Acts
13. Cana in Galilee, John 2:1-11.
14. The Good Samaritan, Luke 10:29-37. Who is our neighbor according to this parable?
15. The Prodigal Son, Luke 15:11-32. Why did the elder son have trouble accepting what happened? What does this parable say about the extent of God's love for us?
16. Philemon.
17. 1 Corinthians. See 1 Corinthians 13: 1-13 and 12:4-11.
18. Ezekiel, Ezekiel 37:1-14.
19. The Psalms
20. The Sermon on the Mount, Matthew 5—7 contains the Sermon on the Mount; the Beatitudes are in 5:1-12.

Obviously the exercise would have been easier if done as matching or multiple choice items, but those approaches are not as good a test of knowledge. Our salvation obviously does not rest on intellectual knowledge of Christ or Scripture. Yet our growth in the Christian faith certainly gains as we learn more about the Bible and especially as we seek to apply it to our daily lives.

Most youth respond very positively to Bible study. Some churches have busy youth who want to study the Bible so much that they come at seven in the morning or ten in the evening! Use every opportunity you can to help youth learn more about the Bible and apply that knowledge to the decisions they make.

In the Sermon on the Mount, Jesus speaks about the firm foundation which study of his words provides:

Everyone then who hears these words of mine and acts on them will be like a wise man who built his house on rock. The rain fell, the floods came, and the winds blew and beat on that house, but it did not fall, because it had been founded on rock.

Matthew 7:24-25

As the floods of life come, teenagers receive great help from a firm foundation in God's Word.

3. **We need to take a holistic approach to youth ministry.** The word *holistic* has become part of the jargon of our time, especially in the sense of a holistic view of health—integrating various approaches to physical health, mental health, and spiritual health. Unfortunately the word *holistic* is

thrown about verbally much more than put into practice.

Our society's educational structures are founded on a Newtonian paradigm, which is essentially a parts mentality. Each area of learning (science, art, math, religion, psychology, language) is viewed as a part. As theologian Matthew Fox has expressed it: "No attempt at integration, or the understanding of the whole that is wisdom, is made. The goal of education is not wisdom but getting a job." (*The Coming of the Cosmic Christ*, Harper and Row, 1988, p. 22).

The Christian faith, however, is concerned with true wholeness. The Hebrew and Greek words underlying the words *peace* and *salvation* have a rich history of wholeness—concern for the whole person and the whole of society. While Jesus obviously came with a message about the spiritual condition of people, he did not hesitate to minister to their physical, mental, and social needs. Notice his willingness not only to feed the hungry but even to turn water into wine to enhance a celebration.

The church should be concerned about every aspect of the lives of young people. We need to help them recognize that Christ cares about their physical, mental, and social well-being as well as their spiritual well-being. Indeed, one can't fully separate spiritual health from any other aspect of life.

There has been a great tendency in society and in the church to neglect certain aspects of the education and development of youth. Matthew Fox argues that we have especially failed to help sexuality and aggression develop normally. Children and young people often channel "these powers of sexuality and aggression into self-loathing and self-contempt" (Fox, p. 29). The church needs to be a setting in which young people can talk openly about their developing sexuality and about the problems of finding healthy outlets for natural aggression. As adult leaders, we must set the climate in which that kind of discussion can take place.

A holistic view obviously poses some problems since it may involve us as adult leaders in helping youth deal with issues we would rather avoid. On the other hand, a holistic view opens many programming opportunities, because it means that truly anything happening in the lives of young people is an appropriate topic for program and discussion: MTV, popular movies, school plays, language, physical appearance, sexual feelings, male-female roles, athletic competition, and relationships with parents.

This book attempts to give you good guidance in handling discussions with young people. We'll also refer you to other helpful resources for specific topics. Our special video section provides you with many discussion possibilities based on popular motion pictures.

4. **Youth need help developing strong self-esteem and healthy self-images.** For centuries Christian leaders talked about the sin of pride and the pitfalls of arrogance. Those certainly continue to be problems today, but teenagers are far more likely to suffer from devastatingly low self-esteem than from unhealthy pride or arrogance. Many problems of contemporary teens flow from their fragile self-esteem:

- Depression
- Aggression
- Crime
- Illiteracy
- Illicit drug use
- Early sexual behavior

There are certainly multiple causes of the above problems, but low self-esteem is a major contributor.

The Scriptures affirm to us that we are made in the image of God and that God loves us:

> *God saw everything that he had made, and indeed, it was very good.*

> Genesis 1:31a

> *In this is love, not that we loved God but that he loved us and sent his Son to be the atoning sacrifice for our sins.*

> 1 John 4:10

Teenagers, however, often do not feel that they are made in the image of God and may find God's love a little difficult to believe. They may, in fact, more readily identify with Paul's words:

> *I do not understand my own actions. For I do not do what I want, but I do the very thing I hate . . . . For I do not do the good I want, but the evil I do not want is what I do.*

> Romans 7:15, 19

It seems to some teenagers as though everything they do is wrong. Parents, teachers, and friends often reinforce that concept. Our society continues to act as though strong criticism is absolutely essential to self-development. The ability to accept criticism is a survival tool in our society, and some criticism is helpful. Most of us, however, are subjected to criticism which is destructive rather than constructive.

The church can't protect teens from all the pressures of society. The church can help teens:

- see themselves as the good creation of a loving God,

- form healthy self-images,

- learn how to cope with the criticisms and unrealistic expectations of others,

- by providing reinforcement and appreciation for their positive accomplishments, and

- build supportive community with each other.

For many years I had the pleasure of working with a senior high youth group which had a "Joys and Concerns" time at each meeting. We sat on the floor in front of the church altar with only a few lights on. The sanctuary setting and the lowered illumination created an atmosphere of safety and security. During Joys and Concerns, individuals would simply share whatever had happened during the past week which constituted a "joy" or "concern." Other group members helped celebrate the joys (often with applause) and share the concerns. The group had an agreement that whatever was shared in the group was not discussed outside the group. Nothing was too trivial to be shared, and the results consistently reinforced the self-esteem of the young people. I learned the Joys and Concerns concept from that youth group and have shared it with many other groups, always with great success. Some examples of joys and concerns follow:

- "I finally got up the courage to ask Annie for a date. She said no, but at least I asked her." The speaker received congratulations for having asked her out and sympathy for the result. Others shared similar frustrations.

18

• "I got a B- on my math test. That's the first time I've done better than a D+." Loud cheers!

• "I finally talked with Mom about Dad's drinking. She's been upset, too, and we both cried a lot." Many supportive and empathetic comments.

• "I got in trouble with Mr. Allen. Why do I always get in trouble in that class?" Lots of support and a couple of positive suggestions.

• "I ran two miles every night this week, and I also lost two pounds for the week. I feel so much better!" Loud congratulations.

• "I promised God I was going to stop yelling at my little brother, but I couldn't do it this week. He was like this constant irritation. I shouldn't have made the promise, or I should have tried harder to keep it." Lots of sharing about similar promises made and broken. Also discussion about what kinds of promises one should make and about God's forgiveness.

(As with other examples in this book, the above quotations are all from real group experiences; but names and any identifying information have been changed.)

5. **Young people need experiences of the living body of Christ; they need to experience the kind of community that is only possible in the church.** Young people have an intense need for meaningful community, which can help them build higher self-esteem. The church offers a level of community not available in any other setting, for the church is the body of Christ. Christ is the head of the body, and we are all members of the body.

For just as the body is one and has many members, and all the members of the body, though many, are one body, so it is with Christ.

1 Corinthians 12:12

Verses 14-26 of that same chapter provide a meaningful comparison of the church to the human body. Through their youth activities in the church, young people should experience what it means to be part of Christ's body as they:

• grow closer to Christ through Bible study, prayer, and discussion,

• recognize their own need for support and encouragement from others,

• learn how to express support and encouragement to others,

• develop respect for their own strengths and abilities and for those of other group members,

• learn to trust group members and to be trustworthy,

• share in a whole range of activities including not only study and prayer but also social activities and recreation.

The trust developed in an activity like Joys and Concerns (discussed under guideline four above) deepens young people's sense of the church as the body of Christ. With careful nurture, youth can experience a security and strength in the church which they simply will not find in other organizations in society.

While it is important to include Bible study and prayer, we also need to remember that virtually all shared, positive activities can help group members grow closer to one another. Softball, picnics, parties, and similar events have a place in the church's youth program.

6. **Young people need to develop an appreciation for the natural world as a gift from God.** The land, the air, the sea, plant life, and animal life are all part of God's rich gift to us: the earth! Young people need help recognizing the natural world as a source of revelation of God. They also need to recognize our responsibility for that natural world.

> *Then God said, "Let us make humankind in our image, according to our likeness; and let them have dominion over the fish of the sea, and over the birds of the air, and over the cattle, and over all the wild animals of the earth, and over every creeping thing that creeps upon the earth."*

Genesis 1:26

We live in a time when Mother Earth receives very little respect from those responsible for her and dependent on her. The dominion over the earth which we have received carries with it great responsibility, which we have not met. Consider . . .

● the destruction of the tropical rain forests and all the risk to our future posed by that,

● the mounting problems with nuclear waste,

● the continuing pollution of water and air,

● the needless slaughter of whales and seals.

Young people need help recognizing these as Christian issues and should be encouraged to take positive steps for the improvement of the natural world. Less wasteful and polluting lifestyles are important for all people.

As we look toward the stars, we also realize that the earth is a very small part of a massive, indeed infinite, universe. Space exploration is no longer just science fiction, and today's teenagers could be able to set foot on another planet at some future time. As space travel becomes a viable possibility for ordinary people, we also need to recognize our responsibility to the world outside our own planet's atmosphere. We also need to be concerned about money spent on space exploration while people starve on earth and while we continue plundering our natural resources.

7. **Young people need help developing healthy concern for their neighbors—those close to them and those at a distance.** The sense of community young people develop in the church setting should foster significant concern for one another. We want to help youth express that concern in positive ways, and we also want to help them extend it to a broader circle of people. Learning what it means to care about others can be one of the most valuable results of youth group participation.

Jesus gave a radical response when asked who one's neighbor is. He told the story of the Good Samaritan, which makes it clear that all persons in need are our neighbors; and we are to love them:

> *You shall love the Lord your God with all your heart, and with all your soul, and with all your strength, and with all your mind; and your neighbor as yourself.*

Luke 10:27

You can read the full context and the parable of the Good Samaritan in Luke

20

10:25-37. As familiar as those words are, they merit repetition and discussion in our work with youth because their application is one of the major challenges of the Christian faith. Those who first heard this parable were likely to have had feelings of prejudice toward the Samaritan people, not unlike the strong racial prejudices of our own time. Jesus makes a Samaritan the "hero" of the story, and that heroism is displayed in acts of kindness toward a person not previously known by the Samaritan.

Adults involved in youth work during the 1960s and 1970s may well remember that those teens were more likely than today's teens to (a) resist adult authority and (b) become actively involved in service to others. While there obviously are significant exceptions, youth today are not so likely to challenge adult authority but are also not so likely to reach out to others and to have passion for improving our world. Awareness of Christ's challenge to care for others should lead youth into active involvement in helping meet the needs of others.

Youth class and group programming should include discussion about social problems from a Christian perspective. We should also offer young people opportunities for action projects to help others. Programming examples include:

● A series of sessions on world peace: understanding the USSR and China; what happened at Hiroshima; the current status of nuclear weapons in the world; the biblical call to peace.

● A series of sessions on poverty: the plight of the homeless; local hunger needs; information on poverty around the world; how mission projects are attempting to alleviate hunger; the response of Christ to the hungry.

● A series of sessions on drug problems: factual information about alcohol, marijuana, cocaine, etc.; why people turn to drugs and the problems that result; strategies for reducing drug abuse; a biblical look at responsibility for our bodies and our minds.

● A series of sessions on HIV/AIDS infection: What is AIDS? How is it transmitted? What are the community, state, national, and global facts? What is the role of the individual and of the local church?

● A series of sessions on race relations: understanding the racial tensions which still exist in our country; learning about the ethnic heritage of others; finding ways to improve race relations; understanding the biblical imperative of seeing all people as our neighbors.

● A special program for the whole church to help people be more aware of peace concerns.

● A canned food drive for a local food pantry.

● Distributing information about illicit drugs at shopping malls and other places frequented by teens.

● Having a party or special event with youth from another church that is predominantly composed of members of another race.

● Responding to the needs of others can be the basis for a short term or continuing special interest youth group. Churches have had good success with:

a. A short-term drama group producing a play on peace.

b. A short-term growth group designed to help teens reach out to people suffering from depression (and who are potentially vulnerable to illicit drug use and suicide).

c. A short-term video group using a camcorder to make a film about local hunger problems.

d. A continuing group doing "clown ministry" to nursing homes, shut-ins, the hospitalized, and others.

d. A continuing group operating a food pantry for the hungry in the community.

The "Resources" section provides information on a variety of program resources on the kinds of topics discussed here. You'll also find information on clown ministry and drama.

You'll want to be aware of the programs your church and denomination already support in helping to alleviate poverty, improve race relations, and build peace. Your minister can help you obtain that information. Many denominations have available helpful, attractive materials interpreting various kinds of mission outreach.

8. **Youth need continuing guidance in deepening their spiritual lives.** As the first chapter, "Understanding Young People," discussed, young people are at very different points in their spiritual growth and in their commitment to the church. Some theologians have wisely observed that being a Christian is both a *state* and a *process*. It's a state of having made a commitment to Jesus Christ and wanting to live one's days in service to Christ. It's a process of constantly growing closer to God and striving to live a Christlike life.

Young people, like adults, are filled with questions about the nature of God and how to grow closer to God. In one survey of junior and senior high youth in the late 1980s, 75 percent or more indicated that they . . .

● wanted help growing closer to God.

● didn't understand well the concept of the Holy Spirit.

● wanted to know more about the Bible.

● needed help feeling comfortable with prayer.

● wondered why God permits so much suffering.

● wondered why God seems to heal some people but not others.

● wanted to know if there is a devil and, if so, what the devil is like.

● wondered how God can forgive them for some sins.

● didn't fully understand the concept of "salvation by grace."

In that particular survey, over half the youth indicated that they would like to attend a spiritual life retreat (a result consistent with Gallup polls). Almost half the youth said they would like to be part of a continuing group in which they could freely express their spiritual doubts and concerns.

We in the church have a tremendous responsibility in helping young people grow in the Christian faith and deal with the spiritual issues of concern to them. As adult leaders, we may often feel unqualified to give the help needed, but we should not doubt that God can and will work through us. As discussed at several points in this book, we aren't called upon to have all the answers. We are called to be honest with youth and to help them search for answers.

Achieving balance in the church's youth program is an important task. We can't and shouldn't be serious all the time. The building of relationships that occurs through recreation and social events helps develop Christian community and nurtures the spiritual life. We should, however, be certain that we do provide sufficient opportunities to help young people deal with spiritual questions. Note the Faith Development and Group Life exercise in the chapter on "Evangelism." You should consider using that exercise sometime during the year. Be sure your programming for the year includes time to deal with concerns such as:

- Prayer.

- The nature of God.

- Why people suffer.

- How the Holy Spirit works in our lives.

- How Christ's death and resurrection bring salvation to us.

- The meaning of communion (or the eucharist).

- The meaning of baptism.

- Developing the devotional life.

- Ways to grow closer to God.

- How we experience God through one another.

- How we experience God in the natural world.

- What it means to lead a Christ-centered life.

- How our faith should influence vocational choice.

- The practice of service.

Consider scheduling at least one spiritual life retreat during the year. A time apart from other pressures can greatly help young people in their spiritual search. The "Resources" chapter includes many fine materials to help develop the spiritual lives of youth.

There is no secret formula for successful youth ministry. Every youth group is different from every other one. For this reason, what works well with some youth and some youth groups may be disastrous when tried with others.

Nevertheless, there are some helpful general guidelines, some useful suggestions based on the experiences of people who have spent many years in youth ministry. We offer twenty-five guidelines for your consideration. They do not constitute a panacea or an instant success formula. And the list is by no means exhaustive. You and other youth workers can readily add other guidelines based on your own experiences. The list does contain, however, some tried-and-true suggestions for enriching your youth ministry. We hope that you will find them helpful.

1. **Know yourself—your own faith, your abilities, your limitations; and be honest about who you are.** As a youth worker, you will constantly be dealing with people who are seeking to find themselves. The youth years are an exciting, though often frustrating, period—a time when teenagers are moving from the relatively comfortable security of childhood to the sometimes frightening responsibilities of adulthood. In a sense, the period of years from thirteen to eighteen is one long rite of passage, a time of discovering one's self and one's role in life. Teenagers experiencing this passage need role models; they need to relate to people who have a relatively high degree of certainty about their own personhood. Adult workers with youth, therefore, should have a reasonably clear idea of their own identity, a realistic perspective on where they are in their own development physiologically, mentally, psychologically, socially, and spiritually.

Spend some time in evaluating yourself. Look at where you have been in your own development, where you are now, where you hope to be five, ten, or twenty years from now. Do you feel that you really know yourself? Are you comfortable with the person that you are? Do you have a realistic picture of your abilities? What about your limitations? What are they? Can you accept them? Are you able to see yourself as a good person, a good creation of a loving and concerned God? Evaluate yourself on the basis of these questions and others that you might add. Then resolve to accept and like the person that you are. Such self-acceptance is a necessity if you are to convey to youth the message that they, too, are worthy persons, individuals created and loved by the eternal God.

Spend some time evaluating your own faith. What are your beliefs? What are your doubts? Don't hide from your doubts. Face them squarely. It has been said that "doubt is the beginning of belief." If you have doubts about some aspects of the faith, spend some time praying and reading Scripture. Seek answers. But don't feel that you have to have all the answers. Even Saint Paul spoke often of the "mystery" of the Christian faith; he pointed out that there are some things that we cannot fully understand, some things that we have to accept by a leap of faith. The young people with whom you work will have many doubts. And they will usually relate well to you if you are honest about what you believe and where you have questions.

Identify your strengths and your abilities. Then utilize them. None of us can be good at everything. Some of us are good musicians; some are good at leading recreation; some can speak well in front of groups; some are good listeners. Use your God-given abilities, and then don't hesitate to call on others, adults and youth, to help you in areas where you feel limited. Youth tend to respond well to an adult who comes across as a "whole person," a person with abilities and limitations. Don't fake it. Don't try to appear proficient in areas where you need help. Most young people can spot artificiality quite easily. And they will like you more and respond better to you if you come across as a person who knows and is honest about who he or she really is. On the other hand, be open to possibilities in yourself that you may not have yet discovered. Are there areas in which you can change, areas in which you can improve yourself? Look for these areas. And then make an all-out effort to increase your abilities and skills. You may have many hidden talents that you have not begun to uncover.

2. **Be an adult.** There is a widespread misconception about youth ministry: the belief that youth relate well to adults who assume the role of "big kids" and try to emulate youth behavior. It is true that youth are looking for friends whose attitudes and behavior are similar to their own, but they are looking for these kinds of friends among their own peer group. What they want in an adult youth worker is an adult friend, a grown-up person who cares about them, their interests, and their needs.

So don't try to be a teenager. You are not a youth; you are an adult. And any effort to be an overgrown teenager will come across just that way—as a foolish attempt to be something that you are not. Learn about youth culture. And, more importantly, learn about the youth with whom you work—their needs, interests, motivations, aspirations, and problems. But remember that you have a special perspective to offer them. You are an adult with some insights that you have acquired by living with other adults in the adult world. Much of your effectiveness with youth will be the result of your offering them, in a caring and nonpatronizing way, the benefits of your perspective as an adult. Enjoy your unique opportunity to participate in the freshness and the vitality of the youth world, but give the youth the advantage of reciprocity; give them the gift of an adult friendship and perspective.

3. **Know the young people as individuals.** In youth ministry, many of us make the mistake of relating only to a youth group. The youth with whom you work may be members of a youth group or a youth class, but they are first and foremost *individuals*. They are individual people created in the image of God. Each one of them is a unique creation, a person living a life that no one else in all of history will ever duplicate.

So get to know the young people as individual persons. This process involves more than just being with them one or two hours each Sunday. Visit with them in their homes. Get to know their backgrounds. Talk with individuals during youth group suppers, during recreation periods, or at times when there is a lull in your group's activities. Make yourself available for consultation or counseling. Devise group-building activities that will give you and other adult workers with youth the opportunity to have discussions with small groups (two to nine people). Plan some service projects, a play rehearsal, or some other settings in which you and the youth work together. As any person who has ever been in a play will tell you, there are great opportunities for personal involvement and fellowship when people are working together on an informal basis.

Try to persuade the youth leaders (usually some of the people who are core group members) to draw the fringe people into the main group(s). With a little effort, you can often achieve surprisingly good results with this strategy. In one youth group that I worked with, I persuaded Bill, the group's very popular leader, to work at including Joe, a particularly shy youth, in the main group's discussion. I was so successful that, at one point, Bill shocked the whole group by telling me to quit talking so much so that Joe would have a chance to contribute. And Bill was right in doing so. He very aptly pointed out to me that I needed to listen more in order to do what I am suggesting to you—to get to know the youth as individuals.

Second, keep an accurate attendance record—and utilize it. Give the adult workers and the youth leaders some "pastoral" responsibilities. Assign to each adult and each youth leader the responsibility for relating to several of the youth. Whenever a person shows evidence of a personal problem or stops attending the group's sessions, the adult worker and the youth leader to whom this person has been assigned should make phone calls and visits and offer help and concern.

4. **Care for the young people as individuals.** This guideline cannot be taught. It is something that you have to have or develop, for one of the things that makes a Christian group different from many other groups in our society is the factor of caring. Many of us get so caught up in the goal of having a successful youth group that we lose sight of one of our primary goals: to be a loving, caring community that helps people develop their own potential as individuals.

This aspect of youth ministry was strikingly pointed out to me when we sent a youth ministry questionnaire to all teenagers and parents of teenagers in our church. One very perceptive parent ended her comments with this statement: "In all of our concern about programs, let us not lose sight of persons and their needs." That comment says it all. Programs and group activities are important; but, if we are to be truly successful in our attempts at youth ministry, we must care deeply for the young people with whom we work. That caring must be expressed by the youth and by the church community at large. But you have the primary responsibility for making sure that an atmosphere of caring and concern pervades the youth ministry of your church. It is up to you as a youth worker to set the tone by caring for each young person as an individual.

5. **Discover what the young people want to study and do; and try to set up your programs in response to the young people's needs and interests.** Far too many church youth programs are expressions of what the adults think the youth should be doing. If your youth program is to be successful, you have to get input from the youth themselves about their needs and interests. This is not to say that the programs should be determined entirely by the youth. That can be as great an error as having the adults do all the planning. What is needed is a joint effort. Find out what the youth are interested in and then work with them to plan your program of youth ministry.

How do we discover what the youth are interested in? The number of youth workers who have had terrible results in this regard is legion. Many youth workers just sit down with the young people and ask: "Well, what do you want to do?" Most groups, youth and adults alike, produce a dearth of helpful responses when approached in this manner. A better method is to utilize an "interest finder," which gives group participants the opportunity to rate certain subjects and activities and also allows for participants to add other items that are not included in the questionnaire. For ideas on how to design and utilize interest finders, see our chapters on "The Sunday School," "The Fellowship Group," and "Planning with Young People."

One final note about securing youth input: As a rule, the amount of youth involvement in planning and leading a youth program should increase proportionately as the youth move from the younger teen level to the older teen level. For example, a group of seventh and eighth graders would generally have some minimal input and leadership responsibility, with the adult workers having a large role in program planning and leadership; whereas in a group consisting primarily of eleventh and twelfth graders, the ratio of youth participation to adult participation in planning and leadership should be at least as high as 50 percent.

6. **Plan ahead with the youth.** Good planning is an essential ingredient in any youth program. Plan well in advance. Allow time for "Murphy's law"—for all those things that can go wrong. Usually it is helpful to plan in three phases: general planning on a yearly and quarterly basis; monthly planning; and weekly planning. Whatever you do, don't wait until the last minute. Planning a Sunday evening's program on Sunday morning (or, heaven forbid, on Sunday evening) simply does not allow enough time for discussing goals and plans with leaders, securing

resources, and taking care of all the details that are so important for a successful program.

Unless you are absolutely prevented from doing so, all planning should be done with the youth themselves. And both youth and adults should have responsible leadership roles in the program. As a general rule, youth participation in planning and leadership should increase proportionately from younger teens to older teens—as discussed in the preceding guideline. For more detailed information on program planning, see our chapters on "Planning with Young People," "The Sunday School," and "The Fellowship Group."

7. **Prepare the environment—the room and the setting.** It is often said that in a classroom "the walls talk." There is much truth in this old adage. Walls (and the setting and environment in general) convey subtle messages, both positive and negative. In the church where I recently worked, a church with a very large and ample physical plant, the youth groups had been meeting for years in a huge, cavernous fellowship hall—hardly the ideal setting for youth meetings. It is extremely difficult to achieve a good group feeling when thirty young people are meeting in a hall designed to accommodate supper meetings of two hundred people. On the day I arrived at this church, I began a one-person campaign (soon joined by others) to have new youth rooms built in a large storage area under the fellowship hall. The rooms are now complete and the difference in group spirit is phenomenal. We all need our own space, our own place. And this need is especially strong in teenagers. If you don't have areas that the youth can call their own, look around. Find a place. Generally, even a small room that is theirs alone is preferable to an area that they share with other groups.

If there is no space available in your church, you may even want to "borrow" a basement or a recreation room in someone's house. Try to find a place that can belong to the youth, an area that they can decorate and furnish according to their tastes.

Just as important as the availability of an area for youth is the manner in which that area is prepared for meetings and activities. Bare walls and poorly arranged furnishings convey the message that nothing of importance is going to take place. Work with the youth to prepare their rooms for classes or activities. Put up posters, banners, charts, pictures. Arrange the tables, chairs, and so forth, in a manner that will be conducive to and appropriate for the events that will take place in these areas. And again, as always, do it well in advance.

8. **Have alternative plans; be flexible.** When working with a group of young people, try to have a few extra ideas "up your sleeve." Probably nothing is so deadly in a youth meeting as continuing with a program that is obviously "going over like a lead balloon." You need to have alternative plans. You should try to develop a feel for whether a program is succeeding or "bombing." And you need to be flexible—and freed up—enough to change course in midstream when necessary. If a particular approach is falling flat, don't hesitate to try something else. The worst thing that can happen is that your alternative approach may also fall flat. And, if you have planned enough alternatives, you may hit upon something that will excite the group. The very fact that you do try different approaches will at least add variety which in itself can often save a sinking program.

A related question is what to do when the group veers off the subject and onto something entirely different. Here you must use your own good judgment. If the new subject is of interest and relates to the real needs and interests of the group, it is usually advisable to "roll with the punches" and pursue the new subject. If, on the other hand, the new subject seems to be irrelevant and/or just a waste of time, you should gently and politely urge the group to return to the original subject or to move to an alternative subject that you consider important.

9. **Have realistic goals and expectations.** Many youth workers make the mistake of attempting too much, of trying to achieve goals that are simply unrealistic for the particular group and setting. It is a good idea to have a few very clearly defined goals, rather than a lot of general, overwhelming goals. Remember: There are limits to what you can achieve with youth in the amount of time that you have with them. Although there are many instances in which youth have had life-changing experiences in church meetings, the more common experience is to undergo a series of lesser changes over a more extended period of time.

Most goals can be classified under three headings: cognitive goals, which involve changes in learning and knowledge; attitudinal goals, which involve changes in attitudes and opinions; and behavioral goals, which involve changes in behaviors and actions. It is usually a good idea to limit yourself to no more than three goals for any group session or class. I find it helpful to formulate for each group meeting one very concrete, measurable goal in each of these three categories.

10. **Avoid questions that can be answered only with yes or no and questions that seem to require only right or wrong answers, unless you request further clarification.** A

28

surefire way to end a discussion is to ask a question that requires only a yes or no answer. Very rarely will a youth (or an adult) go a step further and, without prodding, explain why he or she answered affirmatively or negatively. Occasionally it may be necessary to solicit yes-or-no responses. Whenever you do so, however, always have a follow-up question ready. Be prepared to continue the discussion by asking: "Why?" or "Why not?" or "Would you explain your reason for answering as you did?"

An even greater pitfall to avoid is asking the question that seems to require only "right" or "wrong" answers. This type of question can also lead to a dead end in the discussion. What is worse, however, is that such questions tend to imply a dogmatic mind-set on the part of the questioner. When you ask this type of question, you will usually get one of two opposite reactions. Either the young people will tell you what they think you want to hear, thus making any further discussion difficult, or some of the young people will get very argumentative and respond with an answer that is designed to contradict what they think is your opinion, a type of response that often results in a heated and nonproductive dispute.

There are many areas of life in general and the Christian faith in particular in which matters of right and wrong are very appropriate topics for discussion. But, as a general rule, youth (and people in general) tend to relate better to these verities about life and religion and to internalize them in relation to their own experiences when they can be led to make the discoveries on their own rather than having someone lecture them, no matter how subtly, about what they should believe.

11. **Ask open-ended questions.** A basic principle for leading discussions is: Rely mainly on open-ended questions. Ask questions that evoke opinions. Ask questions that will produce disagreement. Although it is good to be able to reach a group consensus on matters being discussed, it is not absolutely necessary. The important thing is to get people talking, to prod people into expressing their own ideas. To create this type of dynamic situation, you must have a climate in which people feel free to express their views. And good, carefully phrased, open-ended questions are your best tools for producing this type of climate.

In addition to using open-ended questions, you should project an open and accepting attitude toward everyone involved in the discussion. Be careful not to inhibit anyone with a put down like "That's ridiculous" or "How could you possibly believe that?" And make sure that the youth themselves do not squelch one another. Politeness, acceptance, and consideration should be the governing guidelines for any group discussion.

One technique for discussion groups is to have each person write down his or her responses to a series of open-ended questions *before* any discussion takes place. Such a procedure will often help to draw the shyer youth into the discussion, since they will have had a chance to formulate their plans privately before exposing their thoughts to the group. In this connection, it is also helpful to monitor the discussion by continually urging the less vocal members to express opinions and by gently restraining those who want to talk all the time. A good technique for increasing participation by the less vocal youth is the "circular response," a procedure by which you begin discussion of a particular question by going around the room and allowing everyone in turn a chance to give his or her response without it being

29

subject to comment by other members of the group.

12. **Begin with general questions, and then move to specific matters.** As a rule, most people are more comfortable with a discussion in which they begin really responding to general, nonthreatening questions and then move to more specific, riskier questions. For example, if you are discussing a movie, begin by asking questions such as: "How was the acting in the movie? Was it generally good or bad?" or "How was the pace of the movie—too fast, too slow and dull, or just about right?" or "What scenes made an impression on you?" Then, after the group has become comfortable with the discussion, move to specific, riskier questions like: "Which character(s) did you identify with? Why?" or "What do you see as the main message of the movie? Do you agree with this message? Why or why not?"

13. **Don't assume that you have all the answers; and don't be judgmental.** Although you may have—and should have—some definite ideas and opinions about topics being discussed by your youth group, try to see yourself as a fellow seeker with the youth. In many cases, you will probably find that the young people will have ideas and beliefs that are similar to yours. But there is also the very real possibility—as many of us youth workers have discovered—that your discussions with young people will lead you to new and better insights. Try to be open to the many sides of truth. Listen as much as—or more than—you talk. And, whatever you do, don't be judgmental. Young people, like all of us, need support in their efforts to discover valid guidelines for living. And they don't need to be told that they are way off target. Such an approach only engenders self-doubt and resentment. What you want to

produce is mutual trust and mutual discovery of how the Christian faith relates to our lives.

14. **Give your witness, ideas, and opinions; but save them until late in the discussion.** Many youth workers make one of two mistakes in leading young people in discussions. Either they are so dogmatic in presenting their views that the youth are absolutely turned off; or they so camouflage their views that the youth end up confused and faced with a lot of alternatives, not knowing where their adult leaders stand on controversial questions. Take a middle course. Don't voice your views so strongly that you inhibit the young people. But, on the other hand, don't be afraid to state where you stand. Lead discussions in an open manner by allowing free and unhampered expression of ideas by all involved, but don't let the youth go away from the discussion with the feeling that you have no opinions of your own. Be sure to state—usually at some point late in the discussion—just where you stand and what your opinions are. But be sure to do so in a way that says: I'm not perfect and I don't think that I have all the answers. I'm open to considering your opinions and other opinions that may differ from mine.

Guidelines 1 through 14 relate to leading discussions—a major part of any youth worker's job. They are given here because we consider them important enough to be listed in any statement on guidelines for youth workers. For more details and some different perspectives on this subject, see our chapter "Leading Discussions and Maintaining Group Life."

15. **Borrow ideas from other youth workers.** Creative youth ministry ideas by the

thousands are floating around throughout the church. Many youth workers often find their creativity is dried up. What can be done when that happens? The answer is simple—borrow. Be constantly on the lookout for a new approach, a creative idea, a different way of doing things. Find something that appeals to you, take a look at your own youth group, and ask: How can I adapt this method to make it meaningful for the youth with whom I work? Most youth workers will be flattered (sometimes even flabbergasted) to discover that you want to use one of their ideas.

16. **Meet with other youth workers for mutual support and exchange of ideas.** Try to make time for regular meetings with other people involved in youth ministry. Such meetings can be real eye-openers. For one thing, you will discover that, in a real sense, you are not alone. Most of the problems and successes that you experience in youth ministry are being experienced by others involved in this endeavor. And it is a great feeling to be able to share ideas and support. The number of resources and activities that you can learn about in such meetings is enormous. So get together with others who share your interest in youth. You will all be better off as a result.

17. **Read and listen; be on the lookout for resources.** Today there is a rebirth of interest in youth ministry. And, along with that renewed interest, there is a multitude of new resources for persons working in this field. Look through your denominational supply catalogues. Take a walk through a local religious bookstore. The resources are there in abundance.

The final chapter is an annotated bibliography of youth ministry resources; it will give you some help in determining the relative value of most of the resources now available in this field.

18. **Keep current on young people's concerns.** There are two main ways to keep up with what is happening with today's youth: through personal experience and through reading and study. Some of our most reliable insights about today's youth come from personal experience. Talk with the youth in your church. Find out what they are interested in. Discuss with them their activities, their interests, their school life, their values, their aspirations. Attend youth functions, such as plays, sports activities, concerts, and dances. If local authorities allow it, spend some time visiting with youth and teachers in the local schools; you can't begin to understand what the youth scene is all about if you do not have some knowledge of the school situation—the environment in which young people spend thirty to forty hours each week. And, if your school situation is anything like the one in my community, it may be a lot different from the situation that you and I knew when we were in junior high and high school.

One note of caution: Remember that most of the resources pertaining to today's youth scene describe the situation in general. You will need to filter these ideas through your own contacts with the youth with whom you work. Local societal, educational, and economic factors may produce a situation in which your youth are quite different from the norms. Even resources such as this book should be read in light of your own experiences with the youth whom you know personally. Read and learn but also be conscious of the fact that resources about youth in general are valuable for their insights about youth in general. They must be supplemented with your own experiences with the youth with whom you work.

19. **Have three-phase meetings and sessions.** It has been said that a good youth group meeting is like a good chess game: it has a beginning, a middle, and an end. First, the beginning. One of the dead spots in many youth programs is the opening. Young people, like adults, do not always arrive on time. Consequently, there is often a period when there are not enough people present for you to begin the main activities, but there are enough people present to constitute a good-sized group of bored individuals. The solution? Devise opening activities that can be experienced by a few people as they arrive and that can serve as lead-ins to the main part of the program. For good transition, these activities should be based on the same theme as the main part of the program.

The middle. This is the main part of your program. This part begins when your whole group is present. The major portion of your activities and discussions should take place during this section of your session.

The ending. The conclusion of a youth session should be easily recognizable as the ending of the program. Too many youth programs are allowed to fizzle out because the time for the session ran out. Plan for a definite ending for your session—and utilize it—even if it involves skipping from an unfinished middle section to the concluding activities. It is usually better to have a clear, definite ending to the session rather than to allow the main discussion to wither away under the pressures of the clock.

20. **Limit activities that require reading.** Some youth are not good readers and are embarrassed by that. Other youth do a lot of reading. Although we do not want to foster programs that have no intellectual content to them, there is a limit to the amount of reading that youth will do productively in a church setting. Some denominational publishing houses are beginning to recognize this limitation. Look at the church school and youth group resources being produced today. In many cases, you will find that the so-called "print content" of some youth resources is now limited to about 50 percent of the overall space in the publications, with much space being given to illustrations and learning activities. Of course, printed material is still of great value for use with youth, so don't hesitate to use printed resources. And don't shrink from asking the youth to do some reading and discussion in your meetings. But, if you want to achieve optimum results, limit this type of activity.

21. **Emphasize activities that can lead to discussion.** There are many springboards to discussion that can be used as alternatives to the read-and-discuss method. Try simulation games, role plays, quizzes, questionnaires, crossword puzzles, and so forth. Ideas on various creative teaching/learning activities for use with youth are given in our chapter on "Teaching Methods." For some excellent ideas on discussion-producing activities, see the sections on "Creative Communications" in the *Ideas* books and the multitude of ideas in the two collections *Recycle Catalogue* and *Recycle Catalogue II*. Further information on these resources is given in the final chapter of this handbook.

22. **Use music.** It is possible to have a successful youth ministry without utilizing music, but it is not easy. Music is a vital part of the lifestyle of today's youth. They listen to it. They dance to it. They study with it blaring in the background. They have it in their cars and in their portable radios and cassette players. And a wise youth worker will take advantage of this ready-made tool for teaching and relating to young people.

For a lot of ideas on this subject, see our chapter titled "Music! Music! Music!"

23. **Use media.** Media is not only one of the primary messages of our society; it is also an essential component of our modern environment. If you have never led young people in making movies, producing slide-and-tape presentations, discussing movies and music, or experimenting with video cassette recorders, you have missed out on one of the best tools available for youth ministry. The field is enormous and growing. And it is a field that the church in general would do well to get more involved with. For many ideas on this subject, see our chapters entitled "Media," "Videos," and "Resources."

24. **Have a way to evaluate and learn from your evaluations.** Many youth workers have an uneasy feeling that something is not right with their attempts at youth ministry. But they have difficulty in determining just what the problem is. There is no guaranteed way to solve this dilemma. But there is a procedure that can help, and that is the process of evaluation.

You should evaluate your youth programs on a regular basis: yearly, quarterly, monthly, and weekly. There should be separate evaluations by the youth and the adults, with each group examining the program on the basis of their own perspectives. But there should also be evaluations by the youth and adults working together.

In an evaluation, you should look back at what has occurred in a particular program; determine which aspects of the program were successful and which were unsuccessful; determine reasons for success and/or failure; and decide, on the basis of the evaluation, what changes should be made

in future programs. Evaluations can be very elaborate, with questions relating to many specific aspects of a program, or they can be very simple, with only a few general questions. The details of an elaborate, comprehensive evaluation would have to be worked out by you and the youth on the basis of the particular program being evaluated. For a simple, basic evaluation, however, a few questions are usually sufficient:

- What were the goals for this program? Were they achieved? Why or why not?

- Which parts of the program were most successful? Why? Which parts were least successful? Why?

- If you could redo this program, which parts would you alter? Why? What alterations would you make?

- What did you learn from planning and leading this program that can be helpful to you in dealing with future programs?

Then celebrate the achievements. Plan a special event or time to recall the "good times." And always thank and acknowledge those who were involved. These acknowledgments should be taking place, of course, throughout the year.

25. **Allow the Holy Spirit to work, do your best, and trust God to fill in the gaps.** It has been said that a great responsibility is taken off our shoulders when we relax and let God run the universe. This old saying is of special value for youth workers. I thank God that I do not have to be dependent only on my own abilities as I work with young people. Our mandate as youth workers is to do our very best. But, in the long run, we

have access to a power that is beyond us. The loving and almighty God is waiting in the wings to help us in our efforts.

So do your best. Examine yourself. Prepare yourself. And work hard. But trust God to work through the Holy Spirit to fill in the gaps in your attempts. Let your work with youth be pervaded by a spirit of prayer and the willingness to rely on God's help. How terrific it is to know that we can say about our work with youth what John Wesley said about his life: "The best of all is: God is with us!"

Almost all successful youth programs rely heavily on youth involvement in the planning and decision-making process. This is true for junior and senior high age levels and for church school and informal (fellowship, recreational, sharing) settings. There are several good reasons for this:

1. **People of any age participate more fully in events and projects which they have helped plan.** Preschoolers have more fun at parties when they have helped make decorations. Elementary children greatly prefer songs which they have selected. Junior highs are much more vocal when they have chosen the topics for discussion. Senior highs will often refuse to participate in activities they have had no share in planning.

The same logic applies to adult groups. I will contribute far more generously to the church budget if I have had a part in developing that budget. If a study group is offered on a broad basis in the church, I will take part *if* the topic interests me and *if* the day and time are convenient. If the study group is offered in response to my own suggestion or if I have helped plan it, I will take part if humanly possible and may even adjust my schedule to do so.

There are few exceptions to this rule: the greater the involvement of people at every point in the planning process, the greater their involvement in the class, group, or event.

2. **Involving young people in the planning process saves adult leaders the frustration of "guessing" what teenagers want to do.** Little is more frustrating than spending hours preparing for a class discussion only to find no one willing to participate because the topic is of no interest. Large sums of money and energy are wasted on parties and youth nights that will be poorly attended.

No matter how closely you work with young people, "assuming" that you know what they want is a needless risk and an affront to their individuality.

3. **If things fail, the whole burden does not rest on the adult leader or advisor!** No matter how careful your planning, some events will not be successful—no one can anticipate every possible variable. If young people are involved in planning, the adult leader is less "on the spot"; and all involved can grow in the evaluation process of understanding why things went wrong!

4. **When events are successful, the youth and adults who helped plan will share the resulting pleasure and satisfaction.** All of us want to feel important and needed. We want to feel as though we are people of worth, whose contributions make life better for others. Be willing to share the credit for well-planned activities!

The Best Way Is Not the Easiest Way

In spite of the obvious advantages, many adult youth workers are reluctant to involve young people in planning and decision-making. While youth involvement in planning is the *best* way to design total youth programs or specific activities, it is by no means the *easiest* way.

1. **Planning with young people involves a great deal of work and frustration.** Planning activities by yourself is almost always less time-consuming. To plan effectively with young people, you will often have to schedule special meetings with volunteers, officers, or committees.

2. **You must also be prepared to live with a certain amount of frustration and failure.** In one of the first youth fellowship

groups I advised, one young person had the responsibility of bringing refreshments each week, and another had the responsibility of arranging the activity for the evening. If refreshments were forgotten or activities badly planned, I always came through and "bailed out" the group. The young people all learned that whether they came through with refreshments or arrangements was irrelevant—if they did not do it, their advisor would! I felt hostile toward the group and badly imposed upon because I had to do so much work for them, but it was really my own fault. After I let the group go without refreshments two weeks in a row, the members learned that they would have to provide them. Young people need the opportunity to assume responsibility in order to grow and mature, but you cannot give them meaningful responsibility unless you are willing to risk occasional failure.

In another church setting, I met with a committee to plan an overnight retreat at the church. The committee members were in too big a hurry and left many details hanging. I resisted the temptation to do everything myself and let the retreat be a disaster. It was the last bad retreat for that group of young people! The next committee was extremely conscious of the disastrous retreat and wanted to prevent a reoccurrence.

3. **You will have to accept some decisions that are inconsistent with your personal wishes.** You may not want to study the topic that is of most interest to your group. If you are morally opposed to a group decision or if there are limitations that make their plans impractical, you should share your concern—and may even have to exercise veto power. You should do so, however, only with reluctance. Unless an ethical issue or overwhelming pragmatic barriers are involved, you should go along with plans which you have permitted the group to make. If you exercise veto power too frequently, the young people will correctly assume that you are playing games with them and are unwilling to give them any significant voice.

Steps in the Planning Process

Readers who have done a great deal of planning in church or professional life may find this section unnecessary. Most of us, however, need to be reminded of planning procedures. Other resources may express the steps differently, but here is the sequence I have personally found most helpful:

1. **Be sure of your overall purpose.** Whether planning for a class, an informal group, or a total church youth program, be certain that you and the young people clearly understand your common purpose. If the group is a Sunday morning educational class, you will want to choose activities and topics consistent with expectations of that class. If the group is a Sunday evening or mid-week, informal group, clarify the reason(s) for the group's existence: sharing, personal growth, recreation, evangelism, etc. Failure to be clear about purpose will often result in choosing activities that are competitive with other groups in the church or that fail to meet the needs of group members. Many fellowship groups have been destroyed by an advisor's insistence that something had to be "learned" each week. Such groups then become competitive with the church school and fail to offer the fun and growth in relationships that young people want and need. In a similar way, some church school classes have become frustrating for serious young people who want to do Bible study and talk about significant issues only to find

the hour continuously consumed by gossip and superficial visiting about the football game.

The purposes of church school classes, informal groups, and other gatherings are not always mutually exclusive, but each group should have a commonly held and identified purpose. Failure to be clear about this will frustrate the rest of the planning process. See the chapter on "What Groups Should We Offer?" for further help with this.

2. **Identify the specific day(s) for which you are planning.** A single class or activity? a month? a quarter? a year? The answer to this determines how specific you must get at any one planning session.

3. **Identify the resources available to you.** Have available copies of curriculum materials and resource books with which the planning group can work. Identify the amount of money available to order film, buy refreshments, etc. Make a list of people who would be willing to help your group.

4. **Brainstorm ideas.** After reviewing your purpose and identifying your target days and resources, share with the young people in listing as many topics or activities as possible. If you are planning for only one or two sessions of a class or group and like the curriculum suggestions, this process may not be a lengthy one. If you have few acceptable curriculum resources, you may need to develop a substantial list of options.

5. **Select the topics or activities that seem most in keeping with your purpose and the needs of the young people.** Members of the planning group may need to vote on their top one, two, three, or more preferences. Another approach to voting is giving each person three symbols to cast as votes, for instance: a square worth five points, a triangle worth three points, and a circle worth one point. This may give you a clearer spread on preferences.

6. **Decide what must be done to implement each topic or activity.** Now you must encourage the group to become extremely specific. Great ideas are of little benefit without a careful strategy for carrying them out. If you are relying in large part on a curriculum resource, you may find adequate steps and instructions developed for you. Generally speaking, you will need to tailor even the best curriculum guides to your situation.

See further suggestions in the subheadings of this chapter on "Planning for Church School" and "Suggestions for Informal Group Planning." Also note the separate chapters related to "The Church School" and "The Fellowship Group."

7. **Assign specific responsibilities to get the job done.** Who will get the refreshments? Who will put the announcement in the church bulletin? Who will ask the minister to visit the class? Who will have markers and newsprint available? Who will give the closing prayer? Who will order the film? Who will recruit homes for the progressive dinners? Who will call ahead to be sure the bowling alley accepts payment by check? Who will give the instructions for the simulation game?

As adult leader or advisor, you can be reasonably sure that if the preceding people are not identified, then *who* will be *you!*

8. **Carry out the plans.** You may have to do some checking and reminding to get this done, but let the young people carry out the responsibilities they have accepted.

9. **Evaluate what happened.** Take the time to think through what happened. What do you and the young people feel good about? Why? What went badly? Why? What persons were uninvolved? How could they have been drawn into the groups. What have you learned that can help you do a better job the next time?

Some Important Guidelines on Planning with Young People

1. **Do not offer problems or opportunities for group decision-making unless you are ready to live with group decisions.** In working with junior highs, you may want to restrict the opportunities offered. If you believe a church school class needs to have a quarter of solid Bible study, do not ask the group "What would you like to study next?" and then complain if no one suggests Bible study. Start by explaining why you think a quarter of Bible study would be good, and then offer some alternative biblical units from which the class can choose.

2. **Be sure that all preferences and desires are expressed.** Silence does not always mean consent. Help with comments and questions such as: "Will people without drivers licenses be able to get to the bowling alley?" "Will movies two weeks in a row be too expensive for some people?" "People who were in confirmation may have spent a lot of time studying that topic last year." "Bill does a good job with posters. Maybe he would help on publicity."

3. **Be certain members understand what responsibilities they have been asked to assume.** If plans are made for a number of weeks in advance, you may want to have a printed schedule that includes the names of people who are to give devotions, provide refreshments, present the session, take reservations, etc.

If group members repeatedly have difficulty remembering to carry through, you may need to help them develop a system of reminding each other through phone calls or some other means. It is best if you can avoid always being the one who reminds others.

4. **Avoid permitting too much responsibility to be pushed on one person.** The same young person should not always be the chief fund raiser, refreshment provider, or discussion director. It is no more healthy for the group to be dominated by one young person than by you as advisor. That young person will feel overworked, and other members will feel left out.

5. **Be sure the young people know that you are willing to help them.** Planning with a group does not mean keeping all your ideas to yourself. They need and want your input and may feel you do not care about them if you never make suggestions. There are some arrangements that an adult advisor may be able to make more easily. Just be sure that you share your ideas as suggestions rather than inflicting your will on the group.

Genuinely work to elicit ideas from everyone. Show your willingness to share in the work and preparation for the group, but be sure you are not doing all the work yourself.

6. **Good planning takes time.** Some groups or classes set aside a periodic meeting for planning. Some have a planning retreat or lock-in once a year. You may also find a need to meet with group officers, class teams, or planning committees. This may seem like a substantial investment of time, but the rewards include a higher sense of group ownership by the young people and a closer link between them and you.

Suggestions for
Informal Group Planning

Informal groups have a variety of purposes. In general, most tend to meet on a Sunday evening and are primarily focused on fellowship and recreation activities. The suggestions which follow may be helpful in planning with such groups.

1. **Unless the group is extremely small, officers should be elected.** Without officers, the group will still look toward one or two people for leadership. Those people may be the most dominating and vocal rather than the most respected members. Without officers, the advisor may be sought out for too much direction.

2. **A group of twenty or more people may well be too unwieldy for detailed planning.** If your group is a large one, you may want to have a planning committee which meets on a monthly basis to evaluate past activities and plan for new events. This group might consist of the officers, the adult advisor(s), and a representative from each age level (seventh grade, eighth grade, freshman, sophomore, junior, senior).

3. **You may want to help the group develop a regular system of sharing responsibilities.**

4. **Be sure group members know what activities or topics are scheduled.** If activities are tentatively scheduled for the entire year, see that each member has a copy of that schedule. Since plans change, a monthly schedule may also be appropriate. The schedule should indicate the nature of the activity, the date, the time, the cost, and the place. Special responsibilities should be clearly indicated.

5. **Make good use of the telephone for communication.** Have someone regularly designated to phone inactives. Have a telephone chain established for active members. The first person in the chain calls the second who calls the third, and so on. The last person calls the first who then knows the chain is complete. The chain can be used to remind the group of regular meetings or to share changes in plans.

6. **Have some form of survey or total group evaluation at least a few times a year.** This can be the basis for profitable group discussion and for future planning. Consider a form like this:

(1) I come to youth fellowship primarily because . . .

___ a. it's a way to get out of the house.

___ b. my friends are here.

___ c. I feel obligated to come because I'm part of the church.

___ d. I like the things we do.

___ e. (other)

(2) I think that . . .

___ a. People should have a right to participate in youth fellowship activities OR to do their own thing as long as they do not destroy stuff.

___ b. People should participate in youth fellowship activities that have been scheduled or NOT COME.

(3) The two most enjoyable youth fellowship activities we've done were:

a.

b.

(4) The two least enjoyable youth fellowship activities we've done were:

a.

b.

(5) How do you feel about gaining new members for youth fellowship?

___ a. I would be willing to help recruit new members by phone calling or visiting.

___ b. I would like to see new members, but I do not want to help recruit them.

___ c. I am really happy with the group as it is and do not particularly want new members.

(6) How much voice do you think you have in determining youth fellowship activities?

___ a. Lots of say.

___ b. Enough say.

___ c. Not very much.

(7) What other suggestions do you have for our group?

7. **Most informal groups find it helpful to have a retreat or lock-in near the beginning of the activity year.** This provides an opportunity to deepen group fellowship early in the year and to lay plans for major events during the year.

Planning for Church School

Involving young people in planning for church school classes is more difficult than for many other groups. Since many churches use a set curriculum for the church school, the number of options available may be few. Many young people anticipate the adult teacher assuming the major responsibility for the church school class.

Detailed help preparing for church school classes can be found in the chapter "The Church School." The following suggestions are concerned with involving young people in the planning process.

1. **Have young people lead *buzz groups* or activity groups during the church school hour.** If questions or instructions for those groups are clearly stated, this does not necessarily require much advance preparation by the youth.

2. **Young people can be involved in preparation by asking them to do specific tasks.** For example, they could interview doctors, lawyers, ministers, or other resource persons during the week.

3. **Planning for special projects during the year should be done with the involvement of the whole class.** Commitments to such things as the all-church Christmas program should not be decided *for* the class but *by* the class.

4. **Even the most rigid educational materials provide at least some flexibility.** Choices are provided for such things as:

● using an audio-visual resource or having a group discussion.

● sharing responses in a total group or sub-group.

● choosing what kind of creative activity to do: collages, banners, posters, paintings.

Whenever your resources and time permit, let the young people make those decisions.

5. **Experiment with class volunteers to help plan and lead a specific session.** This will necessitate your meeting with them during the week. Such an approach is frequently not attempted because of difficulty in finding a common meeting time. If only one, two, or three volunteers are involved, scheduling a meeting is not so difficult as with a larger group. Breakfast or supper meetings ("brown bag") often avoid major conflicts. If the experiment seems successful, you may want to establish a rotating schedule of helpers with the class.

6. **Some classes have had great success in letting class members choose the units of study for the year.** This may not be possible if your church is committed to using a dated curriculum resource. However, many denominations also offer undated study resources on a variety of topics. The topics to be covered in dated resources are usually available a year in advance.

You may want to have a planning committee brainstorm a listing of topics based on denominational resources, nondenominational resources, church resource persons, and community resource persons. Survey active (and inactive!) class members, and then develop a schedule for the year.

The following survey was developed by a church in central Illinois.

POSSIBLE TOPICS FOR THE HIGH SCHOOL GROUP DURING THE CHURCH SCHOOL HOUR

Check the eight or nine topics that would be of the greatest interest to you for study and discussion. Then put a double check by the topic that is of the greatest single interest to you.

____The Sermon on the Mount. (Matthew 5–7. The Beatitudes, the Lord's Prayer, loving your enemies . . .)

____The Second Coming of Christ. (Different interpretations. Solid Bible study to try to eliminate some of the misunderstandings about this.)

____The Occult and the Bible. (ESP, astrology, numerology, etc. What is the biblical witness in relationship to these things? Is there a relationship between biblical prophecy and some psychic phenomena?)

____Bioethics. (Abortion, genetic manipulation, mercy killings, etc. Perhaps involvement of a chaplain and a doctor in discussion.)

____The Racial Situation in Peoria [your community]. (Study of race relationships in Peoria [your community] from a Christian perspective. Perhaps involving the NAACP director and an inner-city project director.)

____Exploration of Our Church. (How does our church function? What is accomplished by the different organizations and boards? Why does our church need to be a more effective agent of Christ's

41

____service? Rap sessions with several church leaders.)

____Dynamics of Change. (How to live in a "Future Shock" world. Coping with technological progress. Effect of change on different generations.)

____Church Renewal. (What should the role of the church in the world be? What are the possibilities of making the church a better change agent in the world?)

____Problems of Senior Citizens. (What problems do the elderly face? How can we better understand them? What could our church do to be of more help to the elderly? How can young people get along better with senior citizens?)

____Poverty in Your Community. (Exploration of poverty in your own area from a Christian perspective. Involvement of various community resource people. Possibility of an action project.)

____World Religions. (Hinduism, Buddhism, Islam, Judaism . . .)

____Sympathy. (How do we express it? Is it good? How do we receive it?)

____Death and Dying. (What is the dying process like? What happens after the event of death? Possibility of some good films, a visit to a funeral home. What is the Christian hope?)

____Building a Personal Faith. (How to relate to God in a confused world. How to cultivate a meaningful prayer life. How to share God's love with others. How to use your faith as a basis for moral decisions.)

____Looking at Yourself. (What are you like? Can you change yourself? How do others see you? How does God see you?)

____Prophets. (Amos, Isaiah, Jeremiah, Micah, and other radicals. What did these men say? Does their message speak to our age as well?)

____Dating and Marriage in Christian Perspective. (The relationship between the sexes. What is proper? What is improper? What builds lasting relationships? How can problems be handled? How much does it cost to get married?)

____Political Life and Christian Faith. (Invite some area political figures such as the mayor and congressional representatives to visit with the group. What are their views on major issues? Do they have a personal faith? Does their faith affect their decisions?)

____The Family. (Relationships between brothers and sisters; relationships between parents and young people. How can love be meaningfully expressed in the family? How to cope with family problems. Perhaps some involvement of parents in the group.)

____Worship as Celebration. (Study of the meaning of Christian worship. Evaluation of what we do in worship in our church. Planning of a service of worship.)

____Contemporary Music and the Christian Faith. (What do the songs of today say to us? Are some of them expressions of faith? Are some the opposite?)

____American Indians and Christian Missions. (Information from class members who visited Indian missions last summer as resource persons. What

42

is the church doing for American Indians? What are the real problems American Indians face, and why are they confronted with them? Did churches help create these problems?)

____South Africa and the Church. (White supremacy is the law in South Africa. The Christian churches there have been opposing many government policies—sometimes at great cost. There are films and other good resources related to this topic.)

____Education. (What makes an educated person? What role is played by the family? the individual? the public school? the church?)

____Film Festival. (Viewing and discussing some of the excellent films available on religious and social issues.)

____Counseling. (Basic techniques in listening to the problems of others. How can you tell if a friend really needs professional help? How to avoid giving the wrong advice. What does the Christian faith suggest about counseling methodology?)

____Your suggestion.

The Youth Council Concept

The administrative structure of local churches varies with such factors as denominational affiliation, geographical location, and membership size. In many churches, youth ministry is largely the responsibility of an education commission, committee, or board. This is particularly true for church school classes which are part of the total educational program of the church. Informal groups are often not directly related to an administrative group in the church but function (begin, grow, fail, and die!) fairly autonomously.

An increasing number of local churches are recognizing the need for an administrative group that looks at the total needs of young people in the church. Such a group is concerned about junior highs, senior highs, and college-age young people. It will be concerned about adequate educational, fellowship, recreational, musical, and service opportunities for these ages. This group, consisting of both adults and young people, may be called a youth board, youth council, or committee on youth ministry. For the purpose of this discussion, the designation youth council will be used.

A youth council insures that the needs of young people are not forgotten in the life of the church. If your church does not have a youth council or has had difficulty making one function effectively, consider these guidelines:

1. **The membership must be carefully chosen and should include representatives of all who are concerned with youth ministry:** one or more church school teachers of youth classes; one or more adult advisors of informal groups; an adult related to music in the church (youth choir director if there is one); one or more parents of teenagers; the minister or a member of the professional staff (employed youth worker, Christian education director). There should be at least as many young people as adults, including: at least one seventh or eighth grader; at least one ninth or tenth grader; at least one eleventh or twelfth grader; at least one college-age person; at least one previously inactive young person.

The youth members of the council may be elected by classes and/or informal groups. However, it is important to include at least one young person who has been relatively inactive. This young person may be chosen by a church nominating committee or the youth council itself.

Some churches choose to relate college-age people to adult classes and groups. The needs of this age level are not directly dealt with in this book and are very complex. Some are in college; some are employed; some are married; some are single; some have children. Ideally, their needs should be dealt with separately from junior and senior highs. They are suggested for inclusion on the youth council for two reasons. First, the needs of this group are too frequently overlooked by the church. Second, people of this age have a great deal to share in the area of youth ministry because of their closeness in age to junior and senior highs.

Small churches may find it impossible to have representatives from each suggested category. In some instances, the youth council may effectively include all the active young people.

2. **Before beginning a youth council, seek approval from the minister and the primary administrative body in the church** (Board of Deacons, Administrative Board, Parish Council). You need their good wishes and their empowerment of the youth council. The youth council needs to be permanently represented on this administrative body.

3. **The youth council should be responsible for and have control of that part of the church budget related to youth ministry.** (See the chapter on funding.)

4. **The youth council needs to meet with regularity in order to function well.** This may be a monthly meeting but should never be less frequent than quarterly. If your church has not had a youth council before and needs a major re-evaluation of youth ministry, weekly meetings could be needed for a time.

5. **The youth council should be making plans for as much as a year in advance.** This is particularly important in making funding requests to the church, which probably sets budget on a calendar year basis. It is also important to allow substantial time to prepare for a summer trip or to promote a new group.

6. **The youth council, like any group, should be careful not to undertake too many projects at once.** Much of the youth council's function will be in coordinating the programs of other groups. However, some projects may involve the council as primary sponsor:

- Sponsoring a film festival for junior and senior highs
- Developing a sex education program
- Starting a new informal group
- Offering special interest groups during Lent
- Remodeling the youth classrooms
- Creating a youth lounge
- Calling on all inactive young people

7. **See the chapter "What Groups Should We Offer?" for further help in evaluating the youth opportunities in your church.**

8. **Develop a simple list of purposes for the youth council and work to keep the youth council and other church groups aware of those purposes.** The youth council will insure that the educational, worship, fellowship, recreational, music, and service needs of junior and senior highs are met in the church by . . .

- evaluating and improving ongoing groups,

44

● making the best possible use of funds available for youth ministry,
● developing a program to reach inactive young people,
● insuring that the needs of young people are remembered by other groups in the church, and
● offering special, short-term opportunities for young people.

Youth Representatives on Other Groups

An important part of youth planning includes having adequate youth representation on any church group concerned with young people. This can include the primary administrative group and also groups responsible for education, worship, property, and even social concerns!

Many churches which have attempted placing young people on a large number of boards and committees have been frustrated. The young people tend to withhold their opinions in those groups and sometimes withhold their presence as well. They often feel overwhelmed by the number of adults present, and they may feel that their representation is token. Some things can be done to help with this:

1. **Never assign only one young person to an adult group.** Assign young people in pairs. If the adult group is a large one, you may need three or four youth representatives.

2. **Provide training for the youth representatives** to help them understand the purposes and procedures of the group to which they have been appointed or elected.

3. **Be certain that the chairperson of the group and the other adult members understand the importance of youth representation.** Encourage these people to genuinely accept and involve the young people but not to put them on the spot with questions like: "Now, what do our young people think?" That question, asked as an afterthought and in a paternalistic voice, will not be appreciated. The youth representatives need to be involved as people in their own right.

4. **Insure that those serving as youth representatives have an opportunity to share their experiences in youth council, church school classes, or informal groups.**

45

5 WHAT GROUPS SHOULD WE OFFER?

A Common Error

In American Protestantism, the focus of youth programming has often been on some kind of Sunday evening fellowship group. In the 1940s and 1950s, many of these groups were well-attended. Relatively small congregations could expect twenty young people to come each Sunday evening, and large congregations might expect as many as a hundred. Comparable Roman Catholic activities were well-attended. The 1960s brought rapid decline in participation for many of these groups, and that decline continued into the 1970s. The 1980s brought slight gains in youth participation for some churches, but the changes were not dramatic. The 1990s need to be a time of major renewal for youth programs.

One of our common errors in church programming has been the failure to adequately define a group's purpose. When our society was more rural in nature and lacking in community activities for young people, the motivation to attend a church youth group was much higher. Today, most communities have ever increasing numbers of scout, school, YMCA, YWCA, and other community programs aimed at teenagers. Many teenagers also have part-time employment.

Opportunities such as going to the movies, bowling, skating, and eating out are readily available; and many young people have adequate financial resources to take advantage of these opportunities. While teenagers living in rural areas may not find such opportunities within their own communities, easy access to automobiles, enough money for gasoline, and improved highways place recreational and social facilities within an hour of all but the most isolated young person. Currently, the so-called energy crunch has not significantly affected teenage driving habits. Most school parking lots are jammed—not with faculty cars but with the cars of students. The competition for young people's time is intense, and the church does not always come out a winner. Many local churches need to take serious inventory of their youth groupings.

Take a few moments to list the youth group opportunities in your church. There may not be any or there may be several. Include classes, fellowship groups, choirs, etc. When does each group meet? Why does it meet at that particular time? What is the group attempting to accomplish? How well does it relate to the needs of teenagers?

Many churches have Sunday evening youth fellowships because "there has always been one" and "teenagers need to be in the church." Such reasons are not precise and probably not adequate justification for the existence of a program. Some careful evaluation of groups offered and more precise definition of group purpose may pay real dividends.

Your church may be one of those which no longer has any classes or groups for youth. If this is the case, you need to determine whether there really are no teenagers in your church or community or whether they are simply inactive in church. In some churches, the excuse is frequently that another congregation has all the young people in the area. "The Baptists (or Methodists or Presbyterians or . . .) have already stolen our young people." Such statements are often loaded with hostility and very often are exaggerations. A careful study of your own church roles may reveal several teenagers who are not involved in another group. A community survey will probably show only a small percentage of young people actively involved in any congregation.

Involve Others in Evaluation

If you believe the youth programming in your church needs a major evaluation, you need to involve others in the process. If a youth council already functions in your church, then that group is the logical one to do a reassessment of your programming. See the chapter "Planning with Young People" for information on youth councils.

If your church does not have a youth council (and most do not), try forming an informal task force. Such a task force should include the minister, a few adults who work directly with young people (teachers, music directors, or group advisors), a few parents, and several young people. If you involve only one or two young people, they may well be too intimidated by the adults present to honestly share their feelings. If your group has twelve people, six of them should be teenagers. Be sure the teenagers are not all the same year in school or the same gender. You may want to ask one or two inactive teenagers to be part of the task force and to help in evaluation and planning.

Begin as a task force or council by examining what your church currently offers. What is the average attendance of each group? What is the commonly understood purpose? What are the strong points? The weak points?

When some consensus has been reached concerning each group, spend some time sharpening the purpose of each group. If you cannot arrive at a clear purpose, that in itself may raise question about continuing the group. Then brainstorm for ideas that could improve existing groups. Select the best ideas and make plans to implement them. You may need the approval of other groups in the church before implementing some changes, particularly those involving financial resources.

Should You Start a New Group?

Once you have considered ways of improving existing groups, you may want to give consideration to new groups that might be offered. Responding to questions such as the following may help you determine whether you need any new groups:

1. **Do young people tend to become inactive in your church when they reach a certain age?** If so, you may need a group that will appeal more to older teens. High school seniors often have different interests and concerns than freshmen.

2. **Do the same groups span both junior high and senior high people?** If so, and if there are enough young people in your church, you may want to create separate groups for junior highs and senior highs. Combining these age levels is possible but should be done only when there is no realistic alternative.

3. **Do you have young people who want a more serious effort at Bible study, prayer, or spiritual growth?** By all means start a group for them rather than have them become church dropouts.

4. **Do your young people have some interests and needs that are not met adequately in the community?** Many school districts, because of financial difficulty, are eliminating drama, art, and music programs. Drama, art, and music can be very appropriate means of expressing the Christian faith and at the same time meeting the creative needs of young people.

5. **Do young people in your church have other special interests?** One youth council decided to offer a midweek film discussion group. Group members met in homes to watch a movie on television and then

47

discussed it from a Christian perspective. Refreshments ranged from popcorn to hamburgers. Once a month the group would attend a movie at a local theater and then go out for pizza. The effort was successful—the teenagers had a great time, and it became the best attended youth activity at the church. The pastor joined the group once or twice a month to share a biblical perspective on the films.

It is important not to begin more than one new group at a time. Careful publicity and personal contacts are crucial if a new group is to be successful. Decide what group would be most beneficial for your church, and then focus on that effort. You should decide in advance what minimal number of people is needed to start the group and what the maximal size should become. A movie discussion group might be permitted and encouraged to be as large as most homes could accommodate. A Bible study group could be cumbersome with over ten people, unless the leader is very skillful or the group is subdivided for discussion. If you are going to set an upper limit on a group, be sure to include that information in your publicity so that no one is offended if he or she expresses interest too late to be included. Save the names of such people, and provide a new group for them as soon as possible.

Publicity about both existing and new groups needs to be as personalized as possible. Bulletin announcements, church newsletters, and mass mailings should be utilized, but don't expect to be swamped with responses. Phone calls and personal visits by both adults and young people will yield far better results.

A Youth Survey

If your church is really serious about evaluating youth programming and initiating some new groups, you may want to try a different strategy. Actually take the time to survey all the young people connected with your church—both active and inactive. Get their feelings about the church, classes, youth groups, etc. Find out what changes would be of interest to them and what new groups would be attractive. A survey can be conducted in several ways. You can do so by mail, but returns are minimal. Be sure to enclose a stamped, addressed envelope for return of the survey.

The survey can be handled more informally and with virtually 100 percent response if done by phone or personal visits. Try involving several active adults and young people in this process, so that no one person has too many contacts to make. Some larger churches might consider employing a college student during the summer to conduct a survey. One of the churches I pastored used a college student two consecutive summers with great success.

Personal visits, whether from the pastor, a college person, adults, or young people, are a way of communicating the church's genuine interest. Mail surveys often hint of trying to "sell" something. A personal visit is an opportunity to show the church's love and to become acquainted with inactive as well as active young people.

Regardless of the manner in which you conduct such a survey, be sure to keep the individual responses. Persons indicating interest in a particular group should be contacted again when that group has been formed.

If you live in a small community, you may want to consider cooperating with other churches in the town in a survey of all the junior and senior highs. Whether this is realistic depends on the spirit of cooperation and amount of trust present among the churches. You may even discover that you can most effectively provide group opportunities by working ecumenically.

In a survey, you should attempt to obtain the following kinds of information:

1. How active or inactive is the young person?

2. If active, why? Parental pressure? Enjoyment of the church? Personal dedication?

3. How does this person feel about existing groups? Try to get specific complaints, suggestions for improvement, etc.

4. What new opportunities would be attractive to the young person? Provide some suggestions for reaction.

5. What are the names of other young people in the church with whom this person would like to be in a group?

6. Are there specific adults in the church that this person believes would make good advisors?

Be sure to interpret any changes which are proposed to the minister and the main governing bodies of the church. If you need financial assistance to conduct a survey or to start a new group, don't be bashful about asking for such help. Most churches are concerned about their young people and simply need encouragement to provide adequate finances for Christian education and youth work. The minister and church nominating committee should be enlisted if new adult leaders are to be obtained. If the young people themselves feel that a particular person would be a good teacher or advisor, you may want to have them make contact with that person. A few years ago, I turned down a social worker who asked me to lead a personal growth group for some teenagers who were on probation. A few days after my visit with the social worker, the six young people who needed such a group came to my home and asked me to help. I was able to tell the social worker I was too busy but not those six young people!

What About Short-term Interest Groups?

Most of the groups discussed thus far involve two assumptions about participating young people. First, they assume that the groups can offer a broad enough range of topics or activities to hold the interest of all those in the group. Second, they assume that the young people are willing to stay committed to the group for several months or, in the case of some classes and fellowship groups, several years. These may be valid assumptions. If young people are intimately involved in planning, if the group purposes are clearly stated, and if topics and activities are changed with reasonable frequency, young people may well enjoy being part of the group for an extended period of time. If many of their own needs are being met, they will "hang in" for activities that appeal more to others.

Every church, however, has young people who are simply not willing to commit themselves to a Sunday school class or fellowship group for months at a time. Certainly commitment is an important part of the Christian faith, but there is a danger in too strongly identifying commitment to

49

Christ with commitment to a particular group.

In adult work, churches have recognized the value of short-term study, prayer, and interest groups. This model, however, has not been carried into youth work. A great many churches offer adults such opportunities as marriage enrichment, Bible study, mission study, heritage classes, etc., for specified amounts of time—generally four to ten weeks. Some people will join a group in which they have a special interest much more readily than a traditional class that involves an eternal commitment.

One reader of an early manuscript questioned the interest group concept: "Our Sunday school class changes topics every four weeks anyway. Why can't people just come in for the period of time they are interested? Why can't people come to fellowship group on the nights there are activities in which they are interested? What difference does it make to offer short-term special interest groups?"

The answer is that it makes a great deal of difference. Consider the barriers involved with enlisting new people in an ongoing group on a short-term or occasional basis:

● You always encounter the problem of integrating new people into the group.

● By the time those people may have become nominally integrated, the topic that drew them will have been abandoned; and they will be ready to leave.

● However, the regular attenders will often resent their leaving—taking it as a personal rejection. The regulars may communicate that resentment, thereby guaranteeing that the short-term visitor will not return.

● Most churches do not have an effective means established to publicize topic changes in existing groups, so usually only regular group members know when special opportunities come.

Young people, like most adults, have a tremendous fear of rejection. Breaking into an existing group poses the threat of rejection and all the accompanying anxieties. High motivation is a necessity for overcoming those anxieties, and most young people who are not regular in attendance do not have that much motivation.

The ongoing opportunities are important and basic to the youth programming of most churches. What is said in this chapter about short-term, special interest groups is not intended as an argument against the ongoing groups. Consider, however, the following arguments for offering special opportunities:

● If such groups are offered out of response to expressed needs and interests (determined from a youth survey or youth visits), they will have appeal to some normally inactive young people.

● Becoming part of a new group is far less threatening to an inactive young person than trying to work into an existing group.

● The short-term nature of such groups helps young people feel more free to commit themselves.

● Adult leadership is easier to recruit for a short length of time (4-10 weeks) than for an entire year. This also permits you to utilize adults with specific skills: doctors, attorneys, the pastor, funeral home directors, teachers, psychologists, etc.

50

• Growth in programming can be accomplished more easily by adding groups than by increasing existing groups. While most interest groups should be intentionally short-term, you may involve young people who will want to form an ongoing group of their own or who will be open to joining a new ongoing group after having had a good short-term experience.

• Interest groups will often involve a mixture of previously active and inactive young people. This contact can prove very healthy and helps young people in each category eliminate some of their previous misconceptions about the others: "Those who don't come to youth group are into booze and drugs." "The people in that church think they're better than people like me."

Starting Interest Groups

Just announcing an interest group in the bulletin and church newsletter will not guarantee a successful group. Careful preparation is crucial, especially the first few times an interest group is offered. The following guidelines should be meticulously followed (they are not listed in any particular order—some will overlap, and all are important):

1. **Be sure there really is interest in the topic you are offering.** New groups should be formed on the basis of information from surveys or visits to both active and inactive young people. If you do not have such data, get it before offering a group.

2. **Recruit specific persons for the group.** Contact, by phone or personal visit, the young people who have such an interest.

3. **Determine the minimum number necessary to begin the group and also the maximum the group can accommodate.** The maximum may depend on subject and available leadership.

4. **Be certain you have good adult leadership before recruiting young people.** Ideally, the adult who will be advising the group should be part of the recruiting process.

5. **As you contact the first young people for the group, ask them who else they think would be beneficial.** They may even suggest some young people who have no church connection—GREAT!!

6. **You may want to involve the young people themselves in determining the day and time for group meetings.** This should be established as quickly as possible. If a regular meeting time is established with the first three or four interested people, you will find others whose schedules will coincide. Try to avoid the trap of recruiting twelve young people only to discover there is no time that will accommodate all twelve. If you do encounter young people who wish to participate but whose schedules are in hopeless conflict, keep a record of them—perhaps they can be involved in a future group.

7. **Determine the number of sessions needed, the resources needed, and the cost (if any) before recruiting young people.** They have a right to know as much as possible about the group.

8. **While you should not rely on bulletins and newsletters to recruit the core members for a new group, do take advantage of those means for additional publicity.**

9. **Be sure to include get-acquainted and trust-building activities in the first few sessions, regardless of the topic for the group.** An overnight lock-in at the church or a weekend retreat can be an ideal way to begin a new group.

10. **Only begin one group at a time.** If you discover there are more interested people than one group can accommodate, start another group later. Trying to do too much at once will doom you to failure.

11. **While some initial planning should precede the recruitment of group members, be sure to leave some decisions for the group.** For example, if you are going to offer a "Preparing for Marriage" group, you will want an advisor, a set number of sessions, and a basic resource selected before recruiting group members. The group itself should help determine how much time will be spent on particular issues.

But We're Too Small

Don't be discouraged if your church is so small that you only have five or six young people. Focus on those young people. Find out what they need and want from the church and from life itself. You may have only one group or class, but that group will be successful if it really starts with the needs of your young people. You may be able to expand opportunities by cooperating with another church or churches.

Avoiding the Yes/No
Discussion Syndrome

Many of the frustrations of youth work center around trying to stimulate good discussions. Questions calling for more than a yes or no response bring a depressing stillness to many youth groups. There are other groups in which the bulk of the discussion always seems to be carried by the adult teacher or advisor and one or two young people—with everyone else as spectators.

There are no guaranteed approaches to stimulating meaningful discussions. The following suggestions are offered with the knowledge that they will not work in every situation, but they should help in many.

1. **As much as possible, try to direct discussions toward concerns raised by the young people themselves.** If problems at school or at home consistently are raised, allow time for exploring those concerns.

2. **Attempt to begin any discussion as close as possible to the lives and concerns of your group.** If you want to deal with the story of the Prodigal Son, try beginning by asking the class to share situations in which they have needed the forgiveness of someone. Then look at the biblical account.

3. **Questions calling for a yes or no response are all right if followed by a question calling for why or how or under what circumstances.** Young people do have reasons for their emotions, ideas, and concerns. Give them opportunity to share.

4. **In a small group, you may often want to conduct informal opinion polls:**

   ● "The story of the Prodigal Son features three dominant personalities:

the father, the prodigal son, and the faithful son. Raise your hand if you most strongly identified with the father, the prodigal son, or the faithful son. Why did you respond like that?"

● "I'm interested in knowing how you think unexcused absences should be handled by the schools. Let's go around the circle and share ideas."

● "I've noticed that church attendance seems to go down on the Sundays we have communion. Let's take a class poll: How many try to miss when you know communion will be served? How many make a special effort to come for communion? How many really don't care? Share something of why communion makes you feel comfortable or uncomfortable."

5. **You may want to use opinion polls or attitude surveys that are in your curriculum resources or that have been prepared by you in advance.** These often precipitate good discussions. If the material is especially controversial, you may want to share the survey results in summary form rather than putting specific individuals on the spot for their responses. Some examples may be found in other chapters.

6. **Lack of response to a question may reflect lack of understanding of the material being discussed or of the question itself.** Another minister and I, who are located 500 miles apart, experienced identical problems in discussing a film with high school people. The film, *Fiesta,* is an excellent retelling of the story of the Prodigal Son in a Mexican-American setting. Both of us were unable to elicit discussion because the young people did not remember the biblical story

of the Prodigal Son. Consequently, questions like these had no meaning: "Who represents the prodigal son in the film? How did the film differ from the biblical story of the Prodigal Son?" It was necessary to back up and look at the biblical story before continuing discussion.

When you find it necessary to rephrase a question or to review background information before continuing discussion, be careful not to do so in a condescending or derogatory way. Neither you nor the young people are necessarily at fault when a question is not understood. Just back up good-naturedly and try again!

7. **Don't be afraid to play the "devil's advocate" to provoke discussion.** Views sometimes need to be stated in the extreme to gain reaction. For example:

● "No one seems to care whether people have the right to an abortion. Suppose your sister or girl friend had been raped by a prowler. Should she have a right to an abortion? Why or why not?"

● "Heaven sounds good to me. In fact, I really can't see why a person should bother doing anything in this life except praying and going to church. The best thing that can happen is to die. Isn't that biblical?"

If you do play the devil's advocate, be sure you eventually clarify your own views.

8. **Consistently reinforce sharing in the group.** You don't have to agree with a young person to express appreciation for his or her sharing openly. If group members are very frequently "put down," they will soon learn not to respond. The best way of insuring open discussion is by consistently reinforcing what young people say—by direct agreement, by appreciation for openness, or by asking questions for clarification.

Relating to the "Silent" Member

No matter how skillful you are in group work, there will always be some people who are particularly quiet in any group. You should not simply assume that silence means acceptance of what others in the group have planned or expressed. It is also unfair to assume that silence communicates lack of interest. Some people are by nature quieter than others. The world is not filled with extroverts (you may not be one yourself). We had a foster daughter for several months who was extremely shy in any group situation. She said almost nothing in her school classes and in Sunday school. Yet, she would come home filled with ideas she had gained from listening to others. While she was not verbally active in any group outside of the family, she was mentally active and felt very positive toward most groups to which she belonged. Respect the right of persons to choose how much of themselves they want to share in a group.

Many shy people, however, actually do want to share more of their own questions, doubts, feelings, and opinions. If you and the rest of the group show genuine acceptance of such persons, they will feel more comfortable in self-expression. You should be certain that even the most silent member is asked for his or her opinion on some occasions, or that person may feel conspicuous or excluded. Assist the group with questions or observations such as:

● "The bowling party sounds good to me, but I wonder if everyone here enjoys bowling."

● "Bob, I'd really like to know how you feel about our group visiting a funeral home."

● "There are several in the group who haven't expressed an opinion yet. I wonder if we could just go around the circle and see what everyone thinks."

● "I think these retreat plans are basically good ones, but only three of the ten people in the group have shared opinions. Are there any other suggestions?"

● "Sharon, you have a good scientific mind. What do you think the paragraph about genetic manipulation means? I'm having trouble understanding it."

Cooling the Dominator

The opposite extreme from the silent member is usually a more serious threat to the group. Some people consistently monopolize conversations. It is important to recognize that those who dominate others are often doing so because of deep feelings of insecurity and an intense desire to "prove" personal worth. While one is tempted to put the group dominator "in his place" or to ask him or her to "shut up," that may not be the best solution. A better strategy may be to involve others more fully. If discussion is really being blocked or bogged down by one person, suggest to the group that you would really like to hear everyone's opinion. Going around a circle or table so that everyone shares his or her feelings may seem artificial, but it can be very effective, without directly confronting the dominator.

In some instances, a perpetual dominator may have to be confronted. If this must be done, talk with that person when other group members are not around. Try to be as understanding and affirming as possible, but explain that you would like others to feel more free to express opinions. Remember that dominating people often do have low self-images and need affirmation of their worth.

Conflict Management

During the Vietnam War, some Christian people used their understanding of the Christian faith and the Bible to defend our country's involvement in the war. Other Christian people used the same sources to oppose our involvement. Differences of opinion were strong all across our country. Some people left political parties, churches, and even families because of the intensity of those differences.

Differences of opinion are inevitable within any group, and some conflict is certain to arise. As a group leader or advisor, you should use care in the handling of conflict, but do not be needlessly afraid of it.

In 1 Corinthians, the Apostle Paul speaks at great length about divisions within the early church. The presence of differing views does not make a group un-Christian but reflects the diversity of humankind. You should not be disturbed when some conflict arises. If opinions are not openly expressed within the group, grudges and resentment may be harbored outside of it. When controversial issues arise (whether about war, drugs, salvation, sex, or group decisions), encourage all people to express their feelings. Recognize that the differences will exist even if you do not permit their expression. Urge persons holding strong opinions to explain the reasons for those opinions so that the group may better understand them.

When conflict arises over group decision making, special care should be used. Compromise may be a solution in some instances, but seek "everybody wins" answers when possible. If a youth group is planning a summer trip and members are divided between going to Washington, D.C. and going to Seattle, you cannot pragmatically do both—at least not unless the group is very large and can be split. Most programming decisions, however, are not of that magnitude. If part of a group wants to meet the day after prom and part does not, meet with those who want to and avoid criticizing those who choose not to meet. If part of a group wants to study the Sermon on the Mount and part wants to discuss the Christian implications of rock music, do both. If the group cannot pragmatically be split for a few weeks, schedule one subject at a different time in the year. The latter alternative is often the best—not only because an intentionally small group in the first place may be difficult to divide, but also because young people grow by being exposed to new material and ideas. Most young people will not oppose studying material that is not their top personal preference, as long as they feel their own interests are also being met or will be met.

If conflict arises frequently in your group, you may want to spend some time discussing conflict and divisions as such. Emphasize the reality of humankind's diversity and the fact that the Christian community needs the talents and ideas of many people. The discussion on the nature of the church as the body of Christ in 1 Corinthians 12 may be particularly helpful. Also, lift up the acceptance which Jesus showed to all people, including people with whom he disagreed.

Discipline Problems

Another kind of conflict is also inevitable for many groups. That is the conflict that arises over the behavior of group members: the junior high boy who won't sit still; the two girls who hold a private conversation instead of giving attention to the group; the girl who tells her parents she is at the church but who actually meets a boy of whom her parents disapprove; the fellows and gals who pollute the church restroom with cigarette smoke; the rowdy fellows who sit on ping-pong tables and fence with shuffleboard sticks. All of the preceding problems occur in thousands of church youth groups and classes every week! A great many Sunday school teachers and youth group advisors have quit in frustration over discipline problems. These problems could be discussed in many sections of the book but are especially appropriate here because of the frequency with which they destroy discussions.

Answers to someone else's discipline problems are easier than solving one's own. I grew very impatient with the inability of a junior high class staff to control behavior until I went with the group for an overnight retreat! I lost my temper with the kids (and my impatience with the teachers) when two fellows broke a table at the same moment a girl threw a shuffleboard puck into the glass front of a pop machine!

Similar problems are encountered not only in church groups but also in other voluntary organizations and in the public schools. A committee of Girl Scout leaders in one urban community listed "poor discipline" as the number one reason for losing adult volunteers! Many school teachers resign each year because of discipline problems in school.

I have already hinted at the reality that there are no easy or magical solutions in the area of discipline. The two most common solutions are yelling at offenders and kicking out repeated offenders. Several members of the Girl Scout committee referred to above felt a major solution to keeping adult volunteers in scouting would be to encourage leaders to kick all discipline problems out of the troop. If one were to rigidly apply that standard to some scout troops (and church groups) with which I am acquainted, the result would be no more scouts! In the case of the public schools, the logic is just as poor. Most of those who cause discipline problems at school do so because of real dislike of attending school. When a person who hates school is suspended or expelled for bad conduct, that person has not been punished, but actually rewarded for bad behavior!

I will readily acknowledge that I yelled at the junior highs who tore up the table and pop machine! Unfortunately, my yelling at them accomplished little more than gaining their attention for a few moments. Yelling is generally ineffective and is deeply resented by most young people.

What should you do then? Let a few people destroy the church? Permit each group discussion to end in five different private conversations? Recognizing that our common solutions are ineffective can at least represent the beginning of more productive approaches.

1. **Be sure you understand why discipline problems are occurring.** If you understand the reasons for their actions, you may be able to respond better to the troublemakers. Ask yourself questions like these:

● Are several people really bored with the material or activities being used in the group? If so, you need to talk about this as a group and try some other approaches.

● Are there serious problems in the home of a troublemaker? Many young people whose parents have had a divorce or who have lost a parent by death may be filled with anxiety or even anger and may be starved for attention. Try to relate to those needs and help others in the group to be aware of them.

● Is the group affording adequate opportunities for meaningful participation by group members and real variety in activities? Those who feel shut out of participation may seek attention in other ways.

● Are there friends in the group who haven't had much time earlier in the day to visit with each other? If so, it may be better to permit ten minutes of informal visiting for everyone before trying to initiate serious discussion or planned activities. After all, adults demand the same right to greet friends and share personal concerns!

2. **Take opportunity at least once a year to talk about discipline and expectations of the group.** Rather than beginning with a list of your complaints and demands, try asking the young people to set some standards.

● Why do you think we have so many interruptions of others in this group?

● What do you think are the main behavior problems in this group?

● What do you think you have a right to expect from each other in terms of courtesy and respect?

57

● What do you think I, as advisor, should have a right to expect from the group?

● What do you think you have a right to expect from me as advisor?

Such an approach keeps the stigma from falling too heavily on the one young person acting up on a particular day. If the young people themselves set some rules or expectations, they will be more faithful to them and less resentful of them.

3. **When discipline problems seem to occur on a minor level as attention-getters, try to ignore them!** If someone is starved for attention, negative attention may be preferred to none at all. Your complaint or criticism may be reinforcing a behavior that will disappear if it produces no obvious results. Work just as hard to give positive attention to that person or persons when behavior is satisfactory or good.

4. **If a discipline problem cannot be ignored, handle it as calmly as possible.** If you must yell to get the attention of the group, lower your voice as quickly as possible. Once you have the group's attention, they will be much more responsive to a calm, quiet voice. Remember that people have been yelling at them for years with little result, so why should yelling work any better for you? Call attention to the problem; ask whether there are any reasons for it; and then drop the matter as quickly as possible.

5. **If a specific person continuously causes trouble, talk with that person privately.** If you shame a young person in front of peers, he or she may resent your action so greatly that the importance of the misconduct itself will be minimized. In talking privately with that person, you may discover some reasons for the behavior which you could not have known before.

6. **If an entire group consistently causes trouble even after you have talked with them at length, you either need more help or restructuring of the group.** A single adult with a large group of junior highs will usually have trouble! One of the great advantages of a small group approach is that discipline is usually easier to maintain. At the junior high level, you may need a ratio of one adult for every five young people in the group. For senior highs, you may need an adult for every six or seven young people.

7. **Only as a last resort should you ever ask a young person to leave a group.** Before doing that, be certain the behavioral problem really is intolerable to the group; visit with the young person involved; visit with the parents of that young person; and seek the counsel of your minister or another adult whose judgment you trust. It is certainly better to lose one or two young people than to lose an entire group! But remember that some rowdy young people grow up to be highly respected community leaders and that a young person alienated from the church may never return.

Meeting Your Own Needs in the Group

While all of us have very distinctive needs, the overall needs for intimacy and for growth are common to virtually everyone. I believe it is critical that youth groups relate to the needs of every participant—including the adult leader or advisor. If you do not feel that some of your needs are being met in the group, you will soon become badly frustrated. Avoiding the style of a dictatorial leader does not mean withholding your own opinions and needs.

By cultivating a style of honesty and openness, you will encourage young people to do the same. By letting them know when your needs are not being met, you will help them become more willing to express their own needs and more sensitive to the needs of others. Statements such as the following may be quite appropriate:

● "I was up really late last night, and I'm afraid I feel grouchy and irritable. If you'll try to hold the noise down, I'll try not to be a grump."

● "I appreciate why you dislike rules at home so much. I guess that I feel a little defensive since I'm a parent myself. I would like to share some of my feelings about rules."

● "I feel disappointed and a little hurt when I've worked on a lesson all week and then find people unwilling to sit still during class."

● "This last week was really bad for me at work. I guess I must feel like you do when things pile up at school."

● "I know that a youth group leader should believe in God all the time. There are times when I'm not so sure. When someone I've been close to dies, I either have a period when I doubt God's existence or when I question how good God really is. Has anyone else ever felt that way?"

● "This must sound stupid—but I don't know where the parable of the Ten Bridesmaids is found. Can someone here help find it, or should we ask the pastor?"

● "I sometimes feel like some of you are afraid to trust me. If I've broken your confidence anytime, I'd like to know when. I *want* to be the sort of person you can trust."

Such statements and questions help your group to know that you have times when you hurt, too. If you show enough confidence and trust in the group, you will make it easier for them to trust you. The most meaningful discussions happen in an atmosphere of trust.

Emphasize Relationships More Than Content

I attended Sunday school with some degree of faithfulness in junior and senior high school. Most of my Sunday school teachers were shocked by how little historical or biblical content my friends and I had retained from elementary Sunday school. They attempted to redeem us by having us memorize books of the Bible, familiar Bible verses, and the travels of Paul. Most of us didn't really care whether Paul was first in Rome or Galatia or Chicago or San Francisco! We could see no point in knowing what book came after Acts when our Bibles all contained a table of contents. Their efforts at imparting to us a richer understanding of our denominational heritage were doomed to even greater failure.

I do remember many things from my Sunday school classes. I remember a couple of teachers who always knew my name and who came to visit me when I was sick. I remember competing with the other fellows in a rush for seats to get close to an attractive high school girl. I remember our discussion the Sunday after a high school boy in a neighboring town had been killed in an automobile accident. I remember making paper airplanes out of the Sunday school paper. I also remember some of the discussions about whether a Christian should engage in premarital intercourse and how far a person should go with necking and petting. I remember a discussion about cheating that took place the Sunday before semester exams. My Sunday school experiences were not wasted, but the most significant sessions for me were not always the most significant ones for my teachers.

Take a few moments to reflect on your own Sunday School or C.C.D. experiences. What interested you? Why did you attend? If you didn't attend, do you remember why? What relationships are most prominent in your memory? If you remember having enjoyed memorizing biblical and historical facts, are you really remembering your junior and senior high years—or your elementary years? Don't cheat—put the book down for a few minutes, sit back in a comfortable chair, and reflect on your own Christian education experiences.

I'm not attempting to say that content is unimportant. A good biblical background and an understanding of denominational heritage are important. From our adult perspective, however, we need to remember that adults are far more concerned about that kind of content than most young people are. Further, the basis of salvation is not knowledge acquired but the individual's relationship with God. The Beatitudes do not say: "Blessed are the smart . . . those who study a lot . . . ," etc.

Be certain to place primary emphasis on relationships. By creating a warm, supportive climate in the classroom, you will provide a setting for discussion of personal relationships with God. By being open to the needs and concerns of class members, you will be demonstrating the kind of love which Christ has asked us to share with others. The "word of God" will come alive more in your life than in your verbalizations.

If students sense your genuine concern for them, they will also be more open to discussions of historical or biblical material which you identify as important. When your discussion of biblical and historical material raises contemporary concerns from class members, follow those concerns rather than considering them as tangents to be avoided.

There Is No Substitute for Preparation

The adult leader will have the major responsibility for discussion leadership in most classes and informal groups. Good discussions don't "just happen." Even those that seem serendipitous are the result of a supportive, trusting atmosphere.

When you know you will have responsibility for leading a discussion, take the time to prepare. If you begin preparation only ten minutes before the class or group, don't be surprised if the discussion flops! The chapters on "The Sunday School" and "The Fellowship Group" contain further suggestions for preparation.

Proverbs and Leadership Style

Some of the best guidance for leaders may be found in the Old Testament Book of Proverbs. The following quotations are from the *Today's English Version.*

Rank yourself from "1" to "5" on each of the following statements, with "1" being "this is not at all characteristic of me" and "5" being "this is extremely characteristic of me." Try to avoid the "middle of the road, sometimes yes, sometimes no" response of "3" unless that really is characteristic of you for the particular item.

Never get a lazy man to do something for you; he will be as irritating as vinegar on your teeth or smoke in your eyes (Prov. 10:26).

___1. I avoid selecting people for jobs when I know in advance that the particular individual will not follow through.

___2. I reject the theory of leadership that says most people are basically lazy and must be motivated by strong reward or threat of punishment.

_____

If your goals are good, you will be respected, but if you are looking for trouble, that is what you will get (Prov. 11:27).

___3. I really attempt to influence youth groups or classes to select goals that are for the overall good of the church and the group.

_____

Anyone who loves knowledge wants to be told when he is wrong. It is stupid to hate being corrected (Prov. 12:1).

___4. In my leadership roles, I seek a style of openness that makes others feel free to correct me or suggest alternative approaches.

_____

When a fool is annoyed, he quickly lets it be known. Smart people will ignore an insult (Prov. 12:16).

___5. I don't permit a meeting or my own emotions to be severely sidetracked because someone has said something that is annoying or offensive to me personally.

_____

A gentle answer quiets anger, but a harsh one stirs it up. When wise people speak, they make knowledge attractive, but stupid people spout nonsense (Prov. 15:1–2).

___6. In the face of conflict and opposition, I try to remain calm and rational, basing my responses on logic and fair play rather than emotions and revenge.

_____

When people are happy, they smile, but when they are sad, they look depressed (Prov. 15:13).

___7. As the leader of a group, I try to be sensitive to the emotions that group members are experiencing.

_____

Get all the advice you can, and you will succeed; without it you will fail (Prov. 15:22).

___8. As a leader, I see myself as an enabler, genuinely working to see that the best insights of all people in the group are utilized.

_____

An intelligent person aims at wise action, but a fool starts off in many directions (Prov. 17:24).

___9. I attempt to keep a group task-oriented and on topic, so that time and energy are not wasted in meaningless pursuit of unrelated issues.

_____

Enthusiasm without knowledge is not good, impatience will get you into trouble (Prov. 19:2).

___10. As the leader of a group, I try to insure that all the relevant facts have been examined before decisions are made.

———

People may plan all kinds of things, but the Lord's will is going to be done (Prov. 19:21).

You can get horses ready for battle, but it is the Lord who gives victory (Prov. 12:31).

___11. I function with a sense of humility, recognizing that it is, after all, God's will which a church group should seek and that no group can genuinely succeed without God's guidance.

———

I walked through the fields and vineyards of a lazy, stupid man. They were full of thorn bushes and overgrown with weeds. The stone wall around them had fallen down. I looked around, thought about it, and learned a lesson from it: Go ahead and take your nap; go ahead and sleep. Fold your arms and rest awhile, but while you are asleep, poverty will attack you like an armed robber (Prov. 24:30-34).

___12. I don't put off doing necessary tasks and permit major problems to be created by the failure to do small things.

———

People who promise things that they never give are like clouds and wind that bring no rain (Prov. 25:14).

___13. I don't make commitments to or for a group without being sure those commitments can be honored.

———

Depending on an unreliable person in a crisis is like trying to chew with a loose tooth or run with a crippled foot (Prov. 25:19).

___14. I am not threatened by working with strong people, and I seek the help and involvement of the most capable people available.

———

Singing to a person who is depressed is like taking off a person's clothes on a cold day or like rubbing salt in a wound (Prov. 25:20).

___15. I respect the feelings of others and recognize that personal problems may sometimes make someone dysfunctional in a group.

———

If your enemy is hungry, feed him, if he is thirsty, give him a drink. You will make him burn with shame and the Lord will reward you (Prov. 25:21–22).

___16. I seek opportunities to be helpful even to those who have opposed me.

———

A fool doing some stupid thing a second time is like a dog going back to its vomit (Prov. 26:11).

___17. As a leader, I learn from my mistakes and attempt to help the groups to which I relate learn from group mistakes.

———

Sensible people will see trouble coming and avoid it, but an unthinking person will walk right into it and regret it later (Prov. 27:12).

___18. I attempt to anticipate group problems and do my best to prepare for them or avoid them.

If you churn milk, you get butter. If you hit someone's nose, it bleeds. If you stir up anger, you get into trouble (Prov. 30:33).

___19. While I do not attempt to avoid necessary conflict, I work to bring out the best in others and not the worst—knowing that one often gets what one seeks.

You may want to use the preceding exercise as a basis for discussion with a youth group or with other adult workers.

What Is Evangelism?

Most people understand evangelism as the winning of people to the Christian faith and to active involvement in the church. Many believe that evangelism is the primary (and perhaps only) purpose of the church.

I agree that winning others to Christ and strengthening the church are crucial goals. I prefer, however, a broader definition of evangelism: *Sharing the good news of Jesus Christ with the world.* While that definition certainly includes winning individuals to Christ and working for church growth, it also includes ministering to the needs of others, opposing injustice, meeting personal needs, and making the world a better, safer place in which to live.

The more narrow definitions of evangelism include some potential pitfalls. Those who see the only focus of evangelism as winning people to Christ often become religious scalp hunters who see non-Christians as targets to conquer. Unfortunately, their interest in those people quickly disappears when the scalp has been claimed.

Many ministers and lay people believe the church's survival is at stake unless more active members can be found. This view also runs the risk of treating people as objects. Many people become satisfied if they can "convert" others from a different Christian denomination. This practice becomes proselyting. Baptists steal Methodists; Methodists steal Lutherans; Pentecostals steal Catholics; and so the list continues. I have trouble believing that such changes really build the kingdom of God.

One prominent Christian church in the West did not put a cross in a new sanctuary because "the cross is controversial" and might keep some potential members away. The cross certainly is controversial, and some of Christ's teachings have always been unpopular. Are those teachings to be suppressed as a necessary price to gain more members? I find that position unacceptable because it is inconsistent with the gospel.

In the long run, I believe the broader definition of evangelism is healthier for the individual members of a youth group and for the group as a whole. While most of this chapter will focus on strategies for personal witnessing and for numerically building youth programs, I hope the reader will remember that taking stands on community problems, reaching out to minorities, and fighting world hunger are all means of sharing Christ's good news and thus are important components of evangelism.

Hidden Evangelism

Some of the best evangelistic strategies in this book are not in this chapter. Meaningful, effective youth programming is an evangelistic asset. If you have good youth programming, you will experience numerical growth; and you will have people who are comfortable sharing their faith with others. The chapters which deal with planning, fellowship groups, and church school classes should all help with evangelism.

There is simply no substitute for a well-planned youth program that is supervised by committed, caring adult leaders. Too many youth resources have tried to make youth ministry seem easy and have emphasized strategies for short term success in numerical growth. Getting young people to your church, however, will not keep them there. They must feel that their personal needs are met; that there are group members who care deeply about them; that their own contributions are valuable to the group; that they can discuss issues of deep concern to them; that they can share confidential thoughts and feelings without fear; that they can have an enjoyable time with a church group; that they can continue growing closer to God as a result of their church activity; and that they are part of meaningful service to others in Christ's name. A church that does an effective job meeting those needs cannot help having a growing youth program. Though the rate of growth may not be rapid, the growth will come and new members will stay active.

Some issues and strategies for "sharing the good news" do merit separate consideration in this chapter. There are some issues and strategies that may not automatically be resolved without specific concern for evangelism, regardless of the definition put on that word.

Are Church Members Christian?

Young people are at different stages in their Christian growth. It is equally dangerous to assume that all the people in your group are mature Christians or to assume that they are all immature Christians or agnostics. It is essential that church youth programs continuously be sharing the good news of Jesus Christ. There very often are persons in a church group who enjoy the close relationships and the activities in which the group members share but who have not yet made a commitment to Christ. One of your most important fields of evangelism may be with those who are already active in your group.

Be careful not to fall into the trap of thinking that any young person whose religious experience differs from your own is not a Christian. It is important to respect the individuality of your people and to recognize that God reaches all of us in a variety of ways.

Do provide frequent times in group or class life for young people to share where they are at in the development of their faith: their problems, their hopes, their concerns, their doubts. This kind of sharing creates a climate in which group members may grow in their faith. Affirm those who share fears and doubts as well as those who share joy and faith. Sharing one's doubts takes a greater act of courage in many ways than sharing one's faith. You can help create a climate for this kind of sharing by letting the young people know of your personal doubts and fears. If you can say the words sincerely, statements such as these may open up group discussion and give encouragement to others who have doubts:

- "I usually feel pretty sure about God's existence. But sometimes I wonder if God is really in control or even there. Why does he let people starve? Why does he let so many people be hurt by others?"

- "Becoming a Christian was easy for me because I grew up in a Christian home. My parents read the Bible to me and prayed with me every night. I was as certain of God's existence as I was of my parent's love. I often wonder how it is for people who weren't taught about God as children."

- "The Christian faith didn't make sense to me for a long time. I never could understand how some people could be so certain of God's presence. Have you had that kind of doubt?"

- "I wanted very much to believe in God, but I could not understand why God, if he exists, didn't make his presence obvious. Why doesn't he just boom out orders from the sky and make everyone believe in him?"

Bible study also provides an excellent means for group members who are not committed Christians to be exposed to the main teachings of the Christian faith.

Some teachers and advisors of youth take time for private discussion with individual young people about faith in Christ and feelings for the group. Advisors in one local church have used a form similar to the one which follows as a basis for one-to-one discussions. Much of the secret of getting a young person to talk openly with you is to be personally open with that young person. As you go through the form, share some of your responses and the reasons for them. Try, however, to share your response to an item after the young person has shared his or her response; otherwise, that person may be uncomfortable differing with you. This works best if done as an oral interview. Always give a young person the right to "pass" or make no comment on an item. You can, of course, use this survey for group discussion, but one-to-one conversations with youth can pay high dividends.

FAITH DEVELOPMENT AND GROUP LIFE SURVEY

Indicate whether you *strongly agree (SA), agree (A), disagree (D),* or *strongly disagree (SD)* with each of the following items.

_____ 1. I enjoy being a member of this group (class).

_____ 2. I learn a lot from this group.

_____ 3. I feel comfortable sharing my feelings with the group.

_____ 4. I think that the other group members value my opinions.

_____ 5. I value the opinions of others in the group.

_____ 6. I have times when I feel very uncomfortable in the group.

_____ 7. There are several things which could improve the group.

_____ 8. I could do a better job of contributing to the group.

_____ 9. I'm glad that I belong to the group.

_____ 10. I feel like God is often present with us in the group.

_____ 11. I feel certain about God's existence.

____12. There are some times when I'm not certain about God's existence.

____13. I have really committed my life to Christ.

____14. I probably haven't committed my life as fully to Christ as I should.

____15. The idea of fully turning my life over to Christ scares me.

____16. The group has helped me grow in my Christian faith.

____17. We need to spend more group time helping one another understand the Bible and the Christian faith.

____18. I spend time every day in prayer and Bible study.

____19. I am able to share my Christian faith with others.

____20. I need more personal help in understanding the nature of God.

The survey intentionally avoids words and phrases such as *saved* and *born again*, since those words have different meanings for different people. The statements are good ones to stimulate discussion. The reasons for answering in a particular way are as important as the answers themselves.

Taking time to visit with every group member may seem like a major task, and indeed it is. The potential rewards, however, are great. You will feel much closer to your young people, and they will feel closer to you.

Follow Up on Absences

Most churches confirm young people as members during the junior high years. Some churches do so in the sixth grade or in high school, but these churches are the exception rather than the rule. Though statistics vary from denomination to denomination and from church to church, a year after confirmation normally finds 40 to 50 percent of the group relatively inactive in the church. Another year costs another 20 to 25 percent. Many local churches discover that only 10 to 25 percent of their high school seniors are still active in the church. There are several reasons for this painfully consistent pattern:

● Parents put a high priority on having their young people meet confirmation requirements. Once their offspring are confirmed, parents often feel that they have fulfilled their obligation to the church. Parental encouragement does help get young people involved, and the lack of that encouragement generally hurts. This is especially true if the parents themselves are irregular in attendance.

● Competition with other activities increases markedly in high school. Even highly committed young people find it hard to place priority on church events when faced with pressure from athletic coaches, drama coaches, close friends, and attractive members of the opposite sex.

● Young people do not always establish a close sense of identity with or belonging to the group during the confirmation years. Thus, they may find relatively little which draws them back to the church.

● Interests may change rapidly in the teenage years. Youth groups may do an excellent job responding to the interests of some young people but do a poor job recognizing the interests of others.

The preceding factors all should be recognized in effective youth programming. Other chapters in this book should give help in dealing with those concerns. Regardless of the quality of your programming, some young people will become inactive. Don't wait too long before responding to any change in a young person's attendance or activity pattern. In a local church study which I conducted, I consistently found a direct relationship between the promptness of response to absence and the probability that a child or young person would return to active involvement. If you wait as long as six months to respond to the absence of a high school person, the probability of that young person's returning to regular activity is about 27 percent. If you follow up on the absence within two to four weeks, the probability of return rises to 93 percent. The kind of response chosen is also important. Letters and postcards work fairly well with elementary children but not nearly as well with junior and senior high youth. Phone calls are a good approach, especially when the absence has only been a short one. If the phone call is not effective or if the absence has been a long one, then a personal visit by yourself or a member of the group should be made.

Do not leave follow-up on absences to chance. Keep a record of attendance if your group is not small enough for you to readily recognize an absence. If the same person is absent two consecutive meetings and there is no apparent reason, you or a group member should call. Don't be critical of the absence, but do make it clear that the person was genuinely missed. You do not need to push for a reason in the first contact. Simply affirm your interest in the youth and express your hope that he or she will be present for the next meeting. If a second or third contact becomes necessary, then you need to discover the reason for the change in activity.

These contacts not only reactivate young people but also give you needed feedback about the group. If your approaches or those of your group do not gain a response, then you may wish to contact the young person's parents. You should not contact the parents with the aim of having them make the young person come; the most that will gain for you will be an angry young person. A better approach is to ask the parents if they know why their son or daughter no longer attends and if they have any suggestions for you.

While some group advisors assume some responsibility for follow-up on absences, it is really better if this is a group responsibility. Young people need help building a caring, supportive group. One way of reinforcing that kind of group is to emphasize group concern and responsibility for a young person who is no longer coming.

No single time investment will pay greater dividends on attendance than this kind of prompt follow up. A phone call or visit now can reactivate a person who will be immune to a multitude of visits in a year. Don't lose those you already have!

Attendance at most Sunday schools and at most youth groups follows a clear pattern. Attendance is high in the fall, at the start of the new school year. Interest in the church is often renewed, and churches usually make a special emphasis or push on attendance. As the school year continues, attendance begins to decline. In most churches youth involvement, like congregational involvement, will increase slightly near Christmas but will not make a major increase again until Lent. The weeks leading up to Easter often bring renewal of interest in the church, and youth attendance will often equal that of the fall. There is an important difference, however: the new attenders in Lent are not necessarily the same people who became inactive after attendance in the fall. You can capitalize on this reality by a careful program of follow-up on those who quit coming. Follow-up on nonattendance can yield rich dividends.

Not meeting in the summer months and not following up on summer nonattenders can be a mistake. Attendance will generally be lower in the summer, because of vacations and summer jobs. Young people still need to know that they are missed! Most junior highs will not have summer jobs and are available for church activities. Summer trips and summer camps are usually very successful. If you do not meet during the summer, you need to make a major attendance push in the fall. (Of course, a major attendance push in the fall is always an excellent idea.)

Youth Witnessing

Reaching out to unchurched young people poses a different set of problems than encountered with the inactive of your own congregation. Most of this work must be done by the young people themselves. You should probably spend one or more meetings focusing on ways to win new people to the Christian faith and to involve them in your church. Many young people are not comfortable talking about their faith outside of the church setting, and they need encouragement in order to do so. Other young people, though armed with the best intentions, may give non-Christians just a large enough dose of slightly distorted Christianity to inoculate them forever against the real thing. It is important to be very specific in instructing others to witness. Though the following do's and don'ts are somewhat simplistic, they are still helpful guidelines for youth witnessing. Use them as a basis for discussion in your youth group or class. You may want to make copies for everyone.

1. **Do** consciously identify friends who are not members of a church and give no indication of professing the Christian faith. Almost everyone knows some people in this category.

2. **Don't** attempt to "win" those who are already part of another church or religious community. While the approaches of Lutherans, Roman Catholics, United Presbyterians, Baptists, Pentecostals, and United Methodists may differ, they all profess faith in Jesus Christ as Lord. The churches to which they belong have the primary responsibility for their Christian development. In biblical times, the process of taking members away from another religious community was called proselyting. This approach may help build a local church, but it does not build the kingdom of God. Your energy is better spent on the inactives in

your own church or on those with no church connection.

The matter of witnessing to Jewish people is more difficult to resolve. A distinction should be made between those who are Jewish by race and those who are Jewish in religious faith. Not all members of the Jewish race actively embrace the Jewish faith. While the Jewish faith does not recognize the lordship of Jesus, that faith still incorporates the Old Testament and the historical foundations on which our Christian faith has been built. Some Christians are convinced that Jewish people who do not accept Christ will go to hell. Others, not willing to make that judgment, affirm the common faith and values of both Judaism and Christianity and place their efforts on witnessing to those who have no religious faith. Jewish people who are religiously active generally resent efforts to convert them to Christianity. A Jewish friend of mine in college expressed his feeling this way: "If being a Jew was good enough for Jesus, it's good enough for me." The point is not a bad one; if we attack the validity of Jewish faith, we are attacking the roots of our own faith.

Each person must decide personally to whom he or she should witness. My own preference is to concentrate on inactive church people and on persons with no religious faith.

3. **Do** share what your relationship with Christ means to you at appropriate times in normal conversation. If Christ is the center of your life, then many of your decisions should be influenced or determined by your faith. Let others know when you feel that Christ has helped you make a difficult decision or cope with a significant problem.

4. **Don't** be caught with inconsistency between what you say and what you do. If you smoke, drink to excess, cheat, manipulate others, and do other things which are generally seen as inconsistent with being a Christian, people will have trouble believing your witness for Christ. This does not mean that you adopt a lifestyle which is sickeningly sweet like a mix of honey, maple syrup, brown sugar, and pop. It does mean that your faith in Christ should be influencing your daily habits and decisions. Others cannot help evaluating your faith by your behavior.

5. **Do** build friendships with persons whom you would like to win for the Christian faith. If you come on strongly about Christ to people whom you do not know well, they will assume (perhaps correctly) that your only interest in them is to gain another scalp for evangelism. Your words about Christ will have the most meaning when addressed to persons who know that you like them and care about them.

6. **Don't** drop your friendship with another person when that person accepts Christ and becomes active in the church. If you formed a friendship with that person for the sake of conversion, your losing interest in that friendship will hurt him or her deeply.

You should be careful in building a relationship with a non-Christian that you do not appear to be offering a deeper friendship than you are going to continue. Be sincere in your relationships, and express feelings of genuine concern and appreciation. Do not act like you want another person as your *best* friend unless you really do.

This caution is particularly important in relationships with the opposite sex. It is cruel to date someone for the ulterior motive of converting that person.

7. **Do** follow Christ's example in caring about other people. Be alert to people who are particularly lonely or isolated because of physical handicaps, low incomes, or ethnic background. You should reach out in concern and friendship. As you reach out to such people, you will find that your own life has been enriched.

You may want to do some self-assessment. Make a list of your closest friends, others whom you consider good friends, and people whom you like but with whom you do not spend much time. Are physically handicapped people on that list? What about people whose families have lower incomes? What about people of different races? You may be losing a great deal personally by not having friends from those categories.

8. **Don't** act in a condescending way toward non-Christians. Being a Christian does not make anyone better than other people. All people are children of God and as such are of great worth in the sight of God. Attitudes of arrogance and superiority are inconsistent with the Christian faith, and you will do little to advance the kingdom of God with such an attitude.

9. **Do** ask others to join you at church activities which are open to nonmembers. Many people have developed faith in Christ through contact with a good youth group. Activities like retreats, lock-ins, films, and parties may be especially good.

10. **Don't** invite large numbers of people at the same time. If you invite a person to attend a church activity with you, then you should arrange transportation for that person, stay with him or her during the activity, and provide introductions to other people. You probably can only do this effectively for one person at a time. If you identify a second person who should be invited to a church activity, it is probably best to ask another member of your group to invite that person.

11. **Do** practice talking about your faith with others. Your group should spend time discussing ways of sharing the Christian faith. Practice completing sentences like these:

● I am a Christian because . . . .

● I feel certain of God's presence when . . . .

● I want others to know about God because . . . .

● Worshiping in church helps me by . . . .

● My youth group helps me by . . . .

● I feel closest to God when . . . .

● My faith in Christ has helped me . . . .

Divide into pairs. Have one person role play the part of a non-Christian or inactive church member. The other should interpret the Christian faith or the merits of church involvement to that person. Then reverse roles. Share reflections on the experience. Sentences such as the following are possible discussion openers:

● "My church youth group is going on a retreat this weekend. I'd like to have you go as my guest."

● "I know that some of the *Jesus saves* types have really turned you off to the church. I don't blame you, but I hope you don't think all Christian people are like that."

● "I've not talked about it a lot, but my faith in God has really helped me get through some hard times this year. I'd like to share my experience with you, if you'd be interested in hearing about it."

● "I feel uncomfortable trying to tell someone else about my faith in God. I'd like to talk with you about it."

● "My church youth group is one of the most enjoyable groups of people that I've known. Would you be interested in joining the group or at least in visiting it?"

Talk as a group about the approaches that should be most effective in sharing your faith with others.

12. **Don't** use religious clichés. Most people who aren't active in church (and many who are) have grown weary of phrases like: "Are you saved?" "Have you accepted Christ?" "What would happen if you died tomorrow?" Those phrases have been badly overworked and turn off many people.

13. **Do** seek answers to your own questions about God, the Bible, and the church. You will be better able to interpret your faith if you are growing in your own knowledge and understanding.

Seek help from your minister, group advisor, classroom teacher, or parents.

14. **Don't** feel that you must have all the answers before sharing your faith with others. No one has all the answers! Committed Christian people have strong differences of opinion on such subjects as the literal account of creation, the virgin birth, whether non-Christians will be saved, the nature of heaven and hell, and the nature of miracles. If you wait until you have all the answers, you will end up sharing your faith with no one! If you are convinced of the reality of God and of his love for you

and others, you are ready to share your faith with others. Keep growing, keep learning, and keep caring about other people as Christ has cared for you.

Special Events

Some special events provide excellent opportunities for reaching out to the unchurched and the inactive. Invite people as guests to activities that will give them a positive introduction to the church. Consider possibilities such as these:

1. **Film Festivals**. Many motion pictures make significant statements on issues of concern to Christian people. Films which lift up war and peace issues, racial problems, suicide, and concern for others make excellent discussion starters. Sources for films like these are included in the "Resources" section of this book. Have a series of three or four films on consecutive Sunday or week-night evenings. Have small group discussion following each film. A group of parents or your church men's group or women's group may help you by selling or providing an inexpensive snack supper. Sell tickets in advance (for a minimal charge) to encourage attendance. Devote special effort to recruiting nonmembers.

2. **New Groups**. "What Groups Should We Offer?" gives advice on starting new youth groups. Note that starting a new group can be an excellent way of involving potential members.

3. **Lock-ins, Retreats, and Camps.** These overnight experiences provide excellent opportunities for young people to build close friendships and to share their Christian faith. If a person experiences an overnight event as your guest, he or she is likely to feel more a part of the group and to continue coming.

People who begin to identify with your group will not only want to continue coming but will also want to learn more about the faith which your group shows and shares.

4. **Parties** can also be an excellent opportunity. Don't overlook possible occasions for a party: birthdays, Christmas, Easter, Palm Sunday, Reformation Sunday. Many people who are uncomfortable discussing religious topics will feel safe attending a group party as your guest. They may become interested enough to return for a regular class or meeting.

5. **Concerts** of Christian music can be excellent. Do not hire any group for use in your church unless you have personally heard that group or have a positive report from someone whose judgment you respect. You should evaluate not only the musical presentation but also the theology which the music presents. A well-performed concert may help many people gain a better understanding of God.

Keep Them Involved

If you gain new members for your group and help them recognize God's presence in their lives, you should take steps to insure their continued involvement. Share these suggestions with group members:

1. **Continue your own friendship with such people.**

2. **See that others express friendship in and concern for new members.**

3. **Involve new members in activities besides the church school class or youth group.** You may wish to encourage regular worship attendance, choir, and summer camp.

4. **Share responsibility for fund raising and service projects with new members.** Do not take advantage of them by asking them to do work which you would be unwilling to do yourself, but do not be bashful about asking help from new group members. Work projects provide excellent settings for growth in Christian community.

5. **Let your minister know about a new group member.** There may be a confirmation class or other event which would be helpful. Your minister may wish to call on the young person or his or her parents.

6. **Keep those people in your prayers.**

A classroom can be an exciting place! Or it can be an absolute bore! And in most cases it is the teacher that makes the difference! The best curriculum materials in the world, the most spacious and inviting classrooms, the most advanced audio-visual materials—all these factors put together—cannot insure good classroom experiences. In a teaching/learning situation, the teacher is always the decisive element!

To be a good teacher, you must have certain characteristics: like a concern for students, a knowledge of the material, and an earnest desire to help students learn. These characteristics are generally accepted as givens; you cannot be a good teacher without them. But there is another aspect of the teaching/learning situation that, despite its importance, often gets short shift. And that is the use of a variety of interesting, effective teaching methods.

The failure to use creative teaching techniques seems to be especially prevalent among church school teachers. The situation in a lot of churches may be epitomized by a sign that I saw recently on the door of a church school class: "Be Present Every Sunday for Mr. Smith's Lecture to the Senior High Class." The lecture method is certainly a valid teaching technique, one that can be used advantageously in many situations. But it should not be used "every Sunday." Nor should any other method! A wealth of creative, innovative classroom techniques is available for the teacher who will seek them out and use them. And that's what you should do!

In this chapter, we offer thirty-five teaching methods for your consideration. Some are old, tried-and-true methods. Some are new and different. If you are planning a class session "from scratch," they will give you a wide variety of approaches that may be used in presenting the material that you

are developing. If you are using a standard curriculum resource from your denomination or some other source, they will provide you with many ideas about ways to alter or adapt your resource's suggested procedures.

1. **Studying Scripture.** The Bible is the basis of our faith, and it should be the foundation of any classroom session. Many of the techniques suggested in this chapter can be used in teaching and learning about the Bible, but there is great value to be found also in just plain, old Bible study. Youth and adults need to learn the essentials involved in understanding the biblical message.

As is true with all teaching/learning techniques, there is a right way and a wrong way to go about studying the Bible. Here are a few tips that should make your Bible study sessions more successful:

● Give your students some background information about the book(s) to be studied—or have the students look up this information. As a minimum, this material should include: author; date; purpose; a brief outline of the book(s); and the political, religious, and social situation(s) involved. This type of information is readily available in most commentaries and Bible dictionaries. Especially recommended are: *The Interpreter's One-Volume Commentary on the Bible* (Abingdon, 1971) and *The Interpreter's Dictionary of the Bible* (Abingdon, 1962, 1976).

● Use a modern, easily readable translation. An especially good one is *Good News for Modern Man* (also called *Today's English Version*).

● Choose a fairly good-sized selection for study. As a general rule, Bible study is more effective if you are dealing with a complete section of the Scripture, either a biblical book or a self-contained unit such as a chapter or complete narrative. Avoid using selections consisting of just a verse or a few verses.

● When dealing with a portion of a biblical book, establish the context of the selection being studied. Have students examine the sections that precede and follow the portion under consideration.

● Have students use biblical commentaries as they study. The biblical material comes from a different world, a different social milieu. And no one should be expected to understand biblical words and concepts without help from additional resources. Many study resources provide this information for you.

● If there are more than five or six people in your class or group, have students work in small groups to read and discuss the Scripture. Much mutual benefit will result from the sharing of questions and insights.

● Prepare in advance some guide sheets for the students to use in their study. Include in these sheets questions and remarks about significant words and concepts.

● Use newsprint and/or a chalkboard as tools for getting significant material visually before the class. During discussions, record students' responses on the newsprint or chalkboard.

● Use visual aids such as time lines and maps.

● Use media resources such as films, filmstrips, and songs related to the biblical passages. Have students utilize media tools for self-expression. Especially effective are slide-and-tape shows and cassette recordings made by the students themselves. For more information on these procedures, see our chapter entitled "Media" and some of the media resources listed in the final chapter of this handbook.

● Use a variety of creative techniques to enhance your Bible study sessions. Utilize role plays, simulations, paraphrases, and many of the other techniques discussed in this chapter.

2. **Listening to and discussing audio selections.** We live in an audio world! Music is all around us! And much of the musical output that permeates our environment is worthy of discussion in a church school class. Of particular value are many of the current pop songs and most of the modern folk hymns. For further ideas in this area, see our chapters entitled "Media" and "Music! Music! Music!"

3. **Discussing implications of paintings, sculptures, and other works of art.** Many great works of art convey a religious message. Some are explicitly religious, such as paintings and sculptures based on biblical themes. Others have a more subtle religious message—such as that found in art works that deal with our social, economic, and political values.

A good procedure in discussing such works is to proceed from general questions to specific questions. Begin by asking about impressions of overall mood by asking for general feelings and reactions. Then move to questions about the meaning of specific aspects of the work.

In a discussion of Salvador Dali's "The Sacrament of the Last Supper," for example, the discussion questions might proceed in this order:

What do you see as the general mood of this painting? Why?●What is your first reaction to the painting?●How do you feel about the painting? Explain why you feel as you do?●What do you see as Dali's reason for mixing two scenes together with the painting? What message about the Lord's Supper is conveyed by this mix?●What are your ideas on the headless figure at the top of the painting? Is it supposed to be a particular person or a symbol? Explain your positions.●Which parts of the picture are the most lighted? What significance do you see in the lighting?●Why do you think Jesus is pointing upward?●Where is the focal point of the painting?●What do you see as the meaning of these details of the painting—the broken bread, the single cup, the fact that all except Jesus have bowed their heads? What significance do you see in other details?● What do you see as the overall message of the painting?

4. **Making wall charts.** Student-made wall charts can be a very effective tool for use with youth. Your students will feel a real sense of involvement when they work as a group to prepare a large visual statement of their own ideas. Wall charts can be used for recording students' feelings, their ideas about the most important aspects of a topic, time lines, questions for consideration by the group, and so forth. A particularly good use of wall charts is the creation of a "graffiti board" on which students can record sayings, quotations, or anything that comes to mind.

Here are a few hints about wall charts: Use large sheets of paper; long rolls of Butcher paper or newsprint are especially good for this purpose. Use high-quality, bold-stroke markers so that the results can be seen and read at some distance. Make sure that the markers will not "bleed through" and leave marks on the walls; if necessary, use several "backup sheets" to protect the walls. Leave the charts up for a few sessions—most youth will be proud of their work and will want to have it on exhibit for some time.

5. **Doing matching quizzes, doing multiple-choice exercises, filling in blanks, completing sentences, and so forth.** Questionnaires are great lead-ins for discussion. Giving the young people a chance to respond privately and individually, or in small groups, to a well-designed questionnaire will usually get thoughts flowing more freely than just hitting the youth cold with oral questions. Such questionnaires are easy and fun to create! Just choose your subject, divide it into ten to twenty points or subtopics, and then use these points or subtopics as the basis for your questionnaire.

One of the best questionnaires for securing factual input is the matching quiz. Students usually feel comfortable with this type of instrument because the answers are there, even if they are all scrambled up; thus, there is less risk of exposing one's lack of knowledge about a subject. Here is an example of a brief, matching quiz on Jesus:

___ 1. Town where Jesus was born
___ 2. Town where Jesus grew up
___ 3. Town where Jesus died
___ 4. Father of Jesus
___ 5. Mother of Jesus
___ 6. Jesus' cousin, who baptized Jesus
___ 7. Author of the shortest life of Jesus
___ 8. Man who wrote most of the letters in the New Testament
___ 9. Disciple who betrayed Jesus

___10. Man whom Jesus raised from the dead

A. Paul   E. Nazareth   I. Judas
B. Mark   F. Lazarus   J. Joseph
C. Jerusalem   G. Mary
D. Bethlehem   H. John

The multiple-choice questionnaire is also a popular method for dealing with factual input. This questionnaire can be fun to design, since it offers you a chance to include humorous choices as well as serious ones. Here are examples of the type of item that may be used in this instrument:

___ 1. Most of the letters in the New Testament were written by:
(a) Saul (b) Peter (c) Paul
(d) Ann Landers (e) none of these

___ 2. The man whom Jesus raised from the dead was:
(a) Houdini (b) Darth Vader
(c) Simon Peter (d) Lazarus (e) Mark

Other instruments, such as the fill-in-the-blanks or sentence completion types, may also be used to secure factual input. But they are most useful for discovering student opinions and feelings, as in these examples:

I think that the most serious problem among youth today is . . .

I feel . . . when I try to discuss something controversial with my parents.

6. **Making artistic self-expression creations from paper, wire, cups, clay, etc.** Many young people will balk at such questions as "How do you feel about yourself?" or "What are you like?" But they will often respond enthusiastically when asked to express their own personalities in more subtle ways—such as creating artistic self-expressions.

Choose a particular medium: sheets of construction paper, pieces of wire, styrofoam cups, gobs of modeling clay, or some other neutral substance. Then ask students to use this medium to express themselves—their own feelings, their own personalities. You may wish to give an example—such as tearing a cup into strips to express your feeling of going in all directions or constructing a wire-frame heart to express your love for other people. Or you may do this activity without giving any examples.

Afterward, have students explain their own creations. As an alternative you may prefer to have students attempt to explain one another's creations before asking for an explanation from each "artist." Be sure to "listen with the third ear." Try to be sensitive not only to the stated explanations but also to more subtle personality aspects that may be revealed through this type of exercise.

7. **Doing pantomimes.** This method is particularly effective for helping students "get into" a story, such as a biblical narrative. Try this procedure: Choose several narratives and assign one to each individual or group. Then have the narratives acted out without any words being spoken. Next, have the group try to guess which narrative is being mimed. Then discuss the various actions, gestures, and facial expressions and how they relate to the various parts of the narrative. Afterward, have each narrative read aloud and then discuss the meaning or message of the narrative.

8. **Viewing and discussing movies, filmstrips, slides, and television.** Audio-visual

media should be a regular part of any program of ongoing sessions with youth. All of us are accustomed to living in a media-oriented world. And we are used to getting many of our messages about life from the media. Your youth group or class should be the setting for many intensive discussions of these messages.

Try to tailor your discussions of media to the needs of your group. But also avail yourself of other resources. Use any available, professionally prepared guides, such as those that accompany most religiously oriented movies and filmstrips. And utilize the discussion guidelines in publications such as *Cultural Information Service* and *Mass Media Newsletter.* For general suggestions on using and discussing media, see our chapter on this subject and many of the resources listed in the media section of our final chapter.

9. **Discussing magazine and newspaper clippings.** One of the best methods for relating the Christian faith to our everyday world is through discussions of materials found in magazines and newspapers. Have students bring clippings (or complete issues) to class. Choose articles and news stories that deal with matters that are pertinent to the students and their concerns. Have students discuss how a Christian should respond to the situations and ideas that are found in these print media. Among the subjects that can be approached in this manner are crime, violence, government and politics, the business world, war and peace, lifestyles, and societal values.

A related activity is a discussion of the advertisements that are found in magazines and newspapers. Have students clip some ads at random and paste them on a wall chart. Then consider the composite picture thus constructed. Have students attempt to reach a consensus about the lifestyles and values systems reflected in the commercials. Then discuss the Christian response to such lifestyles and values.

10. **Having outside resource people.** "You don't have to go it alone" when teaching youth. In most churches and communities, there are many people who have expertise in a multitude of areas. Most of these people probably would not consider teaching a youth class on a regular basis, but many of them would agree to come for a session or two and lead a discussion in some specific area that they feel comfortable with. You don't have to be an expert in every area. But you should reach out to others who can provide expertise. For starters, here is a listing of a few of the areas in which outside resource people could be helpful: family relationships, sexuality, race relations, alcohol, drugs, responsible use of automobiles, vocations and careers, marriage, college, other religions, politics, science and religion, ecology, concerns of the aging, religious cults, children's rights, the teenage school environment, death and dying, and psychological development.

11. **Paraphrasing Scriptures.** Paraphrasing is an excellent method for helping people "get inside" the Scriptures. The important thing to remember is not to do this activity in a vacuum. Don't just assign biblical selections and ask students to rewrite them in their own words. Do some basic Bible study—as suggested in the first method above. Then have students work as individuals or in small teams (two to nine people) to rephrase the scriptural selections in today's language and modern concepts. Afterward, have students read their creations to the group and have a discussion of the meaning and message of the selections.

12. **Role playing.** This technique can be used in many ways. You can have students role play a biblical narrative or a scene from a novel. Or you can set up your own situations that relate to the topic you are discussing. Roles may be taken by individuals; or a small team may "group-play" a role, with the groups deciding at each point along the way what the role player's response will be.

Role plays may follow the action of a particular story from beginning to end in the manner in which the action occurs in a given source or narrative. Or the role plays may be open-ended. With this approach, the basic situation and possibly some initial action are designated for the role players, But the progress of the role play and the final outcome are determined by the role players themselves. This latter approach usually results in more originality and more meaningful input by the role players; and it is generally a better vehicle for producing profitable discussion.

A good variant on the traditional role play is the "resonating" approach, in which people assume not only the roles of people but also the roles of material objects. In a role play of the parable of the Good Samaritan, for example, students would not only portray the main characters of the story; they would also assume such roles as the weapons of the robbers, the water jug, the water, the road, the money paid to the innkeeper, and so forth. The key element in this role play is having the participants "resonate" with the characters and the objects that they portray by expressing to the group how they feel about their roles!

13. **Doing evaluative quizzes and questionnaires.** This method provides an excellent tool for discovering student ideas, opinions, and feelings. These instruments are of two basic types: rating questionnaires and prioritizing questionnaires. In a rating questionnaire, students are asked to rate a series of items in regard to importance or preference. Usually a scale such as 1 to 10 is used. Or the rating may be done with letters or symbols, such as: SA=strongly agree, A=agree, NO=no opinion, D=disagree, and SD=strongly disagree. In a prioritizing questionnaire, students are asked to prioritize several items: 1=first choice, 2=second choice, and so forth. Generally, the rating questionnaire provides more reliable input. The prioritizing questionnaire can be useful in some cases, especially when it is desirable to ascertain the relative weight that students give to each of a series of items. For optimum results, a prioritizing questionnaire should be limited to a small number of items, usually no more than ten.

The example given below is a brief prioritizing questionnaire. For samples of rating questionnaires, see the sections on program planning in our chapters entitled "The Sunday School" and "The Fellowship Group."

RELATIONAL SETTINGS: MY OWN PRIORITIES

Rate the following in terms of their importance in your own life. They should be rated from 1 (most important) to 9 (least important).

____ my family
____ my school life
____ my church school class
____ my friends
____ my hobbies
____ my pastor
____ my church
____ my youth group
____ my teachers

14. **Reading and discussing essays and other printed materials.** Although the read-and-discuss method should not be the only method used in a class, it does have certain advantages. It can be a very good technique for providing students with sound, well-thought out information about a subject. And it can help students to learn to think in an orderly, organized manner.

Here are three hints for more successful usage of the read-and-discuss method. Do not spend more than 20 percent of class time in reading activities. Young people do a lot of reading during the school week, and most of them prefer a change of pace in church school. Choose individual selections that are fairly brief, usually no more than three or four paragraphs. Have students respond in writing before they participate in a discussion of the material.

A good technique to use in securing written response is called the "reverse outline." With this procedure students are asked to write in their own words: the main point or idea in each paragraph, and the main point or idea of the selection as a whole.

In the discussion, have students share their thoughts on the main ideas. Try to reach a class consensus on these ideas. Record this consensus (along with any variations) on newsprint or a chalkboard. Then proceed to a discussion of the meaning and message of the selection as a whole and student opinions about what the selection says.

15. **Doing choral readings.** This technique can be an exciting method for helping students interpret Scripture. It is particularly suitable for the Psalms, but it may be used successfully with other parts of the Bible and with nonscriptural poetry and prose.

The key principle in adapting material for choral reading is to be sensitive to the words themselves and to try to use the human voices as instruments in order to give the words the proper rendering and emphasis. With this technique, the class is seen as a choir, and the written material is treated as if it were music. Some sections are read softly, some loudly. There are crescendos and decrescendos. Some phrases are rendered in rapid, staccato-like speech; some are delivered slowly and deliberately. Some parts are read in a high voice, some in a low voice. Pauses, accents, and tempo changes are used to emphasize the mood of the reading. The leader conducts the group much as a conductor would lead a choir or an orchestra.

16. **Having small-team discussions and reporting to the full group.** It is very difficult to secure full participation in a discussion that involves a dozen or more persons. For this reason, teachers of large classes usually find it necessary at times to divide the class into small teams (two to nine people) that can work as "buzz groups" and then report back to the group as a whole. Usually this procedure not only facilitates the discussion process but also results in more viewpoints being aired.

Several guidelines for this type of discussion should be observed. First, make sure that each team contains a mix of "big talkers" and the shy youth. Second, make sure that each team understands its mandate and has clarity about just what the topic(s) of discussion should be. It is usually helpful to write the topic(s) on newsprint or a chalkboard that will be in full view of all groups. Third, make sure that each team chooses a reporter before starting discussion. Fourth, be sure that each team is monitored by an adult leader—even if you have to circulate among the teams. Fifth, use newsprint or a chalkboard for reporting the results of the team discussions.

17. **Brainstorming.** Some teachers refer to this technique as "the popcorn method." In brainstorming, students are encouraged to "pop out" responses to a particular question as they think of them. Responses are to be given without comment or criticism from anyone; and all responses are to be recorded on newsprint or a chalkboard exactly as they are stated—without any editing by the teacher or members of the class. Once all responses are recorded, the class then works as a group to classify the responses, weed out duplicates, and combine responses that seem to fit together. After this process is completed and its results recorded, the group then proceeds to a critique and/or discussion of the responses.

The brainstorming method is particularly effective when you are considering a question that can have a multitude of equally valid responses. Some examples of questions that might be suitable for brainstorming are: What are the characteristics of junior high (or senior high) youth? What are the marks of a Christian? What happens in a typical worship service? What are some ways in which we spend our money? What are some advantages of living in the country (or the city or the suburbs)? What are some ways in which sexism is being combatted today?

18. **Having circular responses.** The circular response technique is similar to brainstorming in that people are allowed to give responses without their responses being subject to immediate comment or criticism. There is an important difference, however. In brainstorming, responses are given voluntarily, and any one person may give as many responses as he or she wishes to give. In the circular response method, you go around the room and each person is allowed to give only one response in turn until all have responded. Also, in the circular response approach, responses do not have to be given "popcorn style." Each person may be allowed to take a few moments to think through his or her answer before responding.

The circular response is a good method for getting a variety of input on a particular topic. It is particularly valuable as a means of securing reactions from shy youth who might not otherwise speak out.

19. **Having simulations.** Simulations—or simulation games—are classroom experiences that reproduce in a simplified manner the major aspects of real life situations. The purpose of a simulation is to help students deal with the problems, questions, and decisions relating to a particular real life situation without actually participating in that situation.

There are many books that provide examples of classroom simulations. We recommend that you examine some of these resources (such as the ones listed in our final chapter) in order to get more ideas about simulation games and some information on simulation theory. Dennis Benson's *Gaming* is especially excellent.

With a little effort, however, you can design your own simulation experiences. The process is fairly simple. Just choose a real life situation that can be of value to your students. Then write out a brief set of instructions in which you state the purpose of the simulation, the situation, and the procedure to be followed.

The possibilities for simulation games are almost endless! Here are a few ideas (along with suggested titles for the games).

81

THE NEW SOCIETY

Purpose: To give students an opportunity to decide which societal rules, norms, and values are most important to them.

Situation: Students are to be shipwreck survivors on a deserted island.

Procedure: Students are to formulate laws, rules, and regulations for a society based on Christian values.

WORLDWIDE SUPERMARKET

Purpose: To help students become more aware of hunger and poverty.

Situation: Students are to be persons from various nations who are spending their weekly grocery money in the same store.

Procedure: Display an assortment of food items ranging from delicacies such as cake and ice cream to bare necessities such as single pieces of bread and bowls of thin, watery soup. Apportion "play money" in such a way that residents of "developed" nations will have enough money to purchase many delicacies whereas residents of poorer nations will have only enough money to buy some unappetizing necessity.

THE OFFICIAL BOARD

Purpose: To give students experience in dealing with the priorities of the church.

Situation: Students are to be members of an official board in a local church. The church has an annual budget of $100,000 apportioned in the following manner: Pastor's salary and benefits=$25,000; Salaries for part-time secretary, custodian, and organist/choir director=$30,000; Building maintenance and utilities=$20,000; Local church programs (worship, education, evangelism, and so forth)=$10,000; Outreach and mission programs=$15,000. Pledging to the church budget is $10,000 short of the $100,000 goal.

Procedure: Students are to decide where cuts totaling $10,000 should be made. The board has the authority to raise or lower the amounts for any items in the budget. The group will proceed by hearing various motions, debating the motions, and voting on the motions.

20. **Doing interviews.** Student interviews of their fellow students, their teachers, and other persons in the church and community have long been a staple of the creative teacher's methods repertory. With the advent of the cassette recorder, this technique has become even more valuable. The procedure is simple. Choose an interesting topic, preferably one that will elicit a variety of responses. Draw up a brief questionnaire. Give the students the questionnaire, pencil and paper, and/or a cassette recorder. Then send them out into other classes, the church, or the community. Interviews may be collected, reported on, and discussed during one class session. Or you may assign the interviews for the coming week and have them reported on and discussed at the next class session.

21. **Having a fishbowl discussion.** With this technique, a small group has a discussion while the rest of the class watches. There are many different ways of designing a fishbowl discussion. Here is one approach (which you should feel free to alter as necessary for your group):

● Arrange four to six chairs in a circle in the center of your classroom. Choose students to sit in this inner circle and to be the initial participants in the discussion.

• Arrange all the other chairs in a larger circle around the inner circle. All students other than the initial participants are to sit in this outer circle.

• State the fishbowl rules:
a. The persons in the inner circle are the only ones who can participate in the discussion.
b. Persons in the outer circle can ask questions of those in the inner circle; but outer-circle people are not allowed to make comments, deliver "speeches," or participate in any way in the ongoing discussion.
c. Any person who wishes to join the inner circle may do so at any time by stepping forward and lightly tapping an inner-circle person on the shoulder. When this happens, the person so tapped must relinquish his or her seat and sit in the vacant chair in the outer circle.
d. There is no limit to the number of times that any one person may go back and forth from one circle to the other.

This technique is particularly valuable as a method for having a large group receive the benefits of a small-group discussion. As a rule, a fishbowl discussion should be followed by a brief full-group session in which the fishbowl discussion is critiqued and amplified through further discussion by the group as a whole.

22. **Making mobiles and stabiles.** A mobile consists of a group of connected objects that are balanced and suspended so as to hang freely in the air. A stabile is a more stable sculpture-like construction. It often consists of objects mounted on pieces of sturdy wire attached to a common base. The components of mobiles and stabiles may be simple undecorated objects, or they may be objects on which words and/or symbols have been inscribed.

The main value of mobiles and stabiles is that they provide a visually interesting method for presenting various aspects of a single unifying topic. A lead-in for a discussion of the "fruits of the Spirit," for example, might be a session in which students make mobiles and stabiles that illustrate the qualities listed in Galatians 5:22-23. Or students might begin a series on "The Christian Faith and My Life" by making mobiles and stabiles consisting of symbolic representations of things that are important in their everyday lives.

23. **Create finger paintings.** This method may seem messy and juvenile at first, but most youth enjoy finger painting. Cover the floor and tables with plastic drop cloths or old newspapers. Do some sample paintings for the class. In finger paintings, one tries to present feelings and emotions more than thoughts and ideas. Some youth will express feelings in this medium which they will not share in any other way. The following would be appropriate themes for finger paintings: how I feel about myself; how I feel about God; hope; love; heaven; hell; grace; God's love; the Holy Spirit.

24. **Doing skits, mini-dramas, and so forth.** There are many ways to use drama and dramatic techniques in the classroom. Students can write and perform skits. They can adapt biblical narratives for presentation to their classmates or the congregation as a whole. The use of this technique can be as simple or as complicated as you wish. Dramatic presentations can be done "readers' theater" style, with little or no use of scenery, props, costumes, music, sound effects, and so forth. For information on

resources related to this classroom method, see the final chapter of this handbook.

25. **Writing poems, songs, and so forth.** These and other similar methods are useful for encouraging students to express their feelings and ideas. Poems may be written in traditional forms with rhyme and meter or in free-verse forms. Two types of poetry that are especially effective in classroom situations are the haiku and the cinquain.

Haiku is a Japanese form that is used to express a single thought or feeling. A haiku poem has seventeen syllables arranged in this manner: five syllables in the first line, seven syllables in the second line, and five syllables in the third line. Here is an example:

> *My life freely flows*
> *through all my experience*
> *reflecting God's will.*

A cinquain is a French form that has five lines. Line one contains one word, the title. Line two contains two words that describe the title. Line three contains three words—action words related to the title. Line four contains four words that describe a feeling about the title. Line five consists of one word that means the same as the title. Here is an example:

> *Jesus*
> *our Lord*
> *showing the way*
> *responding to our needs*
> *Savior*

Most classes have the capability to express their faith and their feelings musically. For ideas on songwriting, see our chapter entitled "Music! Music! Music!"

26. **Making posters.** A walk through the gift and novelty shops in your area should quickly convince you of the power of the poster! If your youth class is like most, it is likely that many of your students have posters on the walls of their rooms. Poster making is an excellent activity for getting students to express themselves, their thoughts, feelings, and ideas. Whether you are making "me-posters" by which students express their own individual personalities, or posters featuring quotations and sayings, you will probably find this activity to be one in which almost all students will readily and enthusiastically participate.

Here are a few hints regarding poster making. Use the best quality materials that you can afford. Newsprint and other coarse materials can be utilized to good effect, but most groups seem to prefer glossy poster board. Also, use high quality, bold-stroke markers; the posters will be more dramatic and visually more appealing. Use a variety of materials. Don't hesitate to mix media. Pictures and words cut from magazines can be used in conjunction with felt-tipped markers to make an arrangement that is usually more interesting than either of these media alone. Think big! Posters utilizing 22" x 28" poster board make a much better impression than posters on 8½" x 11" paper. If possible, leave the posters on display in your classroom for a few weeks before students take them home. Your classroom will be a more interesting place; and the presence of the posters will be a continuing stimulus for discussion.

27. **Debating.** This old tried-and-true method is still a great technique for dealing with controversial subjects. Traditionally, the topic for the discussion is worded in the affirmative, for example: "Resolved: That our church's youth group should be involved in more service projects." You may divide the whole class into two groups, or you may

have two small teams (two to nine people) or two individual persons do the debating. The advantage of using one of the two latter approaches is that you would then have a neutral group (the remainder of the class) who could serve as judges.

A traditional procedure for carrying on a debate is the following: (a) Primary presentation of the pro position (arguments for the resolution); (b) Primary presentation of the con position (arguments against the resolution); (c) Rebuttal by the pro person(s); (d) Rebuttal by the con person(s); (e) Decision by the judge(s).

28. **Writing prayers, creeds, and so forth.** This activity is a ready-made method for use with sessions on worship. It can also be used in various other contexts. Students should be encouraged to write prayers, creeds, litanies, and other worship materials relating to most of the topics dealt with in class sessions. For ideas on how to use this technique, see our chapter entitled "Worship."

29. **Doing puzzles.** Most people enjoy working puzzles. And puzzles can be useful tools for teaching, particularly for helping students learn definitions and other factual material. Why not try your hand at creating some? It's easier than you may think! Three of the most common types of puzzles are the crossword puzzle, the word box, and the word scramble. Here are some ideas on how to create them:

● **Crossword puzzles.** Choose a list of words that denote important aspects of the subject your class is to deal with. Block off a piece of paper with about 30 blocks across and 30 down. Or simply use a piece of graph paper that has fairly large blocks. Choose one of the longer words to go in or near the middle of the puzzle. Then begin adding

additional words so that letters of the new words will overlap with letters in the original word. As a rule, the best procedure is to begin with longer words and then add the shorter, more easily worked-in words later.

When you have placed all your words on the puzzle, shade in the blank spaces. Then number all the blocks containing the first letters of words—beginning at the top left and proceeding left-to-right and toward the bottom of the puzzle.

● **Word boxes.** Make up a box like the one at the end of the chapter (p. 88) with words arranged horizontally (some forward and some backward), vertically (some up and some down), and diagonally (some forward and some backwards). Then fill in the extra spaces with additional letters. The puzzle that you create by this method is called a word box. It is an especially valuable tool for listing various elements that are of the same general type (like books of the Bible or names of biblical characters).

● **Word scramble.** This puzzle is the simplest of all to create. You just make out a list of words and then scramble the letters in each word.

30. **Making slides and slide shows.** Working with slides is an activity that most young people find fascinating! You can create a nearly professional slide-and-tape presentation using slides taken with a high-quality camera and a complex sound-on-sound music and narration track. Or you can do your projects "on a shoestring budget" and still get superb results with homemade slides and a sound track produced on an inexpensive cassette machine! But regardless of whether your

slide projects are grandiose or simple, you are almost always certain to find the youth totally absorbed by the process. This type of multimedia endeavor is one of the best methods around for getting students seriously involved with a variety of subjects! For a lot of information on this technique, see our chapter entitled "Media" and the resources listed in the media section of our final chapter.

31. **Making movies and video productions.** With the advent of relatively inexpensive equipment, these two types of media are becoming more and more accessible to many churches. Drama itself is a powerful tool for classroom teachers! But when students also have the opportunity to view and discuss their own dramatic creations, the medium of drama takes on a new and exciting dimension! So why not give it a try? The technology is not that complicated, and the techniques are easily learned! For information on how to utilize these fascinating media, see our chapters entitled "Media" and "Video."

32. **Having panel discussions.** This technique, like the fishbowl method discussed earlier, provides an excellent means of giving a large group the benefits of participating in a small-group discussion. Panel discussions may involve only members of your class. Or you may prefer to bring in some "outside resource people." A particularly effective use of this method is the combining of the two approaches—having outside people (parents, pastors, church officials, experts in various fields, and so forth) participate in a panel discussion with members of the class.

Here are some hints for panel discussions: (a) Make sure that all participants understand the specific nature of the topic to be discussed. (b) Prepare a sizable list of primary questions and follow-up questions. Give this list to all participants well in advance of the session. (c) Select as your moderator a person who is thoughtful, considerate, impartial, and good at listening to what people are saying. (d) Point out to your students the necessity of being polite and considerate. (e) Begin by allowing each panelist an opportunity to make a prepared statement; then proceed to a discussion among the panelists; and, finally, open up the session for questions from the group as a whole and general discussion.

33. **Doing research.** Your class sessions will be much more effective if the students do some of the preparation. Not only will this procedure help the students to "get into" the subject, it will also help them feel that they have some control over the direction that the class is taking.

Once you have decided on topics for your sessions, you should assign to some of your students the responsibility for basic research on the topics. This research can be done between sessions, but it is also quite feasible to have research done by individuals or small teams (two to nine persons) during the sessions themselves.

To insure the best results, you should observe these guidelines in directing student research: (a) Make sure that students understand exactly what they are to look for. Assignments should be as specific as possible. An assignment like "Drugs" would probably result in the gathering of a large "mixed-bag" of information, much of which might be of no use for the class sessions. Much better results would be obtained from more explicit assignments: the meaning of the term "illicit drugs"; the nature of the main mind-altering drugs in use today; statistics on drug use among various age

86

groups and economic classes; statistics on the relationship between drugs and crime; expert opinions on the effects of particular drugs; the status of attempts to make various illegal drugs legal. (b) Give students a list of specific questions to guide them in their research. (c) Suggest books, periodicals, and other sources from which information might be obtained. (d) Give students specific guidelines as to the form and length of their research reports.

34. **Having field trips and other outings.** Students usually enjoy activities that allow them to go outside the classroom. You can have field trips during the regular class meeting time (for example, visits to other church services or other church school classes). Or you can have special field trips during the week (for example, visits to service agencies). You can have a scavenger hunt in which students work in teams to gather items related to your class sessions. You can have search parties—such as an exploration of the church sanctuary in order to learn more about such things as altar paraments, liturgical colors, the baptistery, the designs and inscriptions on the stained glass windows, and various memorial gifts in the church.

If you do plan such an outing, be sure to make proper preparation and take necessary precautions. Make sure that parents are informed. Get permission statements, if necessary. Line up cars and drivers if they will be needed. If you plan to have your outing in the church building, remind students not to disturb other classes. Be sure to get permission from church officials, and be sure to contact in advance any people who will be working with your group.

35. **A final note.** This chapter is just a beginning! Many books have been written without exhausting the subject of creative teaching methods, so use this chapter as a starting point—and then go on to do more reading and research on your own. Creative teaching is a fascinating subject! And learning about it can be a lifelong process, a process that will continually reward you with the excitement of new discovery! To aid you in this process, we have listed many books on the teaching/learning experience in our final chapter. Examine the list, and examine some of the books. There's a world of ideas waiting for you.

CAN YOU FIND . . .

Sixteen biblical names? Circle them. Words may run horizontally, diagonally, vertically, forward, or backward.

```
S T E A K A N D R E T E P
J U G I N J N N E I W U O
M O S E S E A O B N A F Y
A N B J O S I A H T T I O
H T I V L U W M O H O O G
A H L I O S O O D A V T E
R A C L M C N S A M U E L
B O R D O T E S N A I S C
A D A M N H K J I C H T A
M A E Y N E A A E V E H L
F V D E I R H R L A N E P
E I D R K A S Z T E C R E
C D K F J O S E P H N I S
A L P U L A F R I C A T H
```

This puzzle comes from *The Bible Game Collection* by Don Kreiss and Steve Clapp. The book is available from *faithQuest*.

What do we mean by the term *media*? It's a word that is tossed around quite a lot today, often without any explanation of what the word means. Since our handbook includes this rather sizable chapter on the subject, it seems appropriate to begin with an attempt at a definition.

The word *media* is the plural form of *medium*, which comes from the Latin word *medium*—meaning "the middle; center; interval; intervening space." We use the English word *medium* in this basic sense when we speak of a person of medium height or of a happy medium between two extremes. In this chapter, we will be using the words *medium* and *media* in a very specialized sense. When we use the term *medium*, we will be speaking of a means of communication, a method for conveying a subject or an idea to a person or a group of people.

There are many kinds of media. Strictly speaking, any means of communicating something to someone can be labeled a medium. In this chapter, we will be concerned with these three types of media: (1) print media—those that convey ideas through the written word; (2) audio media—those that convey ideas through sounds; and (3) visual media—those that convey ideas through visual images. Our primary concern will be the latter two, as they are used independently or in combination with each other and usually referred to as audio-visual media or multimedia. Our emphasis will be on electronic media—those media that require the use of electricity. Much of this chapter will deal with the two main components of electronic media: (1) the "hardware"—the machines (projectors, cassette machines, record players, etc.); and (2) the "software"—the components that contain the subject content (films, slides, tapes, phonograph recordings, etc.).

The main subject areas to be covered in the chapter are the following: Audio, Slides, Slide-and-Tape Presentations, Video Making, and Discussing Media. Because of space limitations, the chapter is designed to serve as an introduction to the subject of media. It can be used as a basic manual to guide you in the utilization of media with youth. But it should be seen as a starting point! For suggestions concerning more detailed information on the various aspects of media, consult some of the resources listed in the media section of our final chapter.

Audio

All of us, and particularly young people, live in an audio world! Electronically reproduced sounds are all around us: in the music and announcements that we hear in stores; in the sounds of stereos in our homes and cars; in the sounds of the seemingly ever-present portable radios and cassette players that we hear in public parks, on the beaches, and even on the city streets! Many of our messages about our lives and our lifestyles come to us through audio media. People involved in youth work have a dual responsibility in regard to these media: (1) to utilize the media effectively in conveying the Christian faith and (2) to take the lead in analyzing the messages that we get from the media. The first of these responsibilities is the subject of this section of the chapter. The second will be dealt with in the final section.

Cassette tape. With the advent of the cassette, the medium of tape has become readily available to almost everyone. Your work with young people can be enhanced by this medium, regardless of whether you use the most expensive equipment and the highest quality tape or just a simple portable machine and budget tape bought at a local variety store. As with all electronic media, however, effectiveness is usually in direct proportion to the quality of the hardware and software used.

The quality of reproduction offered by compact disc players and by the new combination players that play both compact discs and videodiscs is truly outstanding. There is every reason to believe that compact discs will replace cassettes and records as a primary audio medium. At the present time, however, most individuals and churches have greater access to cassette recorders, which are extremely inexpensive and versatile. For that reason, our emphasis here is on work with cassette tapes.

What are some of the ways that cassette tape can be used in youth ministry? Here are a few suggestions:

1. **The cassette recorder is an excellent tool to use in doing interviews.** This activity can be done with a cassette deck that is part of an integrated stereo system in the classroom or a home. Usually, however, the procedure involves sending young people out with portable recorders to do interviews in homes, in meetings, in offices, or on the street. Just give the young people a list of questions on a particular topic; show them how to operate the machines; do a practice run to make sure that they are proficient; and send them out with their assignments.

Be sure to tell the young people to pause between their questions and the replies by the respondents. Young people should also be advised to tell the respondents to pause when moving from one part of a statement to another. These pauses will help insure more professional-sounding interviews, and they will be particularly helpful if you should decide to edit the material.

2. **One of the main uses of a cassette recorder is the transferring of music from a phonograph recording to a cassette tape.** Many young people immediately transfer recently purchased records to tape. This procedure has many advantages: tape is more portable than phonograph recordings; it takes up less storage space; and it provides a medium that preserves the sound quality better than records, which—even with the best care—soon develop "ticks" and scratches.

Compact discs are by far the most durable audio medium. You can expect to see far more materials produced on them in the near future. For the present, transfer of recordings from phonographs to cassette tape will continue as a frequently utilized process. If you have the proper equipment, you can also record from a compact disc to a cassette tape. While the cassette tape is not as high quality a medium as the compact disc, it may be more convenient for classroom use. Compact disc players are not yet a common resource in churches, though that may change, especially with the advent of combination players that can also play video discs.

If you use cassette tape in this manner, you should know these guidelines: (a) The best available equipment and tape should be used. (b) If a Dolby-equipped machine is available, use the Dolby setting to reduce background noise on the tape. (c) If possible, you should record directly from one machine to another by using "patch cords" rather than a microphone. (d) Use C-90 tapes. These tapes have a 45-minute capacity on each side, and, thus, they are ideal for recording phonograph albums, most of which do not run more than forty-five minutes.

90

(e) To record, simultaneously depress both the "record" button and the "play" button; run off a few inches of tape; then set the machine on "pause" while you spot-check the audio level of various bands.

If your machine does not have a pause control, you should proceed as follows: Start the record at the beginning or at some other silent play-through band; then simultaneously depress both the "record" button and the "play" button before the music begins.

Turn on the record; then begin recording each side of the record by disengaging the pause button before the music begins. This procedure will help you avoid distortion, "clicks" on the tape, deletions of musical material, and "start-up noise" caused by beginning the tape while the music is playing.

Transferring phonograph recordings to tape is an especially good method to use when you need to use audio material in a presentation to a class or some other group. By recording the material in the order in which you plan to use it, you can avoid the interruptions caused by changing records and cueing the bands that you need.

This method also provides a good medium for presenting the audio material found on the flimsy soundsheets that come from many curriculum publishers and other sources. And it provides a handy way of removing those annoying "beeps" that are found in many recordings designed for use as soundtracks with filmstrips.

3. **Cassette tapes can be used in recording audio scripts for presentation to a class.** Have your students write a play or a skit, or have them adapt a biblical narrative for this purpose. Then have them record the various voice parts as if they were recording a play for radio broadcast.

You can produce an interesting soundtrack by recording on both tracks of the tape with a stereo tape recorder and then playing the tape back on a monaural machine or on a stereo system with the "mono mode" control engaged. The recording thus played back in mono will integrate the two tracks into one. Here is the procedure: Record the voices on one track of the tape and record background music, sound effects, and so forth on the other track. If you have a three-head machine (one with a record head, an erase head, and a playback head), you can record the second track as you listen to the first by setting the first track on "tape monitor" and the second track on "record." Even on a two-head machine, however, you can achieve good results by using a stopwatch to help you determine where to add music and effects.

For best results, make sure that you carefully monitor the audio level of each track as it is recorded so that one track will not overshadow the other. And remember, this whole procedure is one that you have to get used to. With a little practice, however, you should be able to produce some amazingly professional-sounding results!

4. **A cassette tape can be used for leading a class through a programmed classroom experience.** Here's how you do it. Decide on the procedures that you want the students to follow. Write a script giving step-by-step, explicit instructions. (The basic procedure is to give a block of information and some simple instructions and then to write in "stop-the-tape" cues such as "Stop the tape and do this procedure; then turn the tape back on again." Then record the script and have students participate in the experience by listening to the tape and doing the procedures according to the taped

instructions. Here is a sample of how part of a script might appear:

The five main elements in a worship service are: (*pause*) Adoration and Praise of God; (*pause*) Confession of Sins; (*pause*) Thanksgiving to God; (*pause*) Education About the Christian Faith; (*pause*) and Dedicating Ourselves to God. (*pause*)

On the tables in your work areas are copies of the bulletin from last week's service. Working together in teams, go through the bulletins and decide which of these five categories each part of the service belongs in. Then record your decisions on the newsprint posted in your work areas.

Once again, here are the five categories: (*pause*) Adoration and Praise; (*pause*) Confession; (*pause*) Thanksgiving; (*pause*) Education About the Faith; (*pause*) and Dedication. (*pause*) Okay, ready? Stop the tape and do this assignment. When you have finished, turn the tape back on and listen to the instructions for the next assignment.

5. **Cassettes are very useful for providing the audio component of a slide-and-tape presentation.** Although there will be many instances when it is desirable to have a "live" commentary for slides, filmstrips, and other visual presentations, a well-paced, interesting soundtrack is generally a real plus. The use of such a track will give you a chance to prepare the audio in a deliberate, well-thought out manner and will usually result in a more interesting presentation. For detailed information on this technique, see the section of this chapter entitled "Slide-and-Tape Presentations."

6. **Cassette tapes are excellent tools for providing audio materials for use in learning centers.** In the learning center approach, various sections of the classroom are set up as areas where students may work individually or in teams to perform specified learning tasks either on their own or with some assistance and/or guidance by a teacher. Cassette machines placed in these areas can be used to give very simple instructions for specific tasks or very elaborate instructions for programmed experiences, as discussed above.

There are many other ways to use cassettes in learning centers. You can set up several centers in which you have placed cassettes containing interviews of various persons. You can set up music centers with the cassette in each center containing a particular kind of religious music (for example, standard hymns, classical religious music, folk hymns, pop songs with religious themes, and so forth). You can have students record their responses to questions posted in the centers and afterward use these responses as the basis of a full-class discussion. There are many more possibilities. Just do a little brainstorming! You'll probably be pleasantly surprised at what you come up with!

Guidelines for audio recording and playback. Using audio tape is basically a simple process. Cassettes, in particular, provide a simple medium, one that can be used even by young children. Nevertheless, many people run into all sorts of difficulties when making and playing back audio recordings. Here are some guidelines that will help you minimize your difficulties and increase your effectiveness in using audio tape:

1. **Become familiar with the "keyboard" of your tape machine.** Learn what all those knobs or levers are for and how they should be used.

With most machines you begin recording by engaging (usually by depressing) both the "record" button and the "play" button. The "rewind" button rewinds the tape at a fast speed; the "fast forward" button moves the tape forward at about the same speed. The "play" button engages the playback head and allows you to hear what is on the tape. The "stop" button is used to stop the tape when it is being rewound, when it is moving forward at a rapid speed, or when it is playing back the recorded sound. With most machines, the tape will stop automatically when the tape has been completely rewound or when it has proceeded forward (either on "fast forward" or on "play") to the end of the tape.

The "pause" button is a special control found on some machines. It is a very desirable feature, since it not only allows you to stop the tape momentarily but also enables you to produce better recordings—as discussed above. It is usually operated by depressing once to engage the pause control and by depressing a second time to disengage it. If you are planning to purchase or borrow a tape machine, you should try to secure one that has a pause control.

If your machine has an audio level meter (often designated "VU meter"), become acquainted with how this meter works. It controls the volume level of the audio input that is to be recorded. With the machine set for recording and the pause control engaged, spot-check the audio level by playing various sections of the phonograph record to be recorded or—if you are recording "live"—by speaking into the microphone or having the performing group do some sample material. Note the VU meter. Adjust the volume controls up or down until you get a reading that registers on the meter but does not show high distortion level. On most meters, distortion is indicated when the indicator needle moves to the right of the "O" marking (into the "+" area—which is often designated by numbers in a different color from those that mark the "safe" level).

2. **If your machine operates on either AC current (the electricity you get from an electrical outlet) or batteries, do not use the batteries except when absolutely necessary.** AC current is much stronger, and it is not as likely to "foul up" a tape. If you are recording in an area where AC current is not available, be sure to check your batteries before using them. Also, do not leave batteries in the machine when it is not being used. Power will be drained away, and the batteries will wear out faster.

If your machine does not have a pause control, set the machine for recording, spot-check the audio level by recording various parts of your audio material, and then rewind the tape and reset for recording.

3. **Use the best quality tape that your machine will accommodate.** Much of the budget tape available in variety stores and discount outlets is thin, of low quality, and not properly housed in the cassette. Tape of this type breaks easily, is more prone to "foul-ups," and generally produces low-quality recordings. Most budget tape is not suitable for music reproduction, and it should be used for voice recordings only when higher quality tape is not available.

Cassette tape comes in four standard lengths: C-30, C-60, C-90, and C-120—with a recording capacity on each side, respectively, of 15 minutes, 30 minutes, 45 minutes, and 60 minutes. The C-120 tape should be avoided, since it is very thin and therefore easily broken. For most classroom uses, you should choose either the C-60 or the C-90.

4. **For best results in recording music from a phonograph recording, use a high-quality cassette deck rather than an inexpensive portable machine.** Follow the instructions for music recording given in part two above.

5. **Use the best quality microphone that you can afford.** As a general rule, the inexpensive microphones that come with most portable cassette recorders are of very low quality and should be replaced with "dynamic" microphones.

6. **When recording "live," make sure that the area or room in which you are recording is as soundproof as possible.** Listen for noises that may show up unexpectedly on the recording: the hum of an air conditioner, the sound of footsteps outside. Eliminate as many of these as possible. Be aware of the general acoustics of the room. Sound tends to bounce off metal objects and other hard substances. Try to find a carpeted room. Cover metal objects and other sound reflectors with a blanket or a towel.

Give some attention to placement of microphones. Make sure they are neither too close to or too far from the source of your audio. As a rule, hand-held microphones present a problem. You are likely to move them about and create extraneous noise. Mount your mike on a stand or place it on a table with a handkerchief or a towel under the mike. Make sure that your mike faces the audio source. If you use a script, avoid moving or rattling the paper; such movement will produce "paper noise" on the tape.

7. **Try to secure a recorder with a digital counter—and use the counter.** Most high-quality recorders have an indicator of this sort that will help you quickly locate a particular spot on the tape. Set the counter at "000" when you begin recording, and then make notes as to points at which various parts of the recorded material begin. After you rewind the tape for playback, reset the counter at "000" once again. Thus, you will be able to locate any section of the tape by engaging either the rewind control or the fast-forward control and moving the tape quickly to the desired location.

One word of caution: digital counters are not standardized. Generally, the digital readings for any particular machine are effective for that machine only. If you play the tape on another machine, you will need to redo your digital counter notes on the basis of the readings on the second machine.

8. **When recording voices, make sure that the people doing the talking are stationed at the proper distance from the microphones.** Have these people speak directly into the mikes. As a rule, you will get better results if people stand rather than sit; the human vocal apparatus works better and projects more effectively when people are standing. Caution people not to "pop" their p's and to avoid other speaking noises that will produce unwanted sounds on the recording.

9. **When playing a recording for a group, try to secure the best amplification possible.** Even a tape recording made on a very inexpensive machine will sound much better when played back on a system in which a cassette deck is hooked up to a good amplifier and good speakers. If such a system is not available, you can still improve the playback quality by connecting a good

speaker to the cassette machine at the point designated for external or remote speakers. To secure this type of speaker, check with Radio Shack or other companies that sell speakers especially designed for use with inexpensive portable tape machines.

10. **Take precautions to avoid accidental erasure of recorded material.** Remember that when the recorder is operating in the record mode, all previously recorded material will be erased! If you have made a recording on a cassette and you want to be sure that the material will not be erased, use a letter opener or a small knife to pry loose the two plastic squares on the edge of the cassette opposite the open end. If you later decide to rerecord on the tape, just cover the holes with pieces of cellophane tape.

11. **To produce an "edited" tape, hook up two tape machines and play the original tape on the first machine and record the edited version on a new tape in the second machine.** Use the pause control or the stop control on the second machine to interrupt recording on the new tape while unwanted material on the original tape is "played through." Then resume recording the new tape when you reach the next point at which you wish to transfer material.

One word of caution about tape transfer: Each transfer of recorded material will produce a slightly weakened version of the original recording. Recordings thus made are referred to as "generations." A second generation recording will be weaker than the first generation (or original) recording; a third generation will be weaker than the second. Therefore, you should try to minimize the number of generations involved in the editing process. If your machines are of relatively good quality, an editing process that involves only one transfer will generally

produce only a slight deterioration of the sound quality, usually not enough to be noticed by people with average hearing ability.

12. **Become adept at "troubleshooting" with cassettes.** Here are some suggestions:

● If the tape will not move, check first to see if the machine is plugged in or if the batteries are bad.

● If the machine is getting power and the tape still does not work, check to see if you have the cassette in upside down or if the tape needs to be rewound.

● If you have taken the above steps and the tape still does not move, it may be that the tape has gotten into a bind. If this seems to be the case, take the cassette out of the machine and hit the edge of the cassette against a table. If this procedure does not produce the desired results, insert a ball-point pen or a pencil into the sprocket drive of the cassette and rotate the drive a few times to loosen the tape. If all these procedures fail, try playing the tape on a high-quality machine that has a strong drive system.

● If the tape "leaks out" of the cassette and gets wound around the drive mechanism, carefully remove the cassette from the machine and try to disentangle the tape from the drive mechanism without breaking the tape. Then insert a ball-point pen or a pencil into the cassette sprocket and slowly rewind the tape back onto the cassette.

For more ideas on cassettes, see the section of this chapter entitled "Slide-and-Tape Presentations." For general ideas on using the medium of music, see our chapter entitled "Music! Music! Music!"

Slides

Slides are an excellent medium for use in youth ministry. They are relatively inexpensive. They can be shown in any order that you choose. And they can be shown at various speeds to produce effects ranging from a leisurely paced, easy flow to a rapid, frenzied succession of visuals. And, even though slides present still, static images, they can give the impression of dynamic movement.

How do we produce slides? With a high-quality camera in the hands of an experienced, competent photographer? That's one of the best methods. But not the only one, by any means. It is possible to produce very good homemade slides "on a shoestring budget." And this process is one that can offer many advantages, educationally and otherwise. For one thing, homemade slides offer a wide range of possibilities that are usually not available through the use of a camera. You can make homemade slides of people and events that you could not possibly photograph with a camera. Also, making homemade slides is an exciting hands-on activity that can involve all of your students and facilitate group building.

There are many ways to make homemade slides. The following are some of the most widely used methods:

1. **Contact-lift slides.** To make slides by this method, you will need the following supplies: clear, adhesive shelf paper (Con-Tact, Marvelon, or some other brand), fold-over slide mounts (such as Kodak Ready-Mounts), glossy magazines (the ones with a clay-based surface such as *Newsweek*, *Time*, and *Life*), bowls or similar containers, hand soap or liquid dishwashing soap, water (warm to hot), scissors, spoons, and an iron (a photo-tacking iron or just a regular clothes iron). The process for making contact-lift slides is as follows:

● Cut the adhesive shelf paper into 2-inch squares.

● Select a magazine picture that will fit into a slide mount in such a way that the part that you want to use is framed by the opening in the slide mount.

● Peel the backing paper off the 2-inch square of shelf paper.

● Place the piece of shelf paper with the adhesive side down on the magazine picture. Cut out the part of the picture that is attached to the shelf paper.

● Rub the back of the piece of shelf paper with the rounded part of a spoon until you have removed all wrinkles and air bubbles.

● Place the piece of shelf paper with the picture attached in a bowl of warm-to-hot soapy water. Leave it there for about five minutes.

● Remove the shelf paper/picture from the bowl. In many cases, the picture will have separated from the shelf paper by this stage in the process. If this separation has not occurred, very carefully peel the two apart. The image or picture will adhere to the shelf paper to form a transparent picture.

● Using cold tap water, wash the transparency that you have just made.

● Carefully place the transparency in the slide mount. Make sure that the transparency completely covers the opening in the mount and that the part of the picture that you want to use is framed by the opening.

● Fold over the other side of the slide mount and iron the slide mount shut by going around the edges of the mount. Be sure not to touch the transparency with the iron. You now have a slide that is ready for projection.

2. **Write-on slides.** To make write-on slides, you will need the following supplies: clear, 2-inch plastic slide squares or pre-prepared write-on slides (available from Griggs Associates, other nationwide suppliers, and some local art supply stores)—or sheets of clear or frosted acetate; fold-over slide mounts (such as Kodak Ready-Mounts); scissors; an iron; and high-intensity pens and markers (the kind that will write on almost any surface).

The process is very simple. If you use acetate, cut it into 2-inch squares and mount them in the fold-over slide mounts according to directions given in the last two steps of the contact-lift slide process described above. If you use 2-inch plastic slide squares or pre-prepared write-on slides designed for this purpose, do not mount them in slide mounts; just use them as they are. To make slides, simply draw or write on the plastic slide squares or on the portion of the acetate that shows through the opening in the slide mount.

If you cannot secure acetate sheets, plastic slide or write-on slides, you can make your own slide material from an old filmstrip. Just soak the filmstrip in household bleach (such as Clorox) until the images disappear. You will then have a clear piece of filmstrip stock that can be used by turning it sideways and cutting it to fit #127 fold-over slide mounts.

3. **Slides using filmstrip visuals.** Supplies needed for the procedure are: old filmstrips, "half-mount" slide mounts (also called "easy-mounts"), and scissors. The procedure is as follows: Select from old filmstrips several frames that you would like to use in a slide show. Cut out the frames you want. Be sure to cut through the middle of the spaces (usually black or purple areas) that separate the frames from one another. Insert the frames into the slide mounts.

4. **Slides using filmstrip leader.** You will need the following supplies: old filmstrips; #127 fold-over slide mounts (such as Kodak Ready-Mount); a sharp penknife or other sharp, pointed instrument; scissors; and high-intensity pens and markers (optional).

The process is as follows: Cut off a strip of filmstrip leader (the solid black or purple strip at the beginning or end of a filmstrip). Using a penknife or other sharp, pointed instrument, scratch the duller side of the leader in such a way as to create a line drawing or words. If you wish, you may color in the scratched area. Cut the piece of leader to size and mount it in a #127 fold-over slide mount according to the procedure given in the last two steps of the contact-lift slide-making process described above. If you prefer, you may mount the strip before scratching on the design.

This type of slide produces a very unusual special effect. Since most of the material projected is black or dark purple, the image that you have created will glow as if it were a neon sign!

Slide-and-Tape Presentations

Multimedia presentations featuring slides and an audio accompaniment are very popular! And most young people are absolutely fascinated by them! In my own personal experience, time and time again, I have seen a lethargic group of youth suddenly come alive when they get involved in preparing and presenting a production of this sort! At some point in your youth ministry, you should give this activity a try! You will probably find it to be both an educationally sound experience and a superb group-building tool. And you are likely to get good results regardless of whether you simply put together a basic production using one slide projector and a one-track cassette tape or "go all out" and produce a very complex show using several projectors and "dissolve" units accompanied by a stereo soundtrack featuring voices, music, and sound effects!

The basic preparation procedure will remain essentially the same whether you are involved with a simple presentation or an extremely complicated one. The main steps to follow are these:

1. **Select a theme for your presentation.** You may start with a topic, such as "Love" or "God's World" or "Poverty and Affluence." Or you may simply begin with a ready-made audio component, such as a recording of a popular song. If you choose this latter approach, skip step 2 and proceed to the second paragraph of step 3.

2. **If you choose the topical approach, write a brief outline that includes the main points that you want to convey in your presentation.** At this stage, you should begin to consider the kinds of visuals that you will use.

3. **Using your outline as a guide, write an audio script/production chart that includes voice parts and notations regarding use of music and sound effects.** A good procedure is to write the script in three or four columns. You should have separate columns for voice, time, and music/sound effects. If you prefer, the music and sound effects may be indicated under separate columns. Leave space in your script for the addition of columns for listing of visuals (usually one column per set of visuals).

If you are using a song as your audio component, you should make up a production script with a column for the song lyrics, a column for tune markings, and columns for visuals.

4. **Prepare your audio track.** The preparation procedure will vary according to the type of track you are preparing. Here are directions for preparing two of the most commonly used types:

● If you are using a prerecorded audio selection (such as a song from a phonograph record), just hook up your equipment and transfer the selection to your tape according to the procedures described in the section on audio.

● If you are recording a voice track only, you may choose one of these three methods:

Procedure #1: Try to record the material with one "pass" by having your narrator(s) record the script from beginning to end without stopping. This method requires much advance preparation and practice and is usually successful only when used with very good professional "talent." Even with professionals, however, this method has many pitfalls. In more than ten years of directing recording sessions with amateurs and professionals, I have had only a couple of experiences in which a narrator was able to go through a complete script without a fumble or a flub!

Procedure #2: A better method is to divide the script into sections and record it a section at a time with the recorder stopped or set on "pause" between the sections. With this method you can rewind the tape and redo sections that are not satisfactory.

Procedure #3: The best method is to record the script a section at a time by the "take" system and then to transfer the satisfactory material to a "master tape" by the editing method described in the audio section. With this system, you keep the tape "rolling" throughout the session and record each section sequentially as many times as necessary to secure a satisfactory recording. In order to provide cues for later editing, you begin each new attempt at recording a section with words such as "page 2—paragraph 3—take 2," and so forth. If you choose to stop the recorder between takes, your editing cue would be worded like this: "We're recording page 2—paragraph 3—take 2."

5. **Edit your audio track according to the procedure described in the audio section.**

6. **Prepare your visuals by making slides with a camera and/or making homemade slides by using one or more of the methods described in the section on slides.**

7. **Select the slides that you will actually use in your presentation.** An inexpensive slide sorter will be very helpful to you as you make your selection. If you have not already listed the slides on your script/production chart, you should list them at this stage in the process.

8. **Sequence the slides by lining them up in the order in which you plan to use them.** Arrange them in that order in your slide projector(s).

9. **Mark timings on your script/production charts.**

10. **Assign responsibilities for operation of machines and practice, practice, practice!**

Guidelines for slide-and-tape presentations. Anytime that you work with electronic media, you run the risk of having something "go haywire"! Part of this risk results from what some wag has called "the innate perversity of inanimate objects—especially machines"! No matter how well you prepare, something can always go wrong.

Although there is no way to guarantee that a particular slide-and-tape presentation will proceed without a hitch, you can minimize the possibility of foul-ups occurring. *First,* check and double-check all major factors involved in the presentation. *Second,* be prepared for specific problems that develop, and when they do occur, don't panic! Have an emergency game plan ready—and use it!

1. **Secure the highest quality slide-projector that you can.** For best results, use a carousel projector (the kind that uses a circular slide tray that sits flat on the top of the projector). This type of projector is much more reliable than those types that use a cube, a cartridge, or a "ferris wheel" tray. Other desirable features include a projection lamp (bulb) that will give you a bright, clear picture on the screen; automatic focusing; a timer for automatic changing of slides at various intervals; and a remote control device. If possible, you should secure extra lenses for projecting the picture at various distances.

99

2. **Slides should be placed in the tray upside down and backwards (as seen from a viewpoint behind the projector).** Once you have lined up your slides for proper placement in the tray, number them with a pencil (not with ink). It is a good idea to write the numbers in the same location—for example, the upper right corner of the back of each slide mount. Numbering the slides before you place them in the tray can lower your panic level considerably in the event that the slides should spill out of the tray. Of course, you can help avoid this mishap by always securing the collar on the top of the tray as soon as you have finished filling it!

3. **Bent or broken slides can get stuck in your projector and ruin your presentation or, at the very least, throw your timing off.** Make sure that slide mounts are sturdy and unbent. Try to keep the mounts from becoming tipped or dog-eared. If a mount does get damaged, remount the slide.

4. **Develop a storage system that will give you ready access to any presentation that you have prepared.** Store slides in carousel trays, and place the trays in their original boxes. Store cassettes in their original boxes or in a shelf unit or a cassette storage case. Be sure to label all trays, cassettes, and containers.

5. **Arrange projectors so that the line of projection will not be blocked by viewers' heads.** If possible, station the projectors six feet or so above the floor. If you do not have a stand designed for this purpose, improvise! Place projectors on the hat shelf of a coat-and-hat rack. Or place them on small tables situated on banquet tables. If you use this latter method, be careful. Most banquet tables are collapsible and have been known to collapse under the weight of would-be projectionists.

6. **Make sure that the room is properly prepared for projection.** Check to be sure that the room can be darkened easily and sufficiently. Make sure that projectors can be situated far enough from the screens to produce an image that is large enough to be seen clearly by all viewers. And use screens that are large enough to accommodate images of that size. Have small penlights on hand so that you can read scripts and operate machines when the room is darkened. Be sure to have stopwatches or watches with sweep-second hands available for use in checking timings.

7. **Make sure that you have access to wall receptacles.** Have on hand several extension cords and two-pronged adapters for three-pronged plugs. Locate your fuse boxes or circuit breakers. Have extra fuses on hand if your electrical system requires them.

8. **Use the best playback system that you can secure.** Place speakers in front of viewers and at or near ear level.

9. **If you wish to make your presentation look more professional, try to secure a dissolve unit that will fade each projected image into the following one.**
Dissolve units are fairly expensive, but you may be able to borrow one. In many communities, it is possible to borrow such a unit (and sometimes even projectors and screens!) from the audio-visual department of a local school or college.

Another helpful, "professional" technique is the utilization of an inaudible electronic impulse to change slides automatically according to preprogrammed electronic "instructions" that you can cue into an audio tape in advance. Here again, a local school or college may be a good source for this type of equipment. Also, in many cases, an audio-visual teacher or technician in a school's media department will give you instructions for preparing and using pre-programmed tapes of this type.

10. **Finally, there is the general rule for audio-visual work: Check and double-check!** Don't leave anything to chance! Prepare well. Then check all aspects of your preparation. Do a run-through. Then reset and recue your equipment. And, just before showtime double-check again!

Video Making

There is probably no media activity that can "turn on" a youth group the way film or video making can! Whenever young people get involved in this medium, there is almost always intense excitement, whether you make a simple, silent film with an inexpensive camera; a sound video; or a complex sound movie complete with fades, dissolves, and all sorts of trick cinematography.

The number of persons with video cameras or camcorders has increased significantly, and many churches are starting to purchase these as programming resources. Prices can be expected to fall dramatically over the next few years. The next chapter, titled "Video," focuses primarily on VCR use in the church, though there are suggestions which will help you in work with video cameras. In this section on "video making," I will be sharing information which can be used, with only slight modification, whether you are using a movie camera or a video camera (or camcorder). For the most part, the words *film*, *movie*, and *video* will be used in reference to essentially the same production process. The context will make it clear when instructions are specifically for movie equipment or video equipment.

As exciting as filmmaking is, however, it is also hard work! Having a group make a film, even a brief one, is an involved, time-consuming process, if you do it right! Preparation for filmmaking requires many hours of intensive work; and the filmmaking process itself involves many more hours. But it's worth it! The finished product can be something that the young people are justifiably proud of! And every session along the way, both in preparation and in production, can be an opportunity for learning, group building, and great fun!

To get the best results, you must prepare a step-by-step plan and urge the youth to be involved at every step! If your group is like those I have worked with, the initial excitement about making a film may turn to impatience quite early in the process! The youth that I am now working with are participating in a ten-week process that will culminate in the making of a 15-minute movie. Many of the young people thought that they would begin making the film at the first session; and they were naturally impatient when I posted the schedule calling for seven preparatory sessions before the beginning of filming. Be prepared for impatience, and be ready to deal with it! Point out to the young people that you can empathize with their impatience and that you, too, are impatient to get on with the filming. Then assure them that they are going to have many exciting, fun-filled experiences along the way. And ask for a pledge of involvement in the whole process.

In the next few pages, we will discuss a basic plan for filmmaking. Although the plan is designed specifically for filmmaking, it can also be used with slight modifications with groups that wish to create a video-cassette production.

101

Equipment and supplies. Few churches have on hand all the equipment and supplies that are needed for filmmaking. Determine what items will have to be bought. Check local sources of rental equipment. And see what equipment can be borrowed from church members and others. In most churches where I have worked with youth, I have been able to find people who had equipment that they would let the group borrow. In some cases, I have been astounded at what I have uncovered! In the church where I now work, I have discovered that equipment owned by members includes a Eumig Super-8 sound camera and projector and three Bolex 16mm cameras—one of which is sound equipped. So scout around! You may be surprised at what you find!

The basic equipment and supplies that you will need are as follows:

- Movie camera (sound or silent) or camcorder

- Tape recorder, microphones, and tape (if you plan to produce a separate soundtrack to accompany a silent film)

- Movie film or video-cassette tape

- Tripod (preferably an adjustable one)

- Dolly (can be improvised in many ways—for example, by using a four-wheeled, cafeteria serving cart or a grocery cart)

- Lights (camera-mounted lights or—better by far—photo floodlights that can be mounted on stands at heights of up to six feet or so)

- Script materials (paper, pens, or pencils, paper clips, and so forth)

- Stopwatch

- Editor/viewer and splicing supplies (splicing tape, scissors, single-edged razor, straight pins)

- Projector (sound or silent—according to the type of film that you plan to make) or video player

- Projection screen

A schedule for a filmmaking workshop. The following is a basic schedule that you may use with a group that has never made a film before. The suggested times may vary, depending on the complexity of your project and the pace and involvement of the group.

Learning about film. Viewing and discussing a professionally prepared movie or TV show.

(1-2 hours)

"Hands-On" experience with a camera. Learning how to "shoot" a film.

(1-2 hours)

General planning. Deciding on the basic theme and general outlines of your film.

(1 hour)

Scriptwriting. Writing of the production script.

(2-3 hours)

Acting practice. Having run-throughs of some of the scenes.

(2 hours)

Production planning. Making plans regarding locales, shooting schedules, and so forth.

(1 hour)

Preparing costumes and props and learning about makeup. An optional step.

(2-4 hours)

Shooting the film.

(4 hours)

Preparing the soundtrack. An optional step.

(2 hours)

Editing the film. Deciding which footage to use and splicing together the selected footage.

(2-4 hours)

Some detailed information. The following guidelines provide some information that may be helpful to you as you lead the group through the sessions of your filmmaking workshop:

Step One: Show a professionally prepared movie to the group or have the group watch a TV show. Select a movie or TV show that will include different types of camera shots, lots of dialogue, and a good soundtrack. As a general rule, a scripted, acted-out movie or TV show is better for this activity than a documentary.

Divide the group into four teams that will analyze four different aspects of the movie or TV show. Give members of each team one of the sets of questions provided below. Have the youth use these questions as the basis of their analyses of the movie or TV show. Have the whole group view the presentation. Then have small-team discussions, followed by small-team reports to the full group.

ANALYSIS OF CAMERA WORK

1. Note from what distance various shots are taken. Does the distance from the camera to the scenes seem appropriate? Why or why not?

2. Note the various angles from which scenes are shot. Are any of these angles especially unusual? What effect is created by the use of unusual camera angles?

3. How are scenes introduced? By establishing shots (ESs) that establish locale? By long-distance shots (LSs)? By medium shots (MSs)? By close-ups (CUs)? Are the various types of shots effective? Why and/or why not?

4. Does the camera zoom? If so, in? out? both? Why is this technique used? Does the camera pan (move from side-to-side)? If so, is the movement left-to-right? right-to-left? both? Which of these movements seems most natural? Why? Why do you think this technique is used?

5. Does the camera ever move? If so, what effect does this produce? Why is this technique used? Can you spot examples of "hand-held" camera work? Why do you think this technique would be used?

6. How is the camera used in introducing the characters?

7. How is lighting used? In front of the scenes? behind them? from above? from the side? Which scenes use natural light? Which use artificial light? What effects does the lighting produce?

8. What special or extraordinary uses of the camera do you note?

9. Is the camera work ever obtrusive? If so, how and why? Does the camera work generally help or hinder the development of the film? Explain your answers.

ANALYSIS OF THE SOUND

1. Is the overall sound quality good? Why or why not?

2. Is music used? If so, how? Does it underline the emotions and actions? Or does it get in the way? Explain your answers.

3. What sound effects (natural and artificial) are you aware of? Do they strengthen the movie? Why or why not?

4. Is the soundtrack too subtle? too obtrusive? just right? Explain your answers.

5. What do you consider the best use of sound in the movie? the least effective use of sound? Explain your answers.

6. How would you have done the sound differently? Why?

ANALYSIS OF THE CHARACTERS AND ACTING

1. Are the people in the film actors? Or are they real persons being themselves in a documentary? Explain your answers.

2. Is the acting good? Why or why not? Who is the best actor or actress? Who is the worst? Name some specific scenes and/or lines that caused you to respond as you did.

3. How is the timing of the actors and actresses? Give some specific examples to substantiate your opinions.

4. How are the gestures? the facial expressions? Are they convincing? Why or why not?

5. Which lines were done especially well? Which were done badly? Explain your answers.

6. Which characters showed character development? In what ways did characters develop? Did the quality of the acting strengthen or weaken the portrayal of character development? Explain your answers.

7. Which scenes were the most believable? the least believable? Why?

8. If you were directing a remake of some of the scenes, how would you advise the people in the film to change their acting? Explain your answers.

ANALYSIS OF THE EDITING OF THE FILM

1. Is the pace of the film too fast? too slow? about right? Does the pace fit the subject matter of the film? Explain your answers.

2. Do the various parts of the film seem to fit together well? Or does the film seem disjointed and disconnected? Explain your answers.

3. Do the scenes seem to be too long? too brief? about the right length? Explain your answers. What about individual shots? Do they last too long? Or are they too brief? about right? Explain your answers.

4. Does the film move well? Or is the film too static? Does one scene seem to follow another in a logical flow? Explain your answers.

5. Are flashbacks used? If so, how are they used? Are they effective? What do the flashbacks contribute to the overall development of the film? Explain your answers.

6. In what ways would you have edited the film differently? Why?

In addition to having the young people view and analyze a movie or TV show, you may also want to show a film that is designed to show various movie-making techniques. Especially recommended are: "Award-Winning Teenage Films"; "Six

Filmmakers in Search of a Wedding"; "American Time Capsule"; and "Braverman's Cream of Beatle Soup." See our final chapter for information on how to order these films.

Step Two: "Hands-on" experience with a camera. Secure a movie or video camera, a tripod, and photo floodlights. Have the young people shoot various scenes. You may wish to plan some situations in advance, but you will probably find that the youth themselves will offer a multitude of suggestions!

Here are some activities that will be helpful: shooting establishing shots; shooting long-distance shots; shooting medium shots; shooting close-ups; panning; zooming; shooting with the camera mounted on a tripod; shooting with a hand-held camera; using an improvised dolly (mounting a camera on a cafeteria serving cart or a grocery cart and moving this makeshift dolly forward and backward as you are shooting); shooting with natural light and artificial light—with the light coming from a variety of directions (from above, from below, from each side, from behind the camera, from behind the scene, and so forth); shooting trick shots—for example, making people "disappear" by stopping the camera and moving people out of a scene before continuing shooting; and shooting scenes by exposing a few frames at a time (with each exposure lasting only a *split second!*).

Steps Three and Four: General planning and scriptwriting. Have a general planning session in which you select the basic theme of your movie and outline the scenes. Then have sessions in which you write the script. A movie script should be written like a play script. It should include: notations about the settings of the scenes; dialogue for actors and actresses; suggestions about gestures, movements, and voice tone; and so forth. In addition, a movie script should have explicit directions regarding camera angles, types of shots, panning, zooming, lighting.

Step Five: Acting practice. Begin by having the young people do role plays and simple skits. Then have them do run-throughs of various scenes by acting them out "readers' theater style," with scripts in hand. Then attempt some scenes by memory. You should have a director or a directorial team that can critique the actors in respect to delivery of lines, movements, gestures, facial expressions, and so forth.

Step Eight: Shooting the film. You should shoot the film *one shot at a time*! Choose a section of the script. Then divide the section into various parts so that each part can be the subject of an individual shot. For each shot, decide on the type and/or location of lighting, the camera angle, and special camera effects (panning, zooming, and so forth). Then set up the scene, have actors and actresses run through the scene, and shoot it.

Most scenes will have to be attempted more than once. The scenes should be done in "takes." Before each attempt at shooting, prepare a sign that will be photographed briefly at the beginning of the take. A typical sign might be worded like this: "Script pages 3-4. Scene 2. Take 2."

Step Nine: Preparing the soundtrack. This step is optional. If you are making a silent movie, you may not need a soundtrack—unless you choose to create a music and/or narration track to provide a general accompaniment for the film. If you are making a "talkie" and you have a sound camera, the sound would be recorded as you are filming.

105

If you decide to create a closely coordinated tape to be played on a separate playback system while your silent film is being shown, you should prepare a tape according to the directions in the audio section of this chapter. To prepare this type of sound accompaniment for a silent film, you should: (a) completely finish your film; (b) time the various sections of the film with a stopwatch or a watch with a sweep-second hand; (c) write an audio production script that will match the timings for the various sections of the film; (d) record your audio component (with the aid of a watch) in such a way as to correlate the audio timings with the film timings; and (e) select "cue points" in the film and the tape so that you will be able to coordinate the film screening with the tape playback. The best cue points are the first film image (usually the first frame of the titles) and the first musical note or the first spoken word on the tape.

If you choose to create a separate audio track to accompany a silent film, you will probably have better results if you do not attempt to coordinate dialogue too closely with specific scenes. As a rule, you should avoid trying to match dialogue with scenes that show close-ups of the people who are speaking. Synchronizing recorded words with lip movements by this method is extremely difficult!

Step Ten: Editing the film. After you have shot all your footage, you will need to assemble the film. Your first step should be to cut out unsatisfactory takes—the so-called "out-takes." Next, you should select the footage that you want to use and arrange it in sequence for assembly. You can either wind the footage onto small reels or—with short sections of film—you can hang the film from a bulletin board by attaching it to the board with straight pins placed through

the film's sprocket holes. Once you have arranged all your footage in sequence, you then assemble it by connecting the various sections with splicing tape (available at photography supply stores).

The editing process can be done with the use of a strong light behind the film and a magnifying glass to help you distinguish the film images. If you decide to do the editing in this manner, you may also want to view the film sections by running them through the projector. The best method for editing film, however, involves the use of a film editor (sometimes called an "edi-viewer") which consists of a small viewing screen, a splicer, and mounts for a loaded reel and take-up reel.

This section on filmmaking is designed to give you some basic information about making a film with a group of young people. More information can be found in filmmaking manuals produced by such companies as Kodak and GAF and books produced by independent publishers. For an excellent resource that is an invaluable aid for church groups who want to get into filmmaking, see the Serendipity book entitled *Festival.* This resource provides step-by-step suggestions for leading a group through a course that includes team-building labs, biblical research, and filmmaking steps.

Discussing Media

The creation of media productions is an exciting technique for use in youth ministry! It can be an excellent means for building group spirit; and it can provide an effective method for getting young people to deal with matters pertaining to the Christian faith. Just as important, however, is the analysis of the media and the messages that they convey to us. Using media items in this manner should be an ongoing part of any youth worker's responsibility! The following are a few guidelines that will help you in presenting, analyzing, and discussing media in your work with youth:

1. **Use both secular, mass-media materials, and materials designed to present various aspects of the Christian faith.** Materials produced by religiously oriented companies and organizations can be excellent tools for conveying the Christian faith. And your youth ministry will be greatly enhanced by use of materials of this sort. But you should also have a keen awareness of the fact that in our media-deluged environment many of our messages about life and living come to us from such secular media as commercial movies, television, pop music, newspapers, and magazines! These messages should be regularly analyzed from a Christian viewpoint in your youth groups and classes!

2. **When using electronic media in the classroom, use the best equipment that you can get.** There is a direct ratio between the quality of the media vehicle and the intensity of the message conveyed! A color TV is usually more influential than a black-and-white set; a large movie screen and good audio reproduction are more likely to make a strong impression than a small screen and inadequate sound reproduction; a good stereo system produces more listener involvement than a tinny, monaural record player. So use good equipment—even if it means having your media sessions in a home where such equipment is available!

3. **Be prepared!** Prepare the room. Make sure that chairs and tables and work or discussion areas are arranged for the best presentation and processing of media selections. Place speakers, screens, and so forth, where they will be most effective. Be sure that the room can be darkened if necessary. Check your hardware. Make sure that all machines are operating properly and that you know how to operate them. Have on hand all necessary equipment and supplies: extension cords; two-pronged adapters for three-pronged plugs; stopwatches; penlights; take-up reels; and so forth. Check fuse boxes and/or circuit breakers. Double-check everything.

4. **Whenever possible, preview a media selection before using it with a group.** Such a procedure will help you eliminate offensive or ineffectual material; and it will give you an opportunity to think through your discussion plans in advance! If it is not possible to preview the selection (which is generally the case with a TV show), try to get as much advance information as possible. A VCR lets you record a TV show or movie, preview it, and then show it to your group.

5. **Vary the approach that you use in presenting and discussing media selections.** Here are three possible approaches:

- Have students view and/or listen to the selection. Then discuss it.

- Have students view and/or listen to a part of the selection. Then stop the machine and have a discussion. Continue to the end of the selection by repeating this process: view and/or listen; stop the machine; discuss. Afterward, discuss the selection as a whole.

- Have students view and/or listen to the selection. Then discuss the selection. Finally, have students view and/or listen to the selection a second time. Discuss how their awareness of the selection may have been altered by the intervening discussion.

6. **Proceed in the following manner from a general, no-risk discussion to a very specific, detailed discussion.** Ask the youth to give personal feelings and opinions about how the media selection might relate to their own lives:

● First, ask general questions that call for no-risk responses. Ask about such matters as overall mood of the selection, techniques used in the selection (for example, camera techniques and sound quality), overall level of performance and production (professional? amateurish?), and so forth.

● Second, ask questions that call for somewhat more specific responses that involve some risk: best acting, worst acting, scenes that were especially good, scenes that were especially bad, lines that made an impression, musical lyrics that made an impression, and so forth.

● Third, ask questions that call for responses involving personal feelings and opinions on more controversial matters: what the main messages of the selection were, whether youth agree with these messages or not, how the selection might influence their lives, and so forth.

7. **Be sure to relate the selection, whether secular or religious, to the Christian faith.** Help the young people to determine what the selection is saying. Ask whether the message is in agreement with the teachings of the Christian faith or not. Help the youth to develop their ability to analyze media messages from a faith perspective.

About 60 percent of American households already own a VCR, and many others are trying to decide whether to purchase a VCR or one of the new videodisc players. Many parishes are recognizing the fantastic church programming possibilities of video and are purchasing VCR equipment.

VCRs are much easier to use than motion picture projection equipment. With motion picture projectors, most churches had only a few trained operators. With VCRs one has a church full of trained operators! While VCR sales have leveled off slightly, it looks like sales of videodisc players will soon soar. Philips, Pioneer, and Sony are introducing new videodisc players which sell for less than $500, and some of these will also play compact discs.

Players for videodiscs and compact discs read the grooves on the platter with a laser beam. The process is very much like the way a phonograph needle traces grooves on a traditional record. Thirty-five hundred videodisc titles are available as this book goes to press, and that number is growing by a hundred a month. Most videodiscs sell in the $25–$30 range, and the price could drop. Both compact discs and videodiscs offer two significant advantages over cassettes: they don't wear out, and they have better quality reproduction.

The only limitation with video cassettes and videodiscs comes in the relatively small size of the average television screen. Unless you have an enormous youth group, this is not likely to be a problem. Large screen, high resolution televisions are becoming more popular and less expensive. The larger the screen, the better a videodisc looks than a videotape. In the following pages, we will speak of video cassettes for the most part because VCRs are more commonly found in churches and homes (as of this writing); but most instructions apply to work with videodiscs as well.

Laws about the video recording of television programs and about group showing of rented video cassettes are in a time of significant transition. Current newspaper articles and *Consumer Reports* can help you know the status of regulations. We recommend that you not charge for the viewing of any video cassette or videodisc unless it is one you produced in the church! If you want to charge admission as a fund-raising project, then order the films or videos through a commercial outlet which rents for group use (see "Resources" for suggested sources).

Equipment Purchases

Technological offerings and their prices change so rapidly that we are reluctant to make specific suggestions on equipment. If you are considering purchase of a VCR, videodisc player, or camcorder, consult the latest issue of *Consumer Reports* and do some comparison shopping. The best buys on video equipment generally seem to be in the middle price range. The most expensive equipment often has features that are not frequently used, but those features can carry a premium price. The most inexpensive equipment will sometimes lack desired features or not be reliable in the long run.

Some of the emerging large-screen televisions are of high quality and are much better for group viewing than standard television screens. Prices seem to be falling rapidly on these.

Use of the VCR in Youth Programming

1. **Make use of the growing number of videos especially prepared for church use.**

Information on Paulist and other excellent suppliers will be found in the "Resources" chapter. Your own denomination no doubt offers high quality videos that interpret various church programs.

2. **Show secular motion pictures, and talk about them from a Christian perspective.** This is one of the most popular ways to use VCRs in youth programming.

3. **Tape television programs for use with youth classes and groups.** What's on television at the time your class or group meets may not be relevant, but VCRs enable you to play back what you taped at an earlier time, for example:

- News shows about weapons, the homeless, race relations, etc. *Sixty Minutes* often has excellent segments.

- MTV music videos for discussion

- Soap opera segments that can stimulate group discussion. *Santa Barbara* and *The Young and the Restless* are particular favorites of many teens.

- *Mash* reruns

- Motion pictures

- Benefit concerts

- Television programs with a message

4. **Put different shows/clips together on a particular issue.** If your class or group is talking about drug abuse, for example, you might put together a program made up of:

- An R.E.M. video with an anti-drug message (R.E.M. is a popular music group.)
- A *Sixty Minutes* segment about drugs in public schools

5. **Make your own video using a camcorder.** See suggestions on video making in the "Media" chapter. You can use the finished product not only with your youth group but also with child and adult classes in your church. You may also want to share your video with other churches in the community. If done with sufficient professionalism, your video may qualify for showing on a local cable channel.

The following are possibilities for making your own video:

- What youth think about male and female roles

- What should be done to prevent drug abuse

- A report on poverty in your community

- A retelling of the Good Samaritan in a modern-day setting

- Interviews on how the Bible helps people in their daily lives

- A series of discussion starters on dating, marriage, and sex

- Why people should support the church. Produce this as an aid to your church's fundraising efforts. Show the various groups and services provided by your church.

- A play or drama written by group members

Movie Discussion Guides

The following pages contain discussion guides to 25 popular motion pictures which are available on video cassette. Please note the cautions which are included about the use of some of the films. Each film has been selected for one or more of these reasons:

- The film is very popular with young people, and you can readily use it as a springboard to meaningful discussion.

- The film has a good, positive message, and young people would benefit from the film even without discussion.

- The film does not have a positive message, but we include it because young people need to learn how to view such films critically.

You should review again the suggestions in "Discussing Media" which appear in the chapter on "Media." When using videos with youth classes and groups:

- Always preview the video before showing it to the group.

- Use small groups of three or four people for at least part of your discussion unless your total group is very small.

- Encourage honest expression of opinions and reinforce that by not criticizing youth for what they think and feel. At the same time, be honest about your own opinions.

- Have newsprint and markers or chalkboard and chalk available. You'll want to list some questions and group responses.

- Have extra copies of the Bible available for class or group members who didn't bring their own.

You have our permission to photocopy the guides which follow if that makes it easier to use them in your church. We only ask that you not use a guide outside of your local church programming without the permission of *faithQuest*.

CHARIOTS OF FIRE

Stars: Ben Cross as Harold Abrahams
Ian Charleston as Eric Liddell

Rating: PG

Length: 123 Minutes

Summary: This is the story of two young and gifted British athletes at the 1924 Paris Olympics. Both are outsiders as far as the British class system is concerned: one a Scot who is the son of missionaries in China; the other a Jew whose father is an immigrant from Lithuania. Liddell, the Christian, sees his running as a gift of God and has to explain to an annoyed Prince of Wales why it is not possible to run on the sabbath. This movie has magnificent music, shows running as celebration, and raises meaningful issues for discussion. It is a wonderful movie!

Scripture:
Isaiah 40:27-31
But those who wait for the LORD shall renew their strength, they shall mount up with wings like eagles, they shall run and not be weary, they shall walk and not faint (40:31).

Exodus 20:10-11 (on the seventh day as the sabbath)

Philippians 3:12-16
Forgetting what lies behind and straining forward to what lies ahead, I press on toward the goal for the prize of the heavenly call of God in Christ Jesus (3:13b-14).

Materials: Note cards, envelopes, and pencils

111

DISCUSSION SUGGESTIONS

Before the video: Have group members read Philippians 3:12–16. Suggest to them: "As you watch the movie, think about some of the reasons why Paul used athletic competition as an analogy for the Christian faith."

After the video:

1. Have group members list the ways in which Abrahams and Liddell were alike. Then list ways in which they were different. Why were they both outsiders? How did you feel about the British class distinctions? What are comparable problems in our own society?

2. What was the effect on Liddell of believing so strongly that his running was a gift from God? Would it still have been a gift if he had made second or third place?

3. Have group members look at Isaiah 40:27-31 and again at Philippians 3:12–16. Why did Paul use athletic competition as an analogy for the Christian life? How does the Lord renew our strength? What are the limitations of the athletic analogy? (Not everyone can win a race, but we all are accepted by God. We are challenged to do our best, whatever that means.) Does the movie put too much emphasis on winning?

4. Would someone of Liddell's stature who refuses to compete on the sabbath cause the same controversy today? What kind of courage does it take to make such a stand? Look at Exodus 20:10–11. In what ways do we take the sabbath commandment too lightly today? What are the purposes of that commandment? (The need for rest; respect for God; the need to show ourselves as God's people; the need for physical, mental, and spiritual renewal.)

5. Give each person an envelope, two note cards, and a pencil. Explain: "Many of you may feel motivated to make some significant change in your lives in response to this video and to our discussion. Carrying out change, of course, isn't always easy. Write on both note cards one specific change you would like to make. Be sure to put the same change on each card. Keep one card as a reminder to yourself. Seal the other card in the envelope, and write your name on the outside of the envelope. I'll collect the envelopes but leave them sealed. A month from now, I'll return the sealed envelopes to you as another reminder of the change you wanted to make."

6. Close with prayer, offering God thanks for witnesses such as Eric Liddell.

HOOSIERS

Stars: Gene Hackman as Norman Dale
Barbara Hershey as Myra Fleener
Dennis Hopper as Shooter

Rating: PG

Length: 114 Minutes

Summary: A scandal in Norman Dale's past leads him to a coaching job in a small Indiana high school. His team ends up going all the way to state finals (in the days when schools of all sizes played in the same tournaments). The movie is really a story about three comebacks:

1. The Hickory Huskers (school team)
2. Norman Dale (coach)
3. Shooter (town drunk)

This outstanding movie is guaranteed to make you feel good and think about life.

Scripture:

1 Corinthians 9:24–27

Athletes exercise self-control in all things; they do it to receive a perishable wreath, but we an imperishable one (9:25).

Philippians 3:12–16

Forgetting what lies behind and straining forward to what lies ahead, I press on toward the goal for the prize of the heavenly call of God in Christ Jesus (3:13b–14).

Hebrews 12:1–2

Therefore, since we are surrounded by so great a cloud of witnesses, let us also lay aside every weight and the sin that clings so closely, and let us run with perseverance the race that is set before us (12:1).

DISCUSSION SUGGESTIONS

Before the video: Explain to the group that this movie depicts a time when schools of all sizes competed in the same tournaments. Tell them that this is a movie about comebacks, and ask them to be alert for examples as they view the film.

After the video:

1. Ask group members to share what comebacks they observed in the film. They should at least identify with the team, Norman Dale, and Shooter. They may also identify with some of the young people and Myra Fleener. Have them list factors that make comebacks possible (for example: hard work, a second chance from another person, courage . . .).

2. Point out that Scripture often uses athletic imagery to reflect growth in the Christian faith. Divide into three groups, and assign one of the three passages of Scripture to each group. Put the questions for each group on chalkboard or newsprint. Have each group answer its questions about the passage of Scripture and report back to the total group.

1 Corinthians 9:24–27. Why is self-control so important in the Christian life? How was self-control important in *Hoosiers*?

Philippians 3:12–16. Why is it important not to be enslaved and held back by the past? What characters in the movie had to break free from the constraints of the past?

Hebrews 12:1–2. How can witnesses or heroes help us live as we should? How did the example of others help people in *Hoosiers*?

3. How would you respond if told your school was going to hire a teacher who had been dismissed from his or her previous job? What about hiring a teacher who served a prison sentence for a nonviolent crime? What about hiring a teacher who has a history of alcohol problems but who has remained sober for the last year? Why is our society so reluctant to give second chances? Why is it important for us to extend second chances to others?

4. Close with prayer, thanking God for the second chances given to all of us.

TOP GUN

Stars: Tom Cruise as Maverick
Kelly McGillis as Charlie
Val Kilmer as Iceman
Tom Skeritt as Viper
Anthony Edwards as Goose

Rating: PG

Length: 109 Minutes

Summary: I hated this movie. It's actually not the only one included that I personally dislike, but you'll have to guess the others. I can't write anything about this film without clearly stating my utter contempt for it. Tom Cruise and Kelly McGillis are real heartthrobs for teens (and many adults), and this is precisely the kind of movie teens need help evaluating. Cruise has never been known for socially responsible roles (though I've enjoyed him more in other films), but McGillis has shown better taste and should be ashamed of herself for this one.

Maverick's father was an accomplished Navy pilot who disappeared in unexplained circumstances. Maverick follows after him professionally but shows immense immaturity as a pilot—immaturity that his superiors feel could get himself and others killed. McGillis is an instructor with whom he forms a relationship. The movie glorifies aggression and shows people successfully manipulating each other without questioning the aggression or the manipulation. The movie was also a tremendous box office hit.

Scripture:

Micah 4:1–4

They shall beat their swords into plowshares, and their spears into pruning hooks; nation shall not lift up sword against nation, neither shall they learn war any more (4:3b).

Matthew 5:21–26

But I say to you that if you are angry with a brother or sister, you will be liable to judgment; and if you insult a brother or sister, you will be liable to the council; and if you say, "You fool!"

you will be liable to the hell of fire (5:22.)

DISCUSSION SUGGESTIONS

Before the video: Have group members read Micah 4:1–4. Ask them as they watch the film to think about the extent to which this movie does or does not advance the cause of peace.

After the video:

1. Have group members list the reasons why this movie has been so popular. You may wish to put the reasons on chalkboard or newsprint. Do the best movies always achieve great popularity?

2. Have group members read again Micah 4:1–4. What would be the judgment of this passage on war and violence? To what extent did the movie advance or harm the cause of peace? What dangers come when a popular movie glorifies violence and aggression? Why do we sometimes find ourselves powerfully attracted to scenes of combat and violence? How might the plot of this movie have been more responsibly developed?

(Note: Some teens may feel the movie pushes a strong national defense and actually helps set the stage for peace. That view rests on some faulty assumptions. It's more than a little unsettling to think about people like Maverick making decisions that could lead to World War III. You may not be able to change the minds of those teens, but you will be able to expose them to other ideas. Many in the group will be uncomfortable with the strong militarism of the movie. I have friends who are professionals in the military who wish the film had never been made.)

114

3. Maverick and Charlie developed an intimate relationship which is, of course, no surprise. Why are they attracted to each other? In what ways do they manipulate each other? Were they really ready for an intimate relationship?

4. Have group members read Matthew 5:21–26. This passage says that it isn't enough to simply avoid killing others. Christ warns us that even bitter words and angry feelings are matters of concern. The words of Christ, in fact, seem almost too strong. All of us have feelings of anger. Yet Jesus is telling us here how we should truly live. God's forgiveness still touches our lives as we find ourselves unable to meet such high standards. Why is Jesus concerned about angry feelings as well as outward actions? In what ways do our feelings eventually control our actions? In what ways can harsh words do violence to others? What words spoken in the movie needlessly hurt others? How does our ability to control our own actions relate to world peace?

5. Close with prayer, seeking God's help in the development of a more peaceful world.

ORDINARY PEOPLE

Stars: Donald Sutherland as Calvin
Mary Tyler Moore as Beth
Judd Hirsh as Berger
Timothy Hutton as Conrad
Elizabeth McGovern as Jeannine

Rating: R (Some strong language, but don't let that keep you from using this powerful movie.)

Length: 125 Minutes

Summary: This motion picture, directed by Robert Redford, is based on Judith Guest's novel of the same title. Conrad and his brother are in a tragic boating accident. Conrad survives; his brother dies. The loss inflicts enormous damage on the family. Calvin, the father, tries desperately to hold together his wife Beth and his son Conrad. Beth was closer to the deceased son, and she is unable to show the warmth or concern Conrad needs. Conrad, with some justification, feels that his mother would have preferred that he die and his brother live. Because of his severe depression, Conrad sees a psychiatrist who does help. This is a painful but beautiful movie. Calvin, forced to choose between his wife and his son, chooses his son. Conrad begins to heal; we wonder if Beth ever will.

Scripture:
Ecclesiastes 3:1–15
For everything there is a season, and a time for every matter under heaven (3:1).

Matthew 7:1-5
Do not judge, so that you may not be judged. For with the judgment you make you will be judged, and the measure you give will be the measure you get (7:1–2).

Materials: Note cards, pencils

DISCUSSION SUGGESTIONS

Before the video: Give each person a note card and a pencil. Explain: "Put numbers 1, 2, and 3 on the note card. I'm asking you to make a yes or no response to three questions, writing your answers on the card. Don't put your name on the card. I'll collect all the cards and immediately shuffle them thoroughly so that it's impossible for me or anyone else to know who responded in a particular way." You may want to put the three questions on chalkboard or newsprint:

1. Do you know someone who has attempted suicide?

2. Have you ever felt deeply depressed?

3. Have you ever *considered* a suicide attempt? Note that the questions do not ask the young people to say if they personally have attempted suicide but only if they have considered it. Even with the anonymous note cards, asking for information about personal suicide attempts is requiring too much revelation. Some group members may later acknowledge having attempted it, but that will be in response to a supportive atmosphere in the group. During the video, tally responses to the three questions.

After the video:

1. Have group members share a few key words or phrases to describe each of these characters:

- Conrad
- Jeannine
- Calvin
- Beth
- Berger

Who do you think did the most to help Conrad? Why? Could anything more have been done to help Beth? Why, or why not? Why was Calvin's position so difficult?

2. Share the results of the anonymous note card exercise. Is it abnormal to feel deeply depressed? Why is it important to remember that there is a clear difference between feeling suicidal and acting on that feeling? Why is it important for people who are deeply troubled to seek help? What help did the psychiatrist give Conrad which Conrad's parents could not give? What help

did his father give which the psychiatrist could not? Why is it important to seek adult help for a teen who is suicidal?

3. Have group members read Ecclesiastes 3:1-15. What happens to a person who becomes trapped in one "time" or cycle of life? In what ways were characters in the movie trapped in "times" of guilt, grief, and anger? What new "times" did characters need to move toward? What new "times" do you need to move toward in your own life?

4. Have group members read Matthew 7:1-5. To what extent did Beth judge others too harshly? Why did she do so? What price did she finally pay? To what extent did Conrad judge himself too harshly? Why? Why does the movie make us feel so negative toward Beth? To what extent does that trap us in judgment?

5. Share with the group the following guidelines for dealing with depressed persons or with depression in ourselves:

- Talking about depression usually helps. You don't have to be a trained professional to listen compassionately.

- Activity always helps fight depression. Being silent, staying alone and doing nothing nurtures depression. Go to a movie, read a book, go for pizza with a friend, go running, go to church, help parents with supper.

- All suicidal threats should be taken seriously. A young person who is considering suicide needs adult help, probably professional help. Don't take the responsibility of being the only emotional support for a person who is suicidal. Get help.

Talk with group members about sources of help for people who are suicidal. (For more information on this, see Sol Gordon's outstanding book *When Living Hurts.*)

6. Close with prayer, thanking God for the gift of life.

THE BREAKFAST CLUB

Stars: Molly Ringwald as Claire Standish (prom queen)
Emilio Estevez as Andrew Clark (jock)
Anthony Michael Hall as Brian Johnson (class brain)
Judd Nelson as John Bender (tough guy)
Ally Sheedy as Allison Reynolds (neurotic)

Rating: R (Very frank language but no nudity or violence)

Length: 105 Minutes

Summary: Five high school students find themselves together in Saturday morning detention as punishment for violation of school rules. They seem to have nothing in common and also don't want anything in common. They start the day displeased at being in detention and displeased with each other. As the movie progresses, they find themselves opening up to one another. A major turning point comes when the "tough guy" starts verbally picking on the "prom queen." The five find they have far more in common than they realized, and a bond begins to form. Don't let the strong language turn you off to this film. The young people are realistically portrayed, and your teens will identify with them. The movie also does an excellent job helping youth get past the stereotypes they often hold about certain categories of people. This is one of the best films of recent years for stimulating youth discussion.

Scripture:
1 John 4:7–12
Beloved, since God loved us so much, we also ought to love one another. . . . God lives in us, and his love is perfected in us (4:11–12).

DISCUSSION SUGGESTIONS

Before the video: Tell the group they will be meeting five very interesting young people in the movie. Ask them to do their best to determine:

- the movie teen with whom they most strongly identify,
- the one whom they would have the most difficulty liking,
- the one whom they would most like to know.

You may want to list those three categories on chalkboard or newsprint.

After the video:

1. Write the following characterizations of the movie teens on the chalkboard or newsprint:

- Claire—prom queen
- Andrew—jock
- Brian—brain
- John—tough guy
- Allison—neurotic

Have group members add other words that describe each character (for example, Claire: beautiful, spoiled, lonely). Ask group members to share how their view of the characters changed as the movie progressed.

117

2. Have group members respond to the three categories discussed before viewing the video. You may wish to do this in groups of three or four if your total group is large. Have people share the reasons for feeling as they do about particular characters.

3. Have group members read 1 John 4:7–12. How has God shown love to us? Why are we supposed to love others? How did the feelings of the characters for each other change during the course of the film? What experiences might make you feel more positive about people you currently dislike?

4. Remind the young people of what the movie characters learned by looking at the contents of a purse. In small groups (unless your total group is small), have people show and talk about the contents of purses and billfolds/pockets. (Don't let anyone be put on the spot to dump everything out—some may wish to retain some secrets.) This can be a very enjoyable and revealing activity.

5. Close with prayer, offering God thanks for the diversity of people.

HEAVEN

A documentary directed by Diane Keaton.

Rating: PG-13

Length: 80 Minutes

Summary: Diane Keaton assembles a large number of people and asks them about heaven. There's also a lot of film footage showing how heaven has been visualized in previous films. This is a thought-provoking film which had only limited commercial success. The perspective is not distinctly Christian, but the movie raises a number of Christian issues.

Scripture:
John 14:1–3
And if I go and prepare a place for you, I will come again and will take you to myself, so that where I am there you may be also (14:3).

Plus:
- Deuteronomy 10:14
- Psalm 14:2
- Psalm 89:6
- Psalm 102:19
- Ecclesiastes 5:2
- Isaiah 6:1
- Daniel 2:28
- Matthew 5:18
- Mark 8:11
- Luke 15:18
- John 1:51
- John 3:13
- Colossians 1:5
- Revelation 21:1

DISCUSSION SUGGESTIONS

Before the video: Have group members share words and phrases that describe heaven. Put them on chalkboard or newsprint so you can review them after viewing the film.

After the video:

1. Now have group members share words and phrases about heaven that come to them in response to the documentary. Write those on chalkboard or newsprint. Put them beside the list developed before watching the video, and point out differences and similarities.

2. Divide into pairs or small groups. Then divide the references (15 of them)

listed under "Scripture" among the pairs or groups. Have each pair or group record what they learn about heaven from the passages and then report back to the total group. Make another list on chalkboard or newsprint, and put that beside the other two lists the group has developed. Again, point out differences and similarities.

3. Explain to group members that the Bible obviously leaves us with many unanswered questions about heaven. Much of what is commonly believed about heaven (and is depicted in books and film) comes from sources other than the Bible. Why hasn't God revealed more about heaven in the Bible? What are the dangers of living focused too much on the life to come? What problems come when people forget that there is life that transcends the present?

4. What does the existence of heaven say about God's love for us? How should a healthy belief in the life to come transform and improve our lives now? How does the death of a friend or a relative make us rethink the way we live?

5. Close with prayer, seeking God's help in our daily lives.

GORILLAS IN THE MIST

Stars: Sigourney Weaver as Dian Fossey

Rating: PG-13

Length: 112 Minutes

Summary: This movie is based on the true story of Dian Fossey who made the study and protection of mountain gorillas her life's work. She developed a close bond with the elusive gorillas and did much to protect them from hunters and collectors. Her dedication to work, however, hurt her relationships with others. The movie portrays her obsession honestly and pays tribute to her heroism.

Scripture:
Genesis 1:24–28
Let them have dominion over the fish of the sea, and over the birds of the air, and over the cattle, and over all the wild animals of the earth, and over every creeping thing that creeps upon the earth (1:26b).

DISCUSSION SUGGESTIONS

Before the video: Ask group members to share what they know about gorillas. You may wish to make notes on chalkboard or newsprint.

After the video:
1. Ask group members to share how their thinking about gorillas has changed as a result of the movie. Why have people had so many misconceptions about gorillas? How do you feel about gorillas being maintained in zoos? What about other animals in zoos? Is it right to interfere with the freedom of any being?

2. Dian Fossey had the opportunity to marry a photographer whom she obviously passionately loved. He was willing to live in the jungle setting with her six months of a year but wanted to spend the rest of the year in a more civilized setting. She would not make that compromise and could not marry him. How do you feel about that? Was her obsession too great, or was it dedication? Why? Does it seem as though some obsession is necessary to accomplish great things?

3. Have group members read Genesis 1:24–28. Some people have interpreted this

119

passage as giving humanity "rights" to all nonhuman life. Close examination, however, shows that the "dominion" given men and women includes great responsibility for the created world. What responsibilities do we have for other forms of life based on this passage? Based on the movie, in what ways would you say we have neglected those responsibilities? Why did gorilla heads and hands become so popular? Why was it so difficult to stop the hunters and collectors? What responsibility do we have as Christians for the endangered species of the world?

4. Dian Fossey became very unpopular for her fierce protection of gorillas. She terrified a small child to find where a gorilla had been taken. She did a mock hanging of a poacher. She stormed into a popular club, carrying an infant gorilla, to confront the man responsible for the infant's kidnapping. In what ways was she justified in her actions? In what ways did even her supporters think she went too far? Would less dramatic methods have succeeded?

5. Close with prayer, thanking God for the world we have been given and seeking help in living responsibly.

BACK TO THE FUTURE

Stars: Michael J. Fox as Marty McFly
Christopher Lloyd as Dr. Brown
Lea Thompson as Lorraine Baines

Rating: PG

Length: 116 Minutes

Summary: Marty has a negative view of his parents at the start of this highly improbable, wonderful movie. Then he finds himself transported back thirty years in Dr. Brown's time machine. People see his goose- down jacket and want to know why he's wearing a life preserver! He meets his parents as teenagers and is enormously distressed to find that the girl who will become his mother is more attracted to him than to the man who will become his father. The film has a happy ending, and his parents are slightly transformed by his intervention.

Scripture:
John 3:1–7

Nicodemus said to him, "How can anyone be born after having grown old? Can one enter a second time into the mother's womb and be born?" (3:4).

Materials: Note cards, pencils

DISCUSSION SUGGESTIONS

Before the video: Give note cards and pencils to group members. Have them write down one thing they would like to change about their parents AND one thing they would like to change about themselves.

After the video:
1. Have group members share words and phrases to describe each of the following characters:

- Marty McFly
- Marty's mother as a teenager
- Marty's father as a teenager
- Marty's mother as an adult at the start of the film
- Marty's father as an adult at the start of the film
- Marty's mother as an adult at the end of the film
- Marty's father as an adult at the end of the film
- Dr. Brown

Talk about the changes in his parents. In what ways did Marty himself change? How might the results of his trip have backfired? How would we feel about the movie then?

2. Have group members look at the changes they wrote on the cards before watching the video. Have those who are willing share what they wrote down. After seeing the movie, how do they feel about those changes? Would they still like to make them? Would they like to make different changes? Why is it important to like and accept ourselves just as we are?

3. In some ways this movie is a lighthearted look at "control." As much as we may want to control what happens in our lives, it isn't always possible to do so. What problems does Marty encounter as he tries to control the future? Would you really want to travel into the past? What would be the dangers of that? the possibilities?

4. In some ways both Marty and his parents seem to be reborn through this experience. Marty certainly comes to see his parents in a very different way than before. Have group members read John 3:1–7. What does it mean to be born anew in Christ? How is spiritual rebirth different from traveling back in time? How does Christ help us in the present?

5. Close with prayer, thanking God for the new life offered to us.

THE COLOR PURPLE

Stars: Danny Glover as Mister
Whoopi Goldberg as Celie
Margaret Avery as Shug
Oprah Winfrey as Sofia
Rae Dawn Chong as Squeak

Rating: PG-13 (Strong language and also a scene in which two women kiss, implying a lesbian relationship)

Length: 155 Minutes

Special Note: Before using this movie with your group, read Alice Walker's book of the same title. The book tells the story through a series of letters (some never sent, some never received). Many of the letters are addressed to God, and you may wish to quote from some of them as you meet with the group.

Summary: Celie is first seen as a child running through fields of purple flowers. She unfortunately is pregnant, made so by her father. She is married to a man who is both charming and cruel, loses her children, and becomes separated from her sister, who is the person she loves most. The turning point comes when Mister (her unfaithful husband) brings home Shug (an alcoholic singer who still has beauty and strength). Shug's influence begins to transform Celie. Oprah Winfrey gives a spectacular performance as Sofia, a woman whose strength is horribly damaged by beating and jailing. The affirmation at the end of the movie is so strong that it will bring tears.

Warning: This movie originally caused considerable controversy because of the supposedly lesbian dimension of Celie and Shug's relationship. That dimension is very subdued in the movie; Shug's kindness to Celie and sharing of strength with Celie is what comes through. The movie also generated controversy because it shows strong black female characters but weaker black males. You may or may not want to pursue these issues in discussion.

121

Scripture:

Philemon

Perhaps this is the reason he was separated from you for a while, so that you might have him back forever, no longer as a slave but more than a slave, a beloved brother—especially to me but how much more to you, both in the flesh and in the Lord (15–16).

DISCUSSION SUGGESTIONS

Before the video: Suggest that group members think about why the film is titled *The Color Purple* as they watch it. They'll see purple flowers at the start, but there may be other reasons.

After the video:

1. Divide into pairs or small groups. Have each pair or small group identify a color to describe each of these characters:

- Celie
- Mister
- Shug
- Sofia

Then have them share the colors and the reasons for selecting them. Why is *The Color Purple* the title given to the movie? (You'll have a variety of responses.)

2. The letters of Celie and her sister reflect an intimacy with God. Most of the letters in the book of the same title are actually addressed to God. How could one have such intimacy with God while living under such difficult circumstances? In what ways do you think God helped Celie?

3. Philemon is the shortest New Testament book. Paul wrote to Philemon about a runaway slave named Onesimus. Onesimus had become a Christian, and Paul wanted Philemon to welcome him back as a brother. Have group members read Philemon. Then have group members list some of the inequalities and injustices shown in the movie. What does it really mean to see others as our brothers and sisters? What forms of injustice today are similar to those portrayed in the movie? What should we do about injustice?

4. Does having faith in God mean that we will necessarily be spared pain and suffering? How does God help us in the midst of difficult times?

5. Close with prayer, seeking help in having the courage to oppose injustice in our own time.

FERRIS BUELLER'S DAY OFF

Stars: Matthew Broderick as Ferris Bueller
Alan Ruck as Cameron Frye
Mia Sara as Sloane

Rating: PG-13

Length: 103 Minutes

Summary: Ferris Bueller skips school for the presumed purpose of helping his friend Cameron win self-respect. The fast-paced day takes place in Chicago with scenes at the Sears Tower, a Dearborn Street parade, the Art Institute, and a Rush Street lunch. Cameron's father has an antique red Ferrari which he seems to love more than his son. Cameron's aggression comes out on the car, but with far worse results than Cameron anticipated. This is a difficult movie for adults to appreciate, but most teens identify strongly with it.

Scripture:
Psalm 88:1–18

> *The Psalmist cries out! "For my soul is full of troubles, and my life draws near to Sheol* (88:3). (Sheol was the place of the dead.)

DISCUSSION SUGGESTIONS

Before the video: Suggest that group members identify for themselves (privately—not for group sharing unless they later want to) a time when they felt especially oppressed and frustrated by life. They can then compare their feelings to those of Cameron in the film.

After the video:

1. Have group members read Psalm 88:1–18. Then have them pick out the verses which seem to best describe how Cameron felt. Note that the psalmists are always honest with God about their emotions. When have you known people who felt like Cameron did? How did Ferris try to help Cameron? To what extent was Cameron helped more by the concern of Ferris than by any particular advice from Ferris? Why?

2. Ferris makes the statement: "Life goes by so fast that if you don't stop and look around you might miss it." That seems similar to the saying: "You've got to stop and smell the roses." What do you think those sayings mean? Does life go by too fast or not fast enough? Why? Why is it important to enjoy the present rather than just living for the future? In what ways do the past and the future affect the present?

3. When Cameron kicked the car, was he symbolically kicking his father? Why do you suppose his father had so much trouble communicating with Cameron? What examples can you provide of people placing greater value on material possessions than on people?

4. What is Sloane's role in the day? How does she help Ferris and Cameron? What kind of person is she?

5. What was good about the response Ferris made to Cameron's problems? What was unrealistic about his response and about the day? How should you respond if you have a friend as upset as Cameron?

6. Close with prayer, asking God's help when we and others are troubled.

RAIDERS OF THE LOST ARK

Stars: Harrison Ford as Indiana Jones
Karen Allen as Marion

Rating: PG

Length: 115 Minutes

Summary: Indiana Jones is an anthropologist who in 1936 gets involved in a search for the legendary "ark of the covenant," which is described in the Old Testament as being very valuable and very powerful. The forces of Hitler are also seeking the ark, hoping to use its power to win the war. This is a fast moving, cliff-hanging adventure. There's a romance between Indy and Marion, and mystery surrounds the power of the ark.

Scripture:
Exodus 25:10–22 (describes the ark)

1 Samuel 5; 6; 7 (Continues the story of the ark. See especially 1 Samuel 5:1–5. The Philistines capture the ark but have so many problems as a result that they give it back!)

Ephesians 6:10–20

> *For our struggle is not against enemies of blood and flesh, but against the rulers, against the authorities, against the cosmic powers of this present darkness, against the spiritual forces of evil in the heavenly places* (6:12).

DISCUSSION SUGGESTIONS

Before the video: Read 1 Samuel 5:1–5 about the power of the ark. Suggest that group members think about that passage as they watch the movie.

After the video:

1. Have group members read Exodus 25:10–22 and look again at 1 Samuel 5. How consistent was the appearance of the ark in the movie with the description in the Bible? To what extent was the power of the ark in the movie consistent with the biblical description? What do you think about how the ark was finally handled in the movie (put in a vast government storage facility)?

2. Point out that Indy and Marion are both extremely attractive characters as portrayed in the film. Why are we so attracted to them? List the strong, positive characteristics of Indy and then of Marion. Then list negative characteristics of each. How realistic are these characters? Why?

3. Have group members read Ephesians 6:10–20. Presently, are there national or world leaders we would speak of as a "world ruler of this present darkness"? God normally does not show his power in as obvious a way as with the ark. Why isn't God more obvious in the use of power? How does God choose to use power in our world? Why do we need God's help in opposing evil? What does it mean to "put on the whole armor of God"?

4. Indy and Marion showed great courage. In what circumstances of daily life do you need more courage? Does courage come primarily from one's own strength or from God? Why?

5. Close with prayer, thanking God for protection.

CROCODILE DUNDEE

Stars: Paul Hogan as Mike Dundee
Linda Koslowski as Sue Charlton

Rating: PG-13

Length: 98 Minutes

Summary: Wealthy, beautiful Sue Charlton travels to the Australian Outback where she meets Mike "Mick" Dundee. Then she brings him back to New York. Both of them experience culture shock—New York is fully as strange a world to him as the Outback is to her. This is basically a love story—there are no great insights or significant statements in this movie; but it's still a refreshing, delightful film. You can also have some worthwhile discussion based on it.

Scripture:

1 Corinthians 12:4–26

> *And if the ear would say, "Because I am not an eye, I do not belong to the body," that would not make it any less a part of the body* (12:16).

DISCUSSION SUGGESTIONS

Before the video: Ask how many group members have seen this film before (the response will be close to 100 percent). Suggest that as group members watch the film this time they be alert for the whole range of cultural differences between Crocodile Dundee and Sue Charlton. They'll have noticed some of those before, but familiarity with the film should make detailed observation easier.

After the video:

1. List on chalkboard or newsprint, as many cultural differences as possible between Crocodile Dundee and Sue Charlton. Include not only Australian–New York differences but also the differences of wealth and social class. Why do people who are so different rarely come in intimate contact? To what extent did the differences of these two characters draw them toward each other? Do people who are so different often fall in love?

2. We find Crocodile Dundee exciting and fascinating. That's not always our response to people of different cultures. Why is it important to have openness toward people who are culturally different from us? Name some nationalities that seem to be considerably different from members in our church? What about people who are different from us in other ways: the homeless, the handicapped, the elderly? Which of these people are hardest to accept? Why?

3. Have group members read 1 Corinthians 12:4–26. What does this passage say about differences within the church? What "gifts" did Mike Dundee have? Sue? What are your gifts? How can you best use your gifts in the church?

4. The scene of the kangaroo "shooting back" at the hunters is a great one. How do you feel about killing kangaroos? whales? seals? Why do we respond differently to the killing of pigs, chickens, and cattle? What is a Christian view of animal life?

5. Close with prayer, thanking God for the diversity of the human community.

HANNAH AND HER SISTERS

Stars: Woody Allen as Mickey
Michael Caine as Elliott
Mia Farrow as Hannah
Carrie Fisher as April
Dianne Wiest as Holly
Max von Sydow as Frederick
Barbara Hershey as Lee

Rating: PG-13

Length: 107 Minutes

Summary: Teens tend to either love or hate Woody Allen movies; it depends on your group. This is a very thought-provoking movie that starts and ends with Thanksgiving dinner hosted by Hannah. During the movie, you'll meet:

● a TV executive who fears he will die,

● a woman whose cocaine habit has filled her life with fear,

● an accountant who is in love with his wife's sister,

● an artist who pretends to be strong but is very dependent on his girlfriend.

All the characters are interesting, and many of their experiences reflect problems which teens need to understand.

Scripture:
1 Corinthians 15:35–50
What you sow does not come to life unless it dies (15:36b).

125

DISCUSSION SUGGESTIONS

Before the video: Put on newsprint or chalkboard the following categories:

- the strongest person
- the most insecure person
- the most loving person
- the most passionate person
- the most dishonest person
- the most neurotic person
- the most neglected person
- the most dependent person

Explain that after the film you'll talk together about the persons in the movie who best fit these categories.

After the video:

1. Have group members nominate movie characters for the categories you put on chalkboard or newsprint before the movie. Have people explain why they nominated a particular person for each category. You can vote on each category, or you can simply discuss the persons nominated. There are certainly no right or wrong answers, and some responses may surprise you.

2. Have group members read 1 Corinthians 15:35–50. Mickey is certain there is no afterlife, and he wonders if this life might be a sham! What logic does the Apostle Paul offer in favor of life after death? Would Mickey accept that logic? Why, or why not? How does a positive view of life after death transform life now?

3. The movie deals in part with the passion, thrill, guilt, and tragedy of adultery. What do the characters gain from their adulterous experience? What price do they pay? How does it affect their primary partners? Why do you think the Bible prohibits adultery?

4. In what ways do Thanksgiving dinners stand as landmarks in our lives? How would your Thanksgiving dinners compare to the two portrayed in the film? What positive things should happen at such experiences?

5. Close with prayer, thanking God for the richness of God's love.

STAR TREK II: THE WRATH OF KHAN

Stars: William Shatner as Kirk
Leonard Nimoy as Spock
Ricardo Montalban as Khan
DeForest Kelley as McCoy
Kirstie Alley as Lt. Saavik

Rating: PG

Length: 113 Minutes

Summary: Khan, an old enemy of Kirk's, attempts to take control of the "Genesis Device." The Genesis Device was designed to create new worlds—to make it possible for the process of life development to be greatly accelerated—indeed, to bring life to barren, lifeless planets. Khan, however, also sees the destructive, military potential of this technological breakthrough. In the course of the adventure, Kirk meets a son he didn't know he had, a son who initially hates him. In the finale of the movie, Spock sacrifices his own life to save the Enterprise and its crew. At his funeral, his body is sent to the Genesis Planet, and there is just a hint that Spock might somehow come back to life (which he does in Star Trek III).

Scripture:

Genesis 1:1–2:25. Note that there really are two distinct creation stories: Genesis 1:1—2:4a and Genesis 2:4b-25. In the second account, man is created before vegetation, animals, and woman.

> Then the LORD God formed man from the dust of the ground, and breathed into his nostrils the breath of life; and the man became a living being (2:7).

Man (*'adham*) is formed from the ground (*'adhamah*).

DISCUSSION SUGGESTIONS

Before the video: Tell group members that they'll see in this movie something called the "Genesis Device." Suggest that they be alert for all the "new beginnings" that they see in the film.

After the video:

1. Have group members identify the "new beginnings" in the film. The list will probably include the new life from the Genesis Device, Kirk's new relationship with his son, the new crew members of the Enterprise, the new life for Kirk without Spock, the new beginnings which may yet be there for Spock. Why are beginnings so important? Why do we speak about entry into the Christian life as being "born again"?

2. Have group members compare the two creation accounts: Genesis 1:1—2:4a and Genesis 2:4b-25. List on chalkboard or newsprint the similarities between the two accounts. Then list the differences. Note that both passages were considered important enough to be preserved in Scripture, and each passage gives us insights into God's plan for creation. Do you think something like the Genesis Device could become technologically possible. Should people have control of something so powerful?

3. Spock told of one life being sacrificed for the many. How is that view consistent with the Christian way of life? Could you make such a sacrifice? Why, or why not? How is Spock's sacrifice like the sacrifice of Christ? In what ways is Christ's sacrifice radically different from that of Spock? Why should Christians have confidence in life after death, even without a Genesis Device?

4. Khan's life was distorted by anger. How did his anger destroy him? Why are anger and hate such dangerous emotions? In what ways did Kirk's anger help others? How can Christ help us deal with anger in our lives?

5. Close with prayer, thanking God for new beginnings.

STAR TREK III: THE SEARCH FOR SPOCK

Stars: William Shatner as Kirk
DeForest Kelley as McCoy
James Doohan as Scotty
Leonard Nimoy as Spock

Rating: PG

Length: 105 Minutes

Summary: This is a sequel to *Star Trek II* and, in fact, just a little hard to understand if you didn't see *Star Trek II*. Kirk and his close associates return to the Genesis Planet to find out what happened to Spock. It turns out that the "essence" of Spock resides in McCoy and that is a troubling experience for McCoy. They find a young Spock growing rapidly under the influence of the unique Genesis environment. After conflict with a Klingon spaceship, they return to the planet Vulcan with Spock. There, in a mystical ritual, the essence of Spock is passed from McCoy to Spock's new body. If you are a Star Trek fan, this is a wonderful movie. If you aren't, it will seem pointless to you. Most teens will thoroughly enjoy it.

Scripture:

John 15:12–17

> *I am giving you these commands so that you may love one another* (15:17).

1 Corinthians 15:35–50 (on spiritual bodies and life after death)

DISCUSSION SUGGESTIONS

Before the video: Ask group members to summarize what happened in *Star Trek II*. (Even if you didn't show that movie to the group, you'll have enough teens present who can give a good summary.)

After the video:

1. What unexpected things happened in this film? Why was much of the film very predictable to any Star Trek fan? Why do we like these characters so much?

2. Have group members read John 15:12–17. What is the greatest sign of love according to this passage? How had Spock already shown this kind of love? To what extent were his friends willing to do the same? Why are such relationships so rare? What has God done to show love for us? What kinds of relationships can we have with Christ?

3. There's some deception at the start of this film as Kirk obtains a spaceship for the trip. How did you feel about that deception? Why would such actions cause greater problems in real life than they do in this motion picture? Why do bureaucracies have trouble responding to human need?

4. The "essence" of Spock was transferred to McCoy and then returned to Spock's new body. What is the "essence" of a person? What makes you "you"? Have group members read 1 Corinthians 15:35–50. According to this passage, what happens to our bodies at death? What must we do to gain a spiritual body? How does Christ assure us that the "essence" of who we are continues after death?

5. Close with prayer, thanking God for the promise of life which transcends death.

FOR KEEPS

Stars: Molly Ringwald as Darcy
Randall Batinkoff as Stan

Rating: PG-13

Length: 98 Minutes

Summary: Darcy is a popular high school student who gets pregnant and then gets married. The teacher asks Darcy to drop out of school because she's so popular that other girls might imitate her. Darcy's life in many ways is far better than for most girls in her situation. The movie lacks the pain, shame, and suffering that should be present to make this a realistic story. On the other hand, it is clear that Darcy pays a greater price than Stan. She's stuck at their walk-up apartment while her husband has beer with his friends. He has far better options than she for college. The ending of the film seems artificial and contrived—too much comes together too well. Nevertheless, this is a film teens will like; and the movie certainly raises significant issues.

Scripture:

Genesis 2:24–25

> *Therefore a man leaves his father and his mother and clings to his wife, and they become one flesh* (2:24).

1 Corinthians 13:1–13 (familiar verses on love)

DISCUSSION SUGGESTIONS

Before the video: Suggest to group members that they think about what parts of the movie are realistic and what parts are unrealistic.

After the video:

1. List on newsprint or chalkboard what group members thought was realistic and what they thought was unrealistic about the movie. (For example: Unrealistic—too nice an apartment, too few parental problems, too easy a time for Stan. Realistic—the unexpectedness of the pregnancy, life being harder for the woman than for the man.) Talk about those lists.

2. Have group members read Genesis 2:24-25. What does it mean for a couple to become one flesh? The major religious faiths have all taught that sexual intercourse belongs only in marriage. What problems can result from intercourse outside of marriage? Were Darcy and Stan mature enough to sleep with each other? Why, or why not? What should they have done differently if they were going to sleep with each other? Were they mature enough for marriage? Why, or why not?

3. Have group members read 1 Corinthians 13:1–13. Point out that the love spoken of in this passage can apply not only to marriage but to many other relationships. Then have group members develop a list of traits which this passage suggests would be important in a marital relationship, for example: being humble, being patient. Which of these traits did Darcy possess? Stan?

4. Divide into small groups on the basis of sex—males together and females together.

Have each group make a list of characteristics that are important for a husband in a marriage relationship and for a wife. Then have the group compare lists so they can see how the opposite sex felt.

5. Close with prayer, thanking God for good marriages and families.

THE BIG EASY

Stars: Dennis Quaid as Remy McSwain
Ellen Barkin as Anne Osborne
Ned Beatty as Jack Kellom

Rating: R (Quite a bit of violence and a steamy love scene. The love scene does take place without nudity, but there's no question what is happening! For older teens only.)

Length: 106 Minutes

Summary: Remy is a vice cop in New Orleans. He's basically honest, in most ways but has rationalized accepting free meals and the occasional payoff. He's very much a part of the "Widows and Orphans Fund," for which police officers collect money. The fund goes to police officers and families for a lot more purposes than widows and orphans! Anne is a special prosecutor to clean up police corruption. She has a lot of insecurity in relationships with men (particularly sexual relationships), and she surprises herself by becoming intimate with Remy. Then he gets caught accepting a bribe, and she is furious. She prosecutes him and, driven by her anger, she hopes for a stiff penalty. But he manages to get the incriminating video destroyed and goes free. Her continued anger and further developments in the intricate plot cause Remy to reexamine his values. There's more tragedy in the film, but the ending is a happy one for Remy and Anne. The film deals constructively with the issue of integrity and with the impossibility of being "a little bit dishonest."

Scripture:

Proverbs 19:1

Better the poor walking in integrity than one perverse of speech who is a fool.

Proverbs 19:9

A false witness will not go unpunished, and the liar will perish.

Matthew 5:33–37

Let your word be "Yes, Yes," or "No, No"; anything more than this comes from the evil one (5:37).

Materials: Note cards, pencils

DISCUSSION SUGGESTIONS

Before the video: Give a note card and pencil to each group member. Have them number the cards one through five and respond with yes or no to each of the following questions. Tell them not to put their names on the cards.

1. Have you ever cheated on homework or a test?

2. Do you think most (over half) of the students you know have cheated at some time?

3. Have you ever been deeply hurt by a lie someone told?

4. Have you ever told a lie that hurt another person?

5. Have you ever told a lie that hurt yourself?

Collect the cards and tally the yes and no responses to each question during the video.

After the video:

1. Ask group members to list the instances of dishonesty and deception that occurred in the film. Why did some of those appear to be humorous? What was the film's message about dishonesty? Why is it easy to get caught up in dishonest activity as Remy did?

2. Share the responses to the five questions answered "Before the video." Then talk together about the responses. Why do many people cheat at school? How is that similar to the dishonest practices in which Remy got involved? Why do we sometimes ridicule people like Anne who seem so rigid in their integrity? Why do we need people like that? What additional examples can you give of dishonest statements or practices which have hurt yourself or others?

3. Have group members read Proverbs 19:1 and 19:9. How do these verses relate to the movie? Then have them read Matthew 5:33–37. Why does Christ actually discourage us from taking oaths? Why is it sometimes difficult to keep one's word even with the best of intentions? Why is it important to keep promises once they have been made?

4. In what ways did Remy change during the film? In what ways did Anne change? Why is it important to remember that we always have the ability to change how we respond to a situation even if we cannot change the situation?

5. Close with prayer, seeking God's help in living with integrity.

MASK

Stars: Cher as Rusty Dennis
Eric Stolz as Rocky Dennis
Sam Elliott as Gar
Laura Dern as Diana

Rating: PG-13

Length: 120 Minutes

Summary: Rocky suffers from craniodiaphyseal dysplasia, a disease that causes calcium deposits on the skull and forces his face out of shape. Rocky has remarkable ability to cope with the disfiguring condition. He says: "What's the matter? You never seen anyone from the planet Vulcan before?" His mother Rusty is a complicated woman. She loves her son and nurtures him; but she rides with a cycle gang, abuses drugs, and sleeps with gang members. In the course of the film, we see Rusty initiate changes in her life—primarily as the result of her son's encouragement. Rocky helps as a counselor at a camp for the blind where he meets beautiful camper Diana. Rocky and Diana grow close to one another—partly because of their respective handicaps and partly in spite of them. One of the beautiful things about the film is that viewers begin to forget about Rocky's disfigurement and simply see him as a person.

Scripture:

Exodus 4:10-17 (God calls Moses to his service. Moses feels awkward because of a speech impediment.)

Jeremiah 1:4–10 (Jeremiah finds it hard to believe God has called him. Jeremiah feels that he is too young.)

Isaiah 6:1–8 (Isaiah finds it hard to believe God has called him! Isaiah sees himself as a person of "unclean lips" living among others of "unclean lips.")

1 Corinthians 1:26–31
But God chose what is foolish in the world to shame the wise; God chose what is weak in the world to shame the strong (1:27).

DISCUSSION SUGGESTIONS

Before the video: Tell group members they are going to meet a rather remarkable person in this film. Ask them to be alert to the different ways in which characters respond to Rocky.

After the video:

1. Ask group members to share how each of the following people responded to Rocky's condition. Also talk about the reasons behind each person's response to Rocky.

- Rusty
- friends at school
- Gar
- Evelyn
- Diana
- Diana's parents

2. Point out to the group that God often works through people who have significant problems. In fact, God at times seems to prefer working through such persons. Have members read 1 Corinthians 1:26-31. Why might God prefer to work through those who seem weak by the standards of the world? Was Rocky really "weak"? Why, or why not? How did God work through other people in the film?

3. Divide into three groups. Assign one of these passages to each group:
- Exodus 4:10–17
- Jeremiah 1:4–10

- Isaiah 6:1–8

Have each group answer these questions about its assigned passage:

- What did God call the prophet to do?

- Why did the prophet feel unequal to the task?

- How did God help the prophet?

You may want to put the questions on chalkboard or newsprint. Have each group share a summary of its assigned passage and their responses to the questions.

4. Diana's parents are obviously shocked when they see Rocky. That surprises us. Why have we grown to accept Rocky so fully? Why do we find it initially difficult to accept people with handicaps or disfiguring conditions? Would a girl who was not blind have been so likely to accept Rocky? Why, or why not?

5. Ask group members to share words and phrases that describe Rusty. How much do you think drug abuse affected Rusty? In what ways do the motorcycle gang members show more compassion to both Rusty and Rocky than we might expect? In what ways do Rusty and Rocky help each other in the film?

6. Close with prayer, thanking God for diversity in people.

E.T.—THE EXTRA-TERRESTRIAL

Stars: Henry Thomas as Elliott
Dee Wallace as Mary
Peter Coyote as Keys
Drew Barrymore as Gertie

Rating: PG

Length: 115 Minutes

Summary: An alien crew member (E.T.) is abandoned when humans surprise a spaceship whose occupants are gathering plant specimens. Elliott is the small boy who, through the help of Reese's Pieces as bait, finds the alien and establishes a close bond; the creature can share its emotions with Elliott. The story is so heartwarming that it has become a classic for persons of all ages.

Scripture:
Job 38:1–13 (God confronts Job with the reality of Job's limited knowledge.)
Where were you when I laid the foundation of the earth? Tell me, if you have understanding (38:4).

1 John 4:7
Beloved, let us love one another, because love is from God; everyone who loves is born of God and knows God.

Materials: Reese's Pieces as part of refreshments

DISCUSSION SUGGESTIONS

Before the video: Ask how many have seen the movie *E.T.* before. The majority of your group will probably be familiar with the movie. Suggest that as group members watch the film they try to identify why this movie has been a favorite of so many people. Why are we so fascinated by E.T.?

After the video:
1. Ask group members to share words which describe how each of the following responded to E.T.: Elliott, Mary, Keys, Gertie, and the government. Talk about the reasons for those responses.
2. Then discuss the question you posed at the start of the movie: Why are we so

132

fascinated by E.T.? You might try listing reasons on newsprint. Examples could include: our desire for mystery, the attraction of goodness or kindness, protective instincts. Read 1 John 4:7 on love, and talk about that verse in relation to E.T.

3. Point out to the group that not all science fiction depicts aliens as kindly as E.T. The movies *Alien* and *Aliens*, for example, show much more gruesome, malicious creatures. What might the differences in such movies reflect about their makers? About our society? Is there any way to predict what alien life would be like? Why, or why not?

4. Have group members read Job 38:1–13. What is God saying to Job about the extent of Job's knowledge? Why are we so limited in what we know about the universe? Does scientific knowledge change human nature or matters of the heart? Can we expect scripture such as 1 John 4:7 to apply in all circumstances?

5. Close with prayer, seeking God's help in being loving to all people.

ALIENS

Stars: Sigourney Weaver as Ripley
Carrie Henn as Newt
Lance Henriksen as the android

Rating: R (Strong language, considerable violence, and a tight emotional edge. Definitely not for junior highs.)

Length: 135 Minutes

Summary: This is a sequel to the 1979 film *Alien* in which a single alien-creature brought catastrophe to a space vessel and its occupants; Ripley and a cat were the only survivors. *Aliens* takes place 57 years after the events in *Alien*. Ripley comes out of a deep sleep in a specialized capsule and is asked to travel back to the area where the alien was found because a group of colonists (who went there in the intervening years) are no longer being heard from. On arrival at the colony's location, it is evident that the aliens have taken over. Newt, a courageous but terrified little girl, is the only survivor; and Ripley identifies with and protects her. The last hour of this movie is incredibly intense—perhaps the most intense this author has ever seen.

Scripture:
Psalm 27:1–14
The LORD is my light and my salvation; whom shall I fear? The LORD is the stronghold of my life; of whom shall I be afraid? (27:1).

Romans 8:31–39
For I am convinced that neither death, nor life, nor angels, nor rulers, nor things present, nor things to come, nor powers, nor height, nor depth, nor anything else in all creation, will be able to separate us from the love of God in Christ Jesus our Lord (8:38–39).

DISCUSSION SUGGESTIONS

Before the video: Suggest that group members think about these two questions as they watch the film:

1. How do you feel about seeing such a strong female character as Ripley?

2. Why are films that scare us so popular?

You may want to put the questions on chalkboard or newsprint.

133

After the video:

1. Quickly go around the group, and have each person share the scariest moment in the film for himself or herself. Why does watching this film cause so much anxiety and uneasiness? Then talk about the second question posed before the video: Why are films that scare us so popular? How would our feelings for the movie be different if Ripley and Newt had not survived? Why?

2. The movie seems a little unrealistic in Ripley not sharing any regrets about the 57 years she has slept through! How would one feel about 57 years having passed? Would it be almost like a new life since past friends and associates would be dead? Why, or why not?

3. Talk about the first question raised before the video: How do they feel about seeing such a strong female character as Ripley? Newt's tenacity and courage seem at times like a childlike version of Ripley. The men in this film are not the heroes; they are victims. Ripley and Newt are the ones who emerge victorious. How does this challenge our traditional ideas about male and female roles? What maternal instincts does Ripley show?

4. Have group members read Psalm 27:1–14 and Romans 8:31–39. In what ways do these passages have meaning for the kind of situation in which Ripley and Newt found themselves? How do these passages apply to the difficult situations which we face?

5. Close with prayer, seeking God's help and strength.

ON GOLDEN POND

Stars: Katharine Hepburn as Ethel Thayer
Henry Fonda as Norman Thayer
Jane Fonda as Chelsea
Doug McKeon as Billy Ray
Dabney Coleman as Bill Ray

Rating: PG

Length: 109 Minutes

Summary: For many years Norman and Ethel Thayer have gone to a house on Golden Pond for the summer. Norman is a rather crotchety, retired professor, and his age is clearly affecting him physically and mentally. Ethel loves him deeply and is in emotional pain over his difficulties. However, she doesn't take much flack from him! Their daughter Chelsea comes to join them, along with Bill Ray, whom she intends to marry, and his son Billy. Norman and Ethel end up taking care of Billy while Bill and Chelsea go elsewhere for a few weeks. At first we think Norman may murder Billy (or Billy murder Norman!), but they end up forging a friendship that surprises everyone. This movie is, among other things, a beautiful story about the reality that people do change!

Scripture:

Matthew 18:1–6

Unless you change and become like children, you will never enter the kingdom of heaven (18:3b).

Ephesians 6:1–4

Children, obey your parents in the Lord, for this is right. . . . Fathers, do not provoke your children to anger, but bring them up in the discipline and instruction of the Lord (6:1, 4).

DISCUSSION SUGGESTIONS

Before the video: Tell group members that this is, among other things, a movie about the ability of people to change. Ask them to be alert, as they watch the film, for the changes that take place in people.

After the video:

1. Ask group members to share what changes they saw take place in each of the following characters during the film:

- Norman
- Ethel
- Chelsea
- Billy
- Bill

Golden Pond doesn't seem to change. What kind of stability does that setting offer to the characters in the movie? What changes do take place in the natural world in or around the lake? Why is some change an inevitable part of life?

2. Have group members read Ephesians 6:1–4. Why is it important for children to obey their parents? Are there limitations on that obedience? Why, or why not? What responsibility does Ephesians say parents have for their children? To what extent did Norman and Chelsea fail each other? To what extent did they help and enrich each other? Why did they misunderstand each other for so long? Have you had any similar misunderstandings with one or both of your parents?

3. Have group members read Matthew 18:1–6. Why does Christ want us to become like children? In what ways did Billy reach the child in Norman? In what ways did

Norman help the child in Chelsea? What does it mean to come before God as children?

4. Have group members list difficulties people face as they grow older in our society. What things could your group do to help those who are elderly? What might those who are elderly be able to do for members of your group?

5. Close with prayer, thanking God for giving each of us the ability to change.

ROXANNE

Stars: Steve Martin as C. D. Bates
Daryl Hannah as Roxanne
Rick Rossovich as Chris
Shelley Duvall as Dixie

Rating: PG

Length: 107 Minutes

Summary: This film is based on the classic story of *Cyrano De Bergerac*. C. D. Bates has a very long nose! C. D. and Chris both fall in love with beautiful astronomer Roxanne. Chris simply doesn't have the tact or finesse to court her properly. C. D., seeing no hope for his own romantic desires, helps Chris write poetry and court Roxanne. The story has a happy ending. When Roxanne finds out C. D. wrote the letters, she can accept him for his heart, in spite of his nose.

Scripture:
Colossians 3:12–17
As God's chosen ones, holy and beloved, clothe yourselves with compassion, kindness, humility, meekness, and patience (3:12).

DISCUSSION SUGGESTIONS

Before the video: Have group members read Colossians 3:12–17. Suggest that during the film they be alert for those people who exhibit the following characteristics (list on chalkboard or newsprint):

- compassion
- kindness
- lowliness
- meekness
- patience

After the video:

1. Have group members discuss the people who they feel exhibited each of the traits listed in "Before the video." Does our society normally reward those traits? Why, or why not? What rewards inevitably come to people who exhibit those characteristics?

2. Were C. D. and Chris dishonest in their approach to Roxanne? Why, or why not? Why do you think C. D. helped Chris? How did Roxanne feel when she first learned of the deception? Why is it almost always wrong to deceive others?

3. The movie had a happy ending. Would it have ended so happily in real life? Why, or why not?

4. With reliance on the telephone and personal contact today, we don't always think a great deal about the impact of letters. What benefits do letters offer over other forms of communication? Why can some things at times be expressed more easily in letters than in person? What are the limitations on written communication? Who might like to receive a letter from you?

5. Close with prayer, thanking God for the ability to accept others and to be accepted by them.

PRETTY IN PINK

Stars: Molly Ringwald as Andie Walsh
Harry Dean Stanton as Jack Walsh
Jon Cryer as Ducky Dale
Andrew McCarthy as Blane McDonough
Annie Potts as Iona

Rating: PG-13

Length: 96 Minutes

Summary: Andie is a teenage girl living in tight economic circumstances. Her mother has left, and she lives with her unemployed father. In addition to attending high school, she works a lot of hours in a record store in a downtown mall. She likes to experiment with fashions, getting materials from places like Goodwill and the Salvation Army. Ducky is a good friend who wants to be more than a friend to her. Andie herself has a crush on a teenager named Blane who comes from a very wealthy family. Blane does seem to care for her, but his friends are snobs. It's a movie about dreams, self-confidence (and lack thereof), love, cliques, promise, and pain. Your teens will find much to identify with, and the film seriously challenges the too materialistic world of youth.

Scripture:
1 Corinthians 13:1–13 (on the nature of love)

Materials: Note cards, pencils

DISCUSSION SUGGESTIONS

Before the video: Give teens note cards and pencils. Have them number the cards from one through five. Tell them not to put their names on the cards. Then have them write down yes or no responses to each of these questions:

1. Do teens from wealthy families often have friends from poor families?

2. Do you have any extremely close friends who are much wealthier than you?

3. Do you have any extremely close friends who are much poorer than you?

4. Are there many cliques in your school that shut people out?

5. Do you feel you personally are part of a clique that shuts people out?

Collect the cards, and tally the yes and no responses to each question during the film.

After the video:
1. Share the results of the exercise that was done "Before the video." Talk together about the responses. Why are economic factors often a barrier to friendships? To what extent were those barriers overcome in the film? To what extent were they not overcome? Why, or why not? Was the movie realistic in its handling of economic differences and cliques?

2. Have group members read 1 Corinthians 13:1–13. Then have them identify the movie characters who showed the following traits:

- showed kindness
- did not envy others
- did not try to appear self-important
- bore much suffering
- did not fail others
- was patient to others
- truly knew how to love others

Talk about the reasons why group members feel certain characters showed these traits.

3. What dreams did Andie have? Ducky? Blane? Iona? To what extent were their dreams fulfilled? In what ways were their dreams frustrated? Why is it important to have dreams? What danger comes if one lives too much in a world of dreams?

4. Why do people put so much emphasis on material possessions? What do possessions really have to do with one's basic worth? According to 1 Corinthians, does love have anything to do with wealth or status? Why, or why not? What could you do to begin changing attitudes toward wealth and possessions in your schools? What could you do to keep cliques from influencing you too much?

5. Close with prayer, thanking God for all people—rich and poor, popular and unpopular.

SIXTEEN CANDLES

Stars: Molly Ringwald as Samantha Baker
Anthony Michael Hall as The Geek
Michael Schoeffling as Jake Ryan
Gedde Watanabe as Long Duk Dong
Paul Dooley as Jim Baker

Rating: PG

Length: 93 Minutes

Summary: Samantha's sixteenth birthday has some problems. Her family forgets it. Her grandparents say: "Look, she's finally got boobies!" A lot more goes wrong. This is a movie about teenage anxiety! Samantha takes everything too seriously with the possible exception of herself. The young people in the film spend a lot of time thinking about sex but are very insecure and uncertain about it. The day does improve for Samantha, and the movie is pleasant and refreshing.

Scripture:

Matthew 6:25–34

And can any of you by worrying add a single hour to your span of life? (6:27).

DISCUSSION SUGGESTIONS

Before the video: Have group members read Matthew 6:25–34. Point out that this passage reminds us that anxiety doesn't prolong our lives or help us deal with difficult situations. Christ was talking specifically about anxiety over material things, but the passage can well be applied to other situations. Of course, we can't help being anxious about many things. Suggest that group members be alert as they watch the video for things that characters are anxious about.

After the video:

1. Have group members list characters in the movie who displayed anxiety. In what situations did they show anxiety? To what extent was the anxiety inescapable? To what extent did characters worry too much? In what instances did anxiety actually keep people from responding as well as they might have to others?

2. Have group members look again at Matthew 6:25–34. How can confidence in Christ lower our anxiety? Are there some things we should be anxious about? Why, or why not? Why are we so often anxious about the wrong things?

3. When the Geek and Samantha are in the shop room, Samantha really puts the Geek down for acting so sex-mad. Do you agree with the way she responded to him? Why, or why not? What direction did their conversation take then? In what ways did they find they were alike?

4. How did you feel about the Geek selling looks at a pair of panties? Why do people do such weird things connected with sex? Why are we so uncomfortable dealing with our own sexuality? In what ways is it impossible to avoid some discomfort in this area?

5. Close with prayer, seeking God's help in dealing with anxiety.

STAR WARS

Stars: Mark Hamill as Luke Skywalker
Carrie Fisher as Princess Leia
Harrison Ford as Han Solo
Alec Guiness as Obi-Wan Kenobi
David Prowse as Darth Vader
James Earl Jones as Vader's voice

Rating: PG

Length: 121 Minutes

Summary: This is a classic story about good and evil, set in another galaxy and a future time. Princess Leia leads a struggling remnant who opposes Darth Vader's Imperial forces. Luke Skywalker trains under Yoda to become a Jedi knight and joins in the battle. Han Solo seems to be an irresponsible space privateer but comes through at the times of greatest need. The movie has a happy ending and hints of the other episodes to come.

Scripture:

Psalm 27:1–14

The LORD is my light and my salvation; whom shall I fear? The LORD is the stronghold of my life; of whom shall I be afraid? (27:1).

John 1:1–18

The light shines in the darkness, and the darkness did not overcome it (1:5).

DISCUSSION SUGGESTIONS

Before the video: Ask how many persons have seen the movie before (the percentage will be large, and that won't prevent them from enjoying it again). Suggest that, as they watch the film this time, they think about the extent to which the "Force" is and is not like God.

After the video:

1. Have group members list the ways in which the Force is like God (for example: all around us, all-powerful, helps people). Then have them list the ways in which the Force is not like God (for example: used as a weapon, has a dark side, doesn't offer a personal savior). What would be wrong with understanding the Force to be the same as God? What aspects of God are revealed in the Force?

2. Have group members read Psalm 27:1–14 and John 1:1–18. What is the light that shines in the darkness? What is the darkness that attempts to overpower the light? In what ways is the struggle between good and evil just as real in our time as in the motion picture?

3. *Star Wars* talks about good and bad as being opposite sides of the same Force. While we do not believe as Christians that good and bad are equivalent forces, we do recognize that a thin line is often all that separates good from bad. Darth Vader speaks of "the power of the dark side" of the Force. What is the power of evil? How should we resist evil?

4. Yoda is certainly an unlikely looking hero! Why is it hard for Luke to accept him as a great warrior? What similar preconceptions do we have about the appearance and manner of people? In what ways does God use unlikely people to further God's work?

5. The scene in the bar on the planet Alderaan is a classic. Talk about diversity of life! Could there be that many different life forms in the universe? What factors in our world suggest that God likes diversity? How can we better protect diversity in our world?

6. Close with prayer, thanking God for the light which shines in the darkness.

11 THE SUNDAY SCHOOL/CHURCH SCHOOL

"The Sunday school is dead." That's what many experts in Christian education have been saying off and on for the past twenty years or so. Lately, however, some of them have been revising their opinions. It now appears that the two-hundred-year-old institution known as the Sunday school refuses to roll over and expire. If we are going to speak of the death of the Sunday school, we should probably say it in the same way that the British speak of the death of one monarch and the rise to power of another: "The Sunday school is dead. Long live the Sunday school."

In the Sunday school movement, old ways are perishing and new ways are being born. In some very important respects, the venerable, old establishment known as the Sunday school has undergone substantial changes. And many of the changes are very exciting.

One important area of change is the youth class. New research, new methods, and new approaches are causing significant changes in the youth classes in many churches. And these changes have not come a moment too soon. On the basis of my experience in conducting dozens of seminars for teachers of youth, my own personal reading in this field, and my own work with teachers and youth in local churches, I am convinced that the youth Sunday school class is an area in which many people are desperately crying for help. In many churches the pattern is this: the children's classes are usually successful, often innovative and exciting; the adult classes are generally on a fairly even keel; but the youth classes are a source of almost constant frustration. It is often quite difficult to recruit teachers of youth; and those who attempt the job are frequently baffled, exasperated, even despondent.

Simple arithmetic will readily point up one of the main difficulties in teaching youth in the Sunday school. The amount of time that is available for Sunday school classes is usually no more than one or two hours per week—or about one percent to two percent of a young person's waking hours. When we compare this figure with the 30 percent or so spent in public school education (class time plus homework time), we are immediately confronted with the problem of deciding on a viable educational model that would be suitable for the limited time frame of this "other school system."

There is no instant panacea that will cure all the ills of the youth class situation. But there is hope. It is possible to have a successful, exciting youth class. What is required is a good understanding of the situation and the possibilities, diligent and thorough preparation, creative and educationally sound teaching methods, a real concern for the students, and a willingness to work. This chapter is an attempt to help you with these and other important factors related to the task of teaching young people in the Sunday school.

Teachers

As is true with any kind of teaching/learning situation, the teacher is the key element in a Sunday school class. No other factor is as important. Well-equipped classrooms, educationally sound curriculum, top-notch audio-visual resources—as important as all these factors are, they are virtually useless without a competent teacher. So, if you want to have successful youth classes, make sure that you have good teachers.

What makes a good Sunday school teacher? A combination of many positive characteristics. For starters, here are a few of the important ones:

1. A teacher should have a deep faith in God.

2. A teacher should have a high degree of self-understanding and be basically comfortable about the person that he or she is.

3. A teacher should be able to relate well to all kinds of people.

4. A teacher should be actively involved in the church.

5. A teacher should regularly study the Bible and other resources dealing with the meaning of the Christian faith.

6. A teacher should care for the students and relate well to them as a group and as individuals.

7. A teacher should be willing to work diligently in preparing for class sessions.

8. A teacher should have a good basic knowledge of the age group with which he or she is working and be able to plan teaching/learning activities that are appropriate for the age group.

9. A teacher should be able to lead discussions in an open, nonpatronizing, nonjudgmental manner.

10. A teacher should understand the overall goals of the Christian education program of his or her church.

11. A teacher should be willing to use a variety of classroom methods and techniques.

12. A teacher should continually work at improving his or her teaching skills through personal study and involvement in teacher training experiences.

This list includes many of the main characteristics of a good church school teacher. For additional ideas, see some of the teaching/learning resources discussed in the final chapter of this handbook and also the material in our chapters entitled "Guidelines for Youth Workers" and "The Fellowship Group."

Groupings

As a general rule, the best grouping for youth classes is a setup in which there is a separate class for each grade level (the grouping). This arrangement is usually found, however, only in very large churches which have a sizable number of young people at each grade level. Other more common groupings include the following: 2-2-2; 3-3; 4-2; and 1.

The grouping that you choose will be determined by several factors: the number of youth at each grade level; the number of classrooms available; the number of persons willing to teach youth classes; and, if standard curriculum resources are used, the grading system used in the resources. If you are not able to have a grouping system in which there is a separate class for each grade level, you should try to set up the next best grouping—the 2-2-2 system. If this system is not possible, you should try to set up your classes by using either the 3-3 model or the 4-2 model. An arrangement in which youth in grades seven through twelve are in one class should be using only when absolutely necessary.

The main factor to consider when grouping students is the wide difference in development and interests that exists between the lower end of the age scale (seventh and eighth graders) and the upper end (eleventh and twelfth graders). If at all possible, these age groups should not be in

141

the same Sunday school class. As is pointed out later in this chapter (in the section on "Planning for Sunday School Classes"), it is possible to have a successful class that includes youth from both ends of the age spectrum. It is, nevertheless, very difficult to accomplish this goal. And, before you give up on the other alternatives and opt for one broadly grouped class, you should make every possible attempt to set up a Sunday school system that includes at least two classes (one for younger youth and one for older youth)—even if you and the youth have to go out and recruit enough additional young people to provide the minimum number (five people per class) necessary for a class at each age level.

Planning for Sunday School Classes

Successful Sunday school sessions do not usually happen by accident. They are generally the result of diligent planning and preparation. In this section, we will consider some aspects of the planning process; and, in the next section, we will deal with some of the main factors involved in preparation for units of study and individual class sessions.

General or overall planning for your Sunday school class should begin well in advance of your first class session. If possible, you should do your overall planning before the church school year begins. In most churches, this means planning in the spring and/or summer for the year that will begin in September.

As a rule, your planning—and your classes—will be more effective if you have students work with you. Students should participate in planning and designing their study program and in preparing and leading units of study and individual class sessions. Generally speaking, the amount of student input and participation should increase

proportionately as the youth move from the younger teen level to the older teen level. A class of seventh and eighth graders, for example, would usually have only minimal input and leadership responsibility, whereas a class made up of eleventh and twelfth graders should have a great deal of input and be responsible for much of the leadership of the class.

There are many different ways to go about planning for your Sunday school class. The following is an outline of a process that we consider especially effective:

1. Determine the needs and interests of the students.

2. Set up overall goals in response to needs and interests.

3. Set up a study program based on needs, interests, and goals.

Step One: Determine the needs and interests of the students. There are many methods for determining the needs and interests of the students. One of the most effective methods is the utilization of "interest finders," questionnaires designed to elicit student responses to a variety of items. For our purposes, two main types of questionnaires should be used: the personal needs questionnaire and the general topical questionnaire. In planning for a church school class, you should begin with the personal needs questionnaire, which will give you information about areas in which students feel needs and/or interests. Data gathered through the use of this questionnaire will help you set up general guidelines for the overall direction and emphases of your class. For an example of a personal needs questionnaire, see the section on "Determining Needs and Interests of the Youth" in our chapter entitled "The

Fellowship Group." For additional information on questionnaires in general, see that section and also the section on "Doing Evaluative Quizzes and Questionnaires" in our chapter entitled "Teaching Methods."

The general topical questionnaire is a particularly valuable tool for use in planning the overall study program of a church school class. Whereas the personal needs questionnaire can provide you with broad outlines in terms of your students' needs and interests, the general topical questionnaire can help you zero in on particular topics that might become the basis of your class study program. An example of a topical questionnaire is given below. You may use it as it is, or you may wish to alter it in view of your own ideas about topics that may be of interest to your students.

SUNDAY SCHOOL CLASS QUESTIONNAIRE

Which of the following topics are you interested in exploring in your class? Mark your questionnaire to show your interest.

5 = A great deal of interest in this topic
4 = More than average interest in this topic
3 = Average amount of interest in this topic
2 = Very little interest in this topic
1 = No interest in this topic

____Bible Study: Old Testament
____Modern Cults
____Bible Study: New Testament
____Judaism
____The Nature of the Church
____Catholicism
____Daily Life as a Christian
____Protestant Denominations
____Death and Dying
____Pop Music and Christianity
____Christian Ethics

____Christian Worship
____Making Decisions
____Politics and Christianity
____Getting Along with Parents
____Science and Christianity
____Getting Along with Peers
____Social Concerns and the Church
____Personal Identity
____The Christian Year
____Poverty and the Christian
____Sexism
____Race Relations
____History of Christianity
____Sexuality
____School
____Dating
____Ecology
____Marriage
____Older People
____Alcohol
____Children's Rights
____Drugs
____Money and the Christian
____Tobacco
____Automobiles and Safety
____Our Denomination
____Vocations and Occupations
____Witnessing as a Christian
____(other)_____
____(other)_____

Collating the Results. Add up the total score for each topic. Then divide the total score for each topic by the number of students who responded to that particular item. Make up a large reproduction of the questionnaire on newsprint or a chalkboard. Record the average scores on this chart and present the results to the class.

Choose a "cut-off point" for determining which topics might be included in your class program. A good cut-off point is 3.0, but you may want to choose another figure based on the wishes of the class. Circle all topics that are at or above the cut-off point. Then prepare a second chart showing the chosen topics in order of preference.

One group obtained the following as the top preferences of the members:

4.4	Vocations and Occupations
4.3	Modern Cults
4.3	Dating
4.1	Pop Music and Christianity
3.9	Death and Dying
3.8	Getting Along with Parents
3.8	Getting Along with Peers
3.4	Race Relations

Step Two: Set up overall goals in response to needs and interests. On the basis of information gathered through the use of questionnaires, you and your students should formulate some general, overall goals for your class. Suppose that your students' responses to the topical questionnaire were the same as those recorded above and that their responses to the personal needs questionnaire indicated strong needs in these areas: having better relationships with parents, having a sense of purpose in life, being part of a caring group, and being more caring people.

Obviously, most of these responses to the needs questionnaire would intersect quite neatly with some of the preferences in regard to topics. The two areas of needs that probably add an extra dimension to the topical data are the last two which, although they are related to the topic "Getting Along with Peers," would nevertheless seem to suggest the need for a separate goal related to these two areas.

The following is an example of an overall goals list that might be compiled on the basis of information gathered in this hypothetical class. The first goal relates to the two special needs indicated by responses to the needs questionnaire. The others relate to the topical questionnaire responses.

OVERALL GOALS FOR OUR SUNDAY SCHOOL CLASS

● To build a more caring, concerned group

● To help students learn more about their own vocational aptitudes and skills and discover facts about various vocations and occupations

● To help students learn about some of the modern cults and increase the students' ability to deal with these cults

● To help students learn how the Christian faith relates to pop music

● To help students gain more factual information about death and dying and develop their ability to deal with these subjects

● To help students make necessary changes in attitudes and behaviors related to people of other races

● To help students grow in their ability to relate well to their parents

● To help students develop their ability to relate well to other class members and other people in their peer group and to feel comfortable in dating situations

These goals should be written on poster board or newsprint and posted in a conspicuous location in the classroom. Having the overall goals visually before the students throughout the year will be a constant reminder of the class's overall purposes.

Step Three: Set up a study program based on needs, interests, and goals. Students should have input at this point in the planning process just as they did in the two earlier steps. Here is a procedure that may be used to secure student input in the designing of your program for the year:

1. Divide your study program into several major topics on the basis of information regarding needs, interests, and goals.

2. Determine as best you can the total number of class sessions that you will have during the year.

3. List your major topics on a handout or post them on newsprint or on a chalkboard.

4. Have students work individually to record their ideas as to the number of sessions that should be allotted to each topic.

5. Collate the results by dividing the total number of sessions for each topic by the number of students who responded in regard to that particular topic. Post the results of your collation.

6. Have a class discussion in which you reach a consensus on the number of sessions that you will allot each topic and the sequence in which the topics will be dealt with.

The results of this type of survey do not usually align themselves into a neat pattern that will tell you exactly how many sessions should be spent on each topic. Nevertheless, the raw scores will give you a good indication of general ideas on scheduling. And it will then be up to you and your class to reach a consensus regarding the exact number of sessions to be spent on each topic

and the sequence in which the topics will be studied.

Curriculum Resources

One of the primary questions that you will face as you do your overall planning is the question of whether or not to use an ongoing series of curriculum resources prepared by your denomination or some other publisher. Before making a decision in this matter, you should carefully consider the advantages and disadvantages of an ongoing curriculum series as well as the particulars of your own situation.

There are many advantages to using a standard series of ongoing curriculum resources. In most cases, this type of material is prepared under the supervision of well-trained professionals in the field of Christian education. As a rule, an ongoing curriculum series will be based on a sound curriculum plan that provides for comprehensiveness, balance, and appropriate sequencing of units of study. Much attention is usually given to such important matters as making sure the reading level is appropriate to the age group; providing the teacher with a variety of suggestions for creative teaching/learning activities; supplying and/or suggesting audio-visual resources related to the print materials; and providing step-by-step lesson plans.

There are, however, some disadvantages involved in relying solely on an ongoing curriculum series. One of the main difficulties, particularly with youth classes, is that the topics dealt with in any given time frame will not necessarily be the topics that are most relevant to the needs and interests of the students at that time. In one senior high class that I was involved with, for example, the young people were feeling a great deal of grief and frustration because two of their classmates had just died in automobile accidents. The curriculum resources for that period dealt with the rise of new religious cults and the history of the church. The next unit on death and dying would not be off the presses until six months after these tragedies occurred.

Other disadvantages of using an ongoing series of resources relate to the difficulties that curriculum planners face when they try to create resources that will be usable and applicable in a variety of types of communities, churches, and classes. I worked for five years as a curriculum resources editor with one of the best religious publishing firms in the country; and my experience taught me all too well the difficulties of producing resources that can be effectively used across-the-board in a multitude of different types of classroom situations. Even the best resources should be seen as providing a starting point—a basic plan that you must adapt to your own particular situation.

All Christian resources reflect to some extent the theology of the authors and editors. This book has an automatic bias. Both authors are United Methodists. We tried to compensate for that by setting up an "editorial board" representing twenty different denominations and churches of all sizes. They've "blown the whistle" on us several times.

Many ecumenical resources do not have that kind of editorial board or gatekeeping system. Thus, the description may be "ecumenical," but you are going to find a major dose of one or two denominational perspectives.

In general, you need to carefully evaluate any Sunday school materials which have not been produced by your own denomination. Be certain that you will not be teaching some other denomination's beliefs. (You do not generally have to be as cautious in choosing resources for fellowship groups, retreats, and other settings.)

If you carefully consider the various resources available and make your choice wisely, a standard ongoing series of resources can provide you with a sound basis for your group's program of study. Just remember: you should feel free to adapt the resources to make them more suitable for your individual situation.

On the other hand, if you have creative educational workers, the willingness to work hard, and an adequate budget, you may wish to design your own study program by using a planning process such as the one suggested above. If you choose this option, you will probably want to use some standard curriculum resources along with other resources. Here are some guidelines for using curriculum resources in the development of your own tailor-made program of study:

1. **Never throw any curriculum resources away.** Store them away—and develop a filing system that will give you quick access to resources on any topic. Over a period of a few years, you will amass a vast collection of resources on a variety of topics. Most of these resources will not become obsolete; and those that do become out-of-date can usually be updated very easily.

2. **Be aware of the difference between these two systems of curriculum resources: the "dining hall" system and the "cafeteria" system.** In the dining hall approach, resources are published at regular intervals (usually quarterly or semi-annually) on an ongoing basis. These resources, usually part of a series, are often referred to as "dated" resources since they are designed for use in

particular sessions on particular Sundays—the dates of which are generally stated in the resources themselves.

Cafeteria-type resources, on the other hand, are usually undated. And whereas dated resources are generally available only during the time period for which they are designed, undated resources are usually available at any time during the period that they are in print. The food analogy works this way: with the dining hall system, you have to take whatever is served up, whether it's what you want or not; with the cafeteria system, you have a wide variety of choices at any given time. The implications are obvious. The undated, readily available resources should be an important source for people who are planning their own study programs.

3. **Try to secure available resources that provide a complete unit of study on topics that are of interest to your class.** If you have built up a library of resources from past years, check these resources to see which ones might be usable in your present study program. When a class that I worked with wanted to spend four sessions on the subject of racism, we located in our back files a very good, ready-made, four-session unit, prepared by our denomination on that subject.

After checking out your own collection, look through catalogues for your denomination and other sources. Also visit a local religious bookstore to see what resources are available there. With most topics, you should be able to secure many helpful resources by looking around this way—cafeteria-style.

4. **Don't hesitate to use various parts of an ongoing series piecemeal.** There is no law that says you have to use all parts of a curriculum unit just as it is given. Feel free

to pick and choose—to select the parts that fit your needs—and leave the rest of the unit unused. In a recent five-session unit on vocations and occupations, for example, a senior high class that I taught used three sessions out of a five-session unit on this subject and used a job aptitude questionnaire and a career counselor as the basic resources for the other two sessions.

5. **Adapt.** Feel free to use a standard curriculum resource as your basic resource and then to add, alter, or delete as appropriate. You should be especially conscious of this guideline as you make decisions about audio-visual resources. Most standard curriculum resources are designed according to the "bare bones" theory. They are developed for use by classes with a minimum of money and materials; and they provide very simple step-by-step plans that should be amplified by creative, innovative teachers and leadership teams. In fact, most curriculum planners not only expect you to modify the resources, they usually suggest that such alterations be made. So feel free to "make the session plans your own."

The One-Youth-Class Sunday School. As stated above, this situation should be avoided if at all possible. For those churches where an alternative is not possible, however, there are some guidelines that can help produce optimum results with a one-youth-class situation. Here are a few ideas:

1. **Examine some "broadly graded" resources to see if they are usable with your class.** These resources, designed for classes made up of youth in grades seven through twelve, will usually have a reading level pitched toward the lower end of the age range. That in itself should not present a

147

problem, however. After all, many successful mass media periodicals are keyed to about a sixth-grade reading level. What you should be more concerned about is the level of suggested activities and procedures. Test them out to determine whether they are either too simple or too complicated for most of your students.

Most curriculum publishers will state in their catalogues the grade level of their resources. If you have questions about whether broadly graded resources are available, write or call the publishers. This type of resource could provide the answer to your needs.

2. **Consider using resources that are graded on a level consistent with the age level of the majority of your students.** A class made up primarily of younger youth may be able to function well with junior high resources. But if most of your students are ninth graders and older, you may want to try senior high resources. Whatever the case, you will probably end up using a trial-and-error method until you determine the level of resources that are best for your class.

3. **Select topics with a wide range of appeal.** Steer clear of such narrow topics as preparing for college or understanding early-teen sexuality. The topics for a one-youth-class Sunday school should deal with matters that are relevant for all ages of young people.

4. **Do not spend more than fifteen to twenty minutes on any one aspect of a topic or any one activity.** Junior high youth have a very short attention span, and when activities and discussions run thirty minutes or so, the younger students will usually get fidgety and start creating discipline problems.

5. **Gear the class sessions toward concrete matters.** As a general rule, junior high youth will not have developed very much capacity for abstract thinking.

6. **Use a variety of activities and methods.** Such an approach is particularly essential when working with younger youth; but older youth (and adults as well) also like to have a lot of variety in class sessions.

7. **Rely mainly on activities that can lead to discussion rather than read-and-discuss approaches.** This guideline should be observed in any youth class, but it is almost mandatory when you have some younger youth in your class.

Preparing for Sunday School Sessions

You should be concerned with two main phases of preparation: (1) preparation for a series of sessions dealing with one unit of study and (2) preparation for individual class sessions. Both of these types of preparation include basically the same elements. The obvious difference is that the first type involves general plans and the second type involves specific, detailed preparation.

Preparation for a series of sessions dealing with one unit of study. As you prepare for a complete unit of study, you should try to get an overall picture of your goals, the topics to be dealt with in the individual sessions, and some of the activities and methods that you will use during the course of the unit. You should give special attention at this time to matters that should be taken care of well in advance: ordering films, gathering hard-to-find additional resources and materials, contacting any outside resource people who will participate, and so forth.

148

One of the best tools for use in this overall preparation is a chart on which you list various aspects of your teaching plan. The chart entitled "Preparing for a Unit of Study" will help you develop a well-organized overall plan and also prod your memory in regard to matters that need special advance consideration. It should be used as you plan an overall course and then referred to and updated as the course progresses.

PREPARING FOR A UNIT OF STUDY

Unit Title:		
Unit Goals:		
Date	Topic	Arrangements Needed

Preparation for individual class sessions. In preparing for a particular class session, you should consider the same factors that were considered in planning the unit as a whole. The preparation for individual sessions should be more detailed, however, and you should also add an additional element: preparation of the classroom.

Here again the use of a chart will help you be more organized in your preparation. The chart entitled "Preparing for a Session" is typical of the type of tool that many successful teachers use in this process.

PREPARING FOR A SESSION

Session Title:			
Session Goals:			
Step No.	Activity Description	Materials	Time Est.

Some hints for successful preparation.
There are many valuable guidelines that will help you to prepare for class sessions. Here are some that you should consider:

1. **Prepare the classroom.** A disorderly room conveys the impression that no one cares about the class and its activities. So make the room as neat and orderly as possible. Give some attention to walls and bulletin boards. In a classroom, it is quite true that "the walls talk." Post class goals, pictures, charts, quotations, maps, and other materials that will make the room attractive and interesting.

Arrange chairs, tables, and other furnishings in a manner that will be both practical and educationally effective. A circular arrangement of chairs is usually better for discussions than a lecture room arrangement. If you plan to have small-team work, be sure that work areas are set up in advance. Have a chalkboard or newsprint available for collating ideas and getting them visually before the class.

2. **Have all resources, materials, and supplies on hand prior to the class session.** Curriculum resources, reference works, pencils, paper, markers, and so forth, should be located so that they are readily available when needed.

3. **Keep the session plan *simple*.** It is generally a good idea to limit the number of classroom activities to no more than five. If you allow this guideline, you will find it easier to remember your plan and students will feel that the session has order and direction.

4. **Give special attention to the beginning and the end of the class session.** Make sure that you plan an "as-students-arrive" activity which can be experienced by a few people as they arrive and then can serve as a lead-in to the main part of the session.

Be sure to end the main part of the session in time to have a purposeful conclusion. Many teachers allow the session to fizzle out at the end because the time ran out. Whenever possible, this kind of chaotic ending should be avoided. Plan for a definite ending to the session—and try to stick to your plan. Such a procedure will help the students feel that they have had a complete classroom experience rather than one that just drifted off into nowhere.

5. **Plan for a session based primarily on activities that can lead to discussion.** Limit read-and-discuss procedures to no more than 20 percent of the class time.

6. **Plan to mix a variety of approaches.** Don't rely too heavily on any one procedure—no matter how good it may be. Think of the class session as a mosaic, a design made up of various pieces that enhance the whole picture through their differences. Intersperse discussion with procedures requiring more activity and movement. Try to achieve a balance among individual activities, small-team activities, and activities for the full class. Have some procedures that you lead and some that are led by the students.

7. **Include alternative procedures in your plan.** Be prepared for those times when a particular activity or approach will fall flat. Always have some optional procedures "up your sleeve."

8. **Have session-plan goals that are specific, concrete, and measurable.** Generally, you should have no more than three goals per session. The goals may all be of one type, but I prefer to try to set up one

goal in each of the three main categories of goals: cognitive goals (changes in knowledge); attitudinal goals (changes in opinions and attitudes); and behavioral goals (changes in actions and behaviors).

It is helpful to have goals for the session posted in a conspicuous place in the classroom so that you and your students will be continuously aware of what you are trying to accomplish. Having goals posted will also facilitate evaluation at the end of the session.

9. Be very thorough in preparing for the use of audio-visual aids. Don't leave anything to chance. Always preview an audio-visual prior to the session. Previewing will help you make sure that the audio-visual resource is appropriate; and it will help you avoid the mistake of using a resource that could be offensive or counterproductive.

After previewing, make sure that you prepare the resource for classroom use. Rewind cassettes or films; reset filmstrips at the beginning; make sure that a slide presentation is reset at the beginning; recue a phonograph recording at the proper band. Make sure that your equipment is in proper working order, and recheck the equipment just prior to the session. Be sure that the classroom is properly prepared for audio-visual use. If you are using slides, a film, or a filmstrip, make sure that the room can be darkened and have a good quality screen set up in advance. If you are using cassettes or phonograph recordings, be sure to check the audio level and the placement of speakers. And always check to see whether you will need an extension cord and/or two-pronged adapter for three-pronged plugs.

Know your equipment. Find out what all those knobs are for. Make sure that you know how to turn the machine on and off,

how to adjust volume and tone, how to focus visuals, and so forth.

And, finally, be prepared for "Murphy's Law": "If something can go wrong, it often will—and usually at the worst possible time." Try to anticipate breakdowns and other emergencies so that you will be prepared to deal with them.

For further ideas on the use of audio-visual aids, see our chapters entitled "Media" and "Music! Music! Music!"

10. Remember the "DAAT Rule": Don't assume a thing. Check and recheck to make sure that you have considered every factor that you possibly can. Good class sessions are largely the result of good, thorough preparation. So do your best to cover all the bases. The effectiveness of your sessions will generally be in direct proportion to the amount of time that you have spent in preparing all the elements of your session plan.

Leading a session. There are many guidelines that will enable you to be more effective in leading youth classes. Suggestions of this sort may be found in various chapters of this handbook. Especially recommended are the chapters: "Teaching Methods," "Leading a Discussion and Maintaining Group Life," "Twenty-five Guidelines for Youth Workers" (especially guidelines 7, 8, 9, 10, 11, 12, 19, 20, 21, 23, 24, and 25), and "Media" (especially the section entitled "Discussing Media").

Evaluation. Many teachers of youth classes have a vague, uneasy feeling that their class sessions are not effective, but they have difficulty in determining the reasons for this ineffectiveness. If you have had this type of feeling, you may be able to gain some helpful insights through evaluation of your sessions.

Evaluations should be a regular part of your work as a classroom teacher. You should evaluate your progress on a continuing basis, with thorough evaluations being made at these times: after each quarter or six-month period (overall, general evaluation); after completion of a unit of study; after completion of each class session. To be most effective, evaluations should include input from teachers and youth. Here are some questions that you should consider in your evaluations:

GENERAL EVALUATION

1. What have students learned during this period?

2. What changes in attitudes and behaviors have occurred?

3. In what ways have behavior patterns been changed?

4. Which students have been involved in activities and discussions? Which students have not been involved? How can we get more students involved?

5. Which objectives and goals have been achieved? Which have not been achieved? What reasons can be given for successes or failures in this regard?

6. Has the group become more of a caring, concerned Christian community? Why or why not? What can be done to help develop more caring and concern?

7. What differences of opinion have surfaced in the sessions? How have these differences been dealt with? How could they be dealt with in the future?

8. Have class sessions provided a balance among various kinds of activities? Have the sessions been interesting? Why or why not? What changes could be made to insure more balanced and more interesting sessions in the future?

9. Are there any relationships among class participants (students and teachers) that need improving? If so, how could these be improved?

10. What general suggestions could be made about ways to improve the class sessions?

EVALUATION OF A UNIT OF STUDY OR AN INDIVIDUAL CLASS SESSION

1. What were the goals for this unit (or session)? Were they achieved? Why or why not? What changes could be made to insure that future goals will be achieved?

2. Which parts of the unit (or session) were the most effective? the least effective? Why? Which parts were the most interesting? the least interesting? Why? What changes could be made in order to make future units and sessions more effective and more interesting?

3. Which students participated? Which students were not involved? What were the reasons for participation or lack of it? How could more participation be achieved in the future?

4. If you could redo this unit (or session), which parts would you alter? Why? What alterations would you make?

5. What did you learn from planning and leading this unit (or session) that can help you to be more effective in the future?

In most churches, the fellowship group is the heart of the youth program. There is a special quality about the fellowship setting that gives young people a chance to grow and develop in ways not provided by other approaches. If your church does not have a fellowship group or some other similar setting for its youth, the establishment of such a group should be one of your top priorities.

What do we mean by a fellowship group? In most denominations, this aspect of youth ministry has been around so long that it needs very little formal definition. Indeed, in many churches, the fellowship group is such an integral part of the youth program that it is accepted as a given—and woe to the person who would attempt to get rid of it. On the other hand, the very fact that the fellowship group is such an accepted fixture suggests the need for clarification of its definition, its purposes, its modes of operation. So let's take a closer look at just what we mean by the term "fellowship group."

Here's an attempt at a definition. A youth fellowship group is an informal setting in which youth and their adult advisors participate on a regular basis (usually weekly) in a program that includes elements such as learning activities, recreation/fellowship, worship, and service projects. Usually, the group has a basic organizational plan that includes regular business meetings led by officers elected by the group. The fellowship group differs from Sunday school classes and other settings in many ways. For one thing, the fellowship group integrates learning activities into an overall program that is less formal than most classroom settings. Also, as a rule, the fellowship group provides more opportunities for youth planning and participation; most fellowship groups operate as a joint effort, with youth and adults sharing on a fairly equal basis in both program planning and the leading of the group.

In most denominations, the fellowship group has a name suggested by the denomination such as Pilgrim Fellowship, United Methodist Youth Fellowship, Catholic Youth Organization. Also, many denominations undergird the fellowship structure with resources and materials ranging from handbooks and program periodicals to T-shirts and official emblems. One of the decisions that you and your youth will have to make is the extent to which you will use suggestions made by your denomination. As a general rule, these suggestions regarding resources, materials, and structure are quite good—the result of research and planning by highly capable national staff people. In many instances, however, fellowship groups can profit from thoughtful consideration of how these suggestions may be adapted for use in a particular local group. Remember that even the best suggestions for general approaches and procedures should be seen as guidelines and that your own creativity in the use of these suggestions can often make the difference between a vital, exciting fellowship group and one that is just run-of-the-mill.

A Balanced Approach

Most experienced youth workers believe that the fellowship group, like youth ministry in general, should provide a balance among certain basic components of the program. A good model is what has been called the "four-square approach" or "the youth ministry diamond." This model calls for a balance among these four elements: (1) Learning Activities, (2) Recreation and Fellowship, (3) Worship, and (4) Service Projects. The scriptural basis for this model is Luke 2:52, which states that "Jesus increased in wisdom and in years, and in divine and human favor." This verse points out four areas of growth and development (intellectual, physical, religious, and social), which correspond in our model to the components of learning, recreation, fellowship, worship, and service.

How do we achieve this balance? Obviously, it is not easy to include each element in every weekly meeting of a youth fellowship group. You may seek to secure this balance through two main approaches. One approach involves having some weekly programs in which all four elements are present. When this approach is used, the service element usually consists of a project that does not consume a lot of time. A good example is a Christmas caroling program, which might include these elements: an opening worship service (10 minutes), a film on the concerns of the aging (20 minutes), caroling at a nearby nursing home (60 minutes), and refreshments and recreation back at the church (30 minutes).

A second approach to achieving this four-component model is one that a group uses more often. In this approach, they plan the fellowship group programs in such a way as to achieve balance in each three-month period. Most meetings include learning activities, recreation/fellowship, and worship; on a regular basis, however, there is a special meeting devoted exclusively to a service project. These service projects are frequently done at a time other than the group's regular meeting time; often they are all-day Saturday events.

There are, of course, other operational models for achieving this type of balance. Regardless of which model you use, you should always make an effort to have a balance among these four components. Most

groups that do not consciously seek such a balance end up with programs that emphasize either study sessions or "game time."

A related matter that is important for fellowship groups is the ratio of regular sessions to special activities. As a rule, the most successful type of scheduling includes some special trips or outings or some other special programs to break the pace of the regular meetings. You have to decide for yourselves what this ratio should be for your group. Many prefer to have a ratio of 3-to-1: three regular meetings in a row followed by one special program. These special programs may be of various types, for example: recreational outings, service projects, learning outings (such as visits to other churches or to service agencies), or special meetings featuring outside resource people who are specialists in areas such as clown ministry, sexuality training, or drug/alcohol problems.

An important key to planning successful youth fellowship programs is the element of variety. Youth (and adults) are easily turned off by a continuing program that is marked by a predictable sameness. But they are usually comfortable with a regular plan if they know that special events will break the pattern from time to time. So strive for balance and variety. Be intentional so that your method and approach will have a sound, well-thought out basis.

The Setting

Most youth fellowship groups meet on a weekly basis, usually on Sunday afternoon or Sunday evening. Some groups have had much success with meetings during the school week or on Saturday. Whether your group chooses the traditional Sunday meeting time or one of the alternatives will depend on local factors—the general view on weeknight curfews, the amount of school homework that is assigned to the youth, the number of young people who have after-school and/or Saturday jobs, the availability of other youth activities in your area, and so forth. Before arbitrarily deciding on a particular meeting time, do some research. Talk with the youth, their parents, the youth group advisors, your church officials. Make sure that you choose a time that will produce optimum results.

The generally accepted time frame for fellowship groups is one to two hours. You should be very careful in deciding on the length of your meetings. You want to have enough time for carrying on a full, well-balanced program without feeling rushed. On the other hand, you do not want to have a time frame that is so lengthy that there is a lot of "dead time"—periods in which the young people just hang around and get bored. A good approach is one that allows for both close scheduling and flexibility. It is a good idea to have all the components of the program mapped out with designated time lengths. But you should also be flexible enough to alter the schedule when necessary.

Beginning the program with a fellowship meal is a real plus for fellowship groups. A fellowship meal provides an opportunity for you and the young people to be together on an informal basis. It also helps solve the problem of how to begin the program when people arrive at different times. Those who come late will be late for the meal, not late for the content parts of the program. Also, if the meals are prepared on a rotating basis by parents and other adults, the use of a fellowship meal can give adults a chance to get better acquainted with the youth and their fellowship program.

There are many different ways to take care of the logistics of your group's fellowship meal. The young people can be asked to pay a small fee. Or the cost of the meal can be covered by parents and other adults on a rotating basis. The cost of the meals can be included in the youth portion of the church's budget, with those preparing the meals being reimbursed by the church. On special occasions you can send out for pizza or burgers. At these times (usually once or twice a quarter), we ask the young people to bring a dollar or so to help cover the costs.

The manner in which the various parts of a fellowship meeting are scheduled will vary from one group to another, and it will also vary from week-to-week in any particular group. Two examples of typical schedules for regular group meetings are given below. Note, particularly, the differences between the two schedules. The key factor in designing the junior high schedule is the interspersing of recreation throughout the program—an approach that many youth workers find especially helpful in their attempts to deal with two characteristics of junior high youth: their exceptionally high energy level and their relatively short attention span (usually a maximum of about 15 to 20 minutes of involvement with one activity).

Schedule 1: A Typical Senior High Fellowship Group Meeting

6:30-7:00 Fellowship Supper
7:00-7:20 Worship
7:20-8:00 Learning Activities
8:00-8:20 Business Meeting
8:20-8:50 Recreation/Fellowship
8:50-9:00 Closing

Schedule 2: A Typical Junior High Fellowship Group Meeting

6:30-7:00 Fellowship Supper
7:00-7:20 Worship
7:20-7:50 Recreation/Fellowship
7:50-8:10 Learning Activities
8:10-8:25 Recreation/Fellowship
8:25-8:45 Learning Activities
8:45-8:55 Business Meeting
8:55-9:00 Closing

An important factor for a youth fellowship group is having "their own place"—a room or area that is used primarily by their group. Many churches have youth rooms that are used mainly for youth groups and classes. If yours does not, look around and see if you can find some available space. Some youth workers have had great success with adapting storage areas for use by youth groups. A lot of churches have areas like this that are not being efficiently used. With very little expense and some good handiwork by the youth and their advisors, you can transform a poorly used area into a place that the youth can call their own. Having such a room can go a long way toward building your group's spirit. I feel so adamant about the youth's need for their own space that whenever I have found absolutely no church space available, I have tried to secure a basement or a recreation room in a church member's home for this purpose. Although this procedure is not as desirable as having space in the church, it is certainly worth trying if no other alternative can be found.

The Structure of the Group

During the late 1960s and early 1970s, some denominations suggested that youth fellowship groups should operate in a very informal way. This "informal group" approach, which usually does not call for election of group officers, has some advantages. When properly utilized, it can allow for more youth participation in leadership roles through the rotation of leadership responsibilities on a weekly or monthly basis. It can be especially useful for a small group that does not have enough members to warrant a full slate of officers. With such an approach, the full group can work as a "committee of the whole" to plan and implement the group's programs and activities.

In most fellowship groups today, however, we have seen a return to the older, traditional model in which a full slate of officers is elected for a complete year or for shorter periods, such as six months or three months. If you choose this model for your group's structure, you should consider electing the following officers: president, vice-president, secretary, treasurer, and class representatives. In some groups, particularly those with memberships exceeding twenty youth, you may also want to elect people for responsibilities in special areas: worship, recreation, learning activities, service projects, fund raising, special events, and publicity.

A structural model that is used by many groups is the fellowship group council model. In this model, all the youth officers and the adult advisors are members of a council that meets (usually at least monthly) for program planning. In addition to meetings by the full council, many groups find it helpful for the youth officers and the adult advisors to have separate meetings on a regular basis. If such separate meetings are held, you should make sure that they do not become adversary undertakings. The purpose of separate meetings is to provide an opportunity for youth and adults to meet and discuss matters that they need to deal with from their own perspectives, not to have each group work out plans for "doing in" the other.

All official planning, however, should be done by the full council, not by the youth or adults alone. And, as a rule, the council should operate in an advisory capacity—working as a small group to make plans that will be considered and acted upon by the fellowship group as a whole. The final approval of the fellowship group's plans and the designation of responsibilities for carrying out those plans should be the task of the whole group. Unless the council operates with this type of open, consultative leadership, council members will soon discover that their leadership is not being accepted or appreciated by the group.

A fellowship group council is not the same group as the youth council which is described in the chapter on planning. A youth council, as the phrase is used in this book, looks at the total youth ministry of the congregation. A fellowship group council only plans for that particular group. A small church does not need both groups.

Advisors

Much of the success of your youth fellowship group will depend on the adults who work with the group as advisors or counselors. There is probably no other job in the church that is as rewarding as the position of youth group advisor. Unfortunately, it is also true that there is no other job in the church that is as time-consuming and exhausting. The burnout rate among youth group advisors is incredibly high. It takes a very special kind of person to fill this role, a person who is willing and able to deal with the time demands, the work load, and the sometimes frequent frustrations that come with this responsibility.

What kind of person should be an advisor to a youth fellowship group? A lot of positive personality characteristics are needed. Here are some of the most important:

1. **A youth group advisor should be a well-integrated, whole person.** You need to have an understanding and acceptance of who you are. You should know your own strengths and limitations and be comfortable with them. If you are to serve as a role model for youth (and that comes with the territory), you should have a stable personality. You should be able to give the youth the advantage of relating to a well-balanced adult who has good feelings about his or her own selfhood. You don't have to be perfect. But you should know and like the person that you are. You should not be dependent on the young people to give you your identity.

2. **A youth group advisor should know and care for the young people as individuals.** Think back about your own days as a youth. Your experiences were probably similar to mine. The adults who had the most important positive effects on me were those who truly and deeply cared for me as an individual. And that's what today's youth are looking for and need in their advisors. They want to relate to adults who know them as they are and care for them as individual persons, adults who will share openly and in a nonpatronizing way the young people's interests, needs, and aspirations.

3. **A youth group advisor should have a strong faith and a heartfelt dedication to Jesus Christ.** You don't have to have all the answers. You can have some doubts. All of us do. But you should know where you stand

in terms of your religion. And you should have a strong compulsion to share your faith with the youth with whom you work.

4. **A youth group advisor should be willing to work.** Being an advisor to a youth fellowship group involves many hours of reading, planning, meeting, leading groups, talking with young people, and performing countless mundane tasks like making sandwiches or working on a car wash. It is not a job for the fainthearted or the lazy. If you accept this responsibility, be prepared to work.

5. **A youth group advisor should be open to youth and be responsive to their ideas, plans, and input.** As an advisor to a fellowship group, you will not be able to function as a dictator—at least not for very long. Working with youth in a fellowship group is a mission of mutuality. You must be willing to listen, to compromise, to plan and work together with the youth. If you're looking for an opportunity to "run" a youth group, to "straighten out the kids," or to be in charge, then look elsewhere. A good youth group advisor is a person who works openly and comfortably with the young people themselves.

Which people make the best youth group advisors? Should we have parents of youth or nonparents? Should youth group advisors be young adults or older adults? If you have a large group, the best approach is to try to secure a mix—some parents, some nonparents, some people in their twenties, some who are older. An advisors' group made up only of parents of youth often ends up being a group that tends toward too much adult dominance of the youth. A group of nonparents, on the other hand, will often lean too much toward doing "whatever the kids want." It is best to have some of each.

If they have the necessary openness, parents and nonparents can serve as checks and balances for each other. Many churches, of course, could not provide that much balance without having more adults than youth. So the final answer is that age and parent/nonparent status are not the most important criteria. Maturity, concern for youth, and communication skills are more important.

There can be a danger in following the route that many churches choose in selecting advisors: recruiting some "young adults who have rapport with the kids." While such people may easily form relationships that encourage the youth to share their concerns with them, sometimes younger adults do not have the life experience that would enable them to give the youth a much needed adult perspective. On the other hand, some "older adults" who can provide a mature perspective may have lost contact with the youth scene.

Being a parent or a nonparent, being young or old—these are not guarantees that a particular person will fit into a general mold. Evaluate each person as an individual. Try to secure people who can give guidance without being domineering, people who can relate to the youth and their interests while still providing the necessary adult perspective. This guideline is important regardless of whether your youth group is to have just one advisor or several.

Just as important as the quality of the people selected as advisors is the matter of training. No one should be allowed to work as a youth group advisor without having at least some minimal training in such areas as characteristics of youth, the current youth scene, program planning, and leading discussions. Ideally, this training should be done by a competent, experienced youth worker. Many denominations provide this type of training by national, regional, or local staff people. Some independent organizations such as Serendipity and Youth Specialties also offer many seminars and workshops that relate to youth ministry and fellowship groups. If such opportunities are not available, you should consider setting up your own professionally led training event. One good approach is to get together with several other churches and share the cost of bringing in a skilled leader in the field of youth ministry.

If you cannot find any opportunities for training by a professional, put together your own local program. Choose some of the youth ministry resources suggested in the final chapter of this handbook. Get together with other youth workers from your church and other churches. Study the resources yourselves. Then plan and implement your own program of training. A good model for designing such a seminar is to choose some of the chapters of this handbook as your main areas for training and then to develop the curriculum for your seminar by using these chapters along with additional resources which we recommend.

One final word about youth group advisors: Allow them some "off time" for rest and recuperation. One way that you can deal with the high burnout rate among advisors (and among youth workers, in general) is by allowing each person to have some time off on a regular basis—a minimum of one meeting per month, if possible. In many churches, of course, it is difficult enough to secure one youth group advisor and nearly impossible to recruit a group of people to share this job. But the effort should be made. Having at least two advisors will allow the advisors to have some relief from the constant demands of this job.

If you cannot recruit more than one person, at least try to secure a part-time substitute. In this job, rest and recuperation are essential.

Another good method for dealing with the burnout problem is to recruit advisors for a set period of time—say, two or three years. When an advisor's time commitment is up, strongly encourage him or her to give up the job for a year or two. This "off time" will usually result in renewed dedication and energy when an advisor returns to the job.

Age Groupings

The best situation is one in which you have separate youth fellowship groups for different age levels. The most common model of this type is a program in which junior high youth and senior high youth have their own separate groups. In some localities, this approach involves having seventh, eighth, and ninth graders in one group and tenth, eleventh, and twelfth graders in another group. In other areas, the groupings in the public school system will necessitate forming one group for seventh and eighth graders and another group for ninth through twelfth graders. The important thing to keep in mind is the wide difference in development and interests that exists between the lower end of the age scale (seventh and eighth graders) and the upper end (eleventh and twelfth graders). If at all possible, these age groups should be in separate fellowship organizations.

A related question is the dilemma faced in some areas where the schools group sixth graders with those who have been traditionally classified as junior high youth. We faced this situation in a church in which I worked. And we decided to keep our age groupings as they had been in the past, which meant not including sixth graders in

159

the youth fellowship program. Because of the difference in maturity between sixth graders and junior high youth, I would recommend this approach, even if it means using a designation other than "junior high" for your younger fellowship group. In our case, we referred to our groups simply as the junior fellowship group and the senior fellowship group.

Although the best situation for fellowship groups is a program in which older and younger youth meet in separate groups, it is possible to have a viable fellowship program in a church where the small number of young people makes it inadvisable to have two groups. If you are in this type of situation, you will have to be especially careful in the planning and leading of your meetings; you will need to make sure that the topics and activities that you choose relate to the younger youth without being on such a simple level that they bore the older youth. You will need to aim the major emphases at the age level that constitutes most of your group. A group consisting primarily of younger youth, for example, may be able to function quite well by using junior high resources. But if most of the youth are ninth graders and older, you may want to try resources designed for senior high youth. Whatever the case, you will probably have to use a trial-and-error method until you find the level of resources and approach that works best for your group.

How do you decide whether to have one group or two? You have to consider each situation on its own. Generally speaking, however, if you have as many as five young people in each of the major groupings (younger and older), you would probably have a more successful program with two groups—even though the groups may be small. If you do not have the minimum number suggested for each group, you will probably find it best to have only one group. Of course, there's always another alternative—you and the youth can go out and recruit enough people to constitute two workable groups. Some churches are large enough to justify having more than two groups. See the chapter "What Groups Should We Offer?"

Planning for Youth Fellowship Groups

Planning for youth fellowship groups should always be a joint effort by the youth and adults. Ideally, much of the basic planning should be done by a group council (as described above) or by some other small group, usually consisting of no more than a dozen or so people. Despite all the "bad press" that committee work has received, there is still much to be gained by having a small, ongoing group doing the planning. In a small group, several people can give input and various viewpoints can be aired without producing the mass confusion that often results from having a large group involved in the planning process.

Planning for a youth fellowship group should be done in several phases. There should be overall planning, usually on a yearly basis. Then there should be more detailed planning, usually quarterly. Finally, there should be the very detailed, specific planning, usually monthly and weekly.

General planning. At some point, usually in the spring or summer before a year's program is to begin in September, there should be a general planning session. Many groups find it helpful to do this type of planning during extended sessions—on a weekend retreat, for example.

160

What procedure should you follow in your overall planning? Don't make the mistake that many groups make. Don't start out by asking: "Well, what do we want to do this year?" A better approach is to begin at the beginning, to start out by considering needs and interests and then to proceed step-by-step to the development of programs and activities. A good process for program planning is one that goes step-by-step through the following procedures:

- Determine what the needs and interests of the youth are.

- Set goals based on these needs and interests.

- Decide on general programs and activities that will be developed to meet these goals.

The main purpose of a general planning session should be the development of broad outlines for the overall program for the group. The only detailed plans to be made at this point might be specific plans for programs for the first month of the year under consideration.

Quarterly planning. The main purpose of quarterly planning is to give your group a chance to evaluate its overall program midstream. Quarterly planning should involve the same type of consideration of needs, interests, goals, and programs that was done in the general planning session, but on a more limited basis. During a quarterly planning session, the focus should be on (a) an evaluation of how the overall program has progressed during the preceding three months and (b) a consideration of how the overall program might be altered during the upcoming three-month period.

Questions that should be dealt with in the quarterly sessions include the following:

1. **Are the needs and interests of the youth group members the same as those discovered in the general planning session?** If not, in what ways have they changed? What new needs and interests might be added to the list?

2. **Are the goals from the general planning session being met?** What new goals should be added? What changes should we make in order to achieve more of our goals?

3. **Which programs and activities have been successful?** Which have not? What are the reasons for success or failure? What new plans for programs and activities should be added? What changes should be made in the ways programs and activities are carried out?

Monthly planning. Your monthly sessions should be concerned with specific plans for programs and activities for a one-month period. These sessions should always deal with the group's plans a month in advance; in the September session, for example, the group should plan programs for October. Specific program responsibilities and assignments should be decided upon during these monthly sessions. As is the case with the quarterly sessions, some time in each monthly session should be given to evaluation of the preceding month's programs and consideration of how this evaluation might cause the next month's program plans to be altered.

Weekly planning. This type of planning session should involve a small group—those people in charge of the program for one meeting. During weekly sessions, final decisions should be made regarding resources, activities, scheduling, and leadership. These sessions should also include some evaluation of the preceding week's program and consideration of how this evaluation might affect the program for the session being planned.

Where to Get Ideas

No youth worker possesses unlimited creativity, so almost all of us need the stimulation of good resources to help with program ideas, recreation, fund raising, worship, and so forth.

Don't overlook the materials provided by your own denomination. Denominational resources tend to be stronger on learning activities than on recreational activities. That makes sense when one considers that the average group can do a better job planning a bowling party than planning a program on drugs or on the use of the Bible.

Youth Specialties publishes a series of nondated paperbacks called *Ideas*. As of this writing, there are around thirty books in the series, simply titled *Ideas # 1, #2, #3*. Youth workers around the country submit games, skits, service projects, discussion starters, publicity approaches, and other IDEAS. Each paperback contains an assortment of these tested activities. These are good planning aids because youth can turn through them and readily identify things they would like to try. You may find that 25 percent of the ideas are not new to you and that 50 percent of them have no appeal to your group. Don't let that discourage you—the books are worth having for the 25 percent that are right for your group. Don't order thirty at once (unless you've seen samples like them and are willing to invest the money).

GROUP magazine provides a variety of suggestions each month, including excellent material for discussions. The magazine is well-balanced theologically, is attractively illustrated, and is generally well-written. Give

serious consideration to a subscription for your group.

If you want the most for your money in creative ideas, buy Dennis Benson's *Recycle Catalogue* and *Recycle Catalogue II*. Both are reasonably priced and are jammed with ideas.

GROUP and *Recycle* books are best for discussion/learning activities. The *Ideas* materials are stronger on recreation and social activities. These are not the only good resources available, however; see the final chapter for more suggestions and for addresses.

Determining Needs and Interests of the Youth

A key step in the planning process—and one that often causes difficulty—is determining the needs and interests of the youth. Most of the difficulties encountered are those that occur when youth group advisors try to determine youth needs and interests in a vacuum. In order to get valid input at this point, you must go beyond merely asking: "What are you interested in?" or "What do you want to do?" You should give the youth some possibilities to choose from. One of the best ways to do this is through the use of interest-finders.

There are many different kinds of interest-finders. For our purposes, we will look at three of the most common types: (1) a personal needs questionnaire, (2) a topical questionnaire, and (3) an activity questionnaire. A simple, personal needs questionnaire follows.

PERSONAL NEEDS QUESTIONNAIRE

This questionnaire is designed to determine the personal needs of the members of our fellowship group. The results of this survey will help the group decide on programs for the coming year. So answer as honestly as possible. Do not put your name on the questionnaire. We want your thoughts—not your identity.

Rate the following on a scale of 1 to 5.

1 = no need at all in this area
2 = a little need in this area
3 = a moderate amount of need in this area
4 = much need in this area
5 = a tremendous amount of need in this area

____to feel better about myself as a person
____to have a stronger faith in God
____to have more friends
____to have a better relationship with my parents
____to feel better about my own sexuality
____to have more of a sense of purpose in my life
____to have more time alone
____to have a better social life
____to improve myself in regard to school
____to get more exercise
____to eat better foods
____to read more
____to have some person care about me
____to belong to a group that cares for me
____to help other people to be more open to criticism
____to be a more caring person
____to have an outstanding achievement in some area
____to relate better to my brother(s) and/or sister(s)
____to improve my personal appearance
____to be more helpful to others in my family
____to have a close relationship with a member of the opposite sex
____to be more careful about my use of time

____to understand "what makes me tick"
____Other:_____
____Other:_____
____Other:_____

The main advantage of a personal needs questionnaire is that it can give you some general ideas about the psychological profile of your group. To some extent, however, it can also provide you with clues concerning possible goals and programs. The questionnaire given above, for example, should help you make some tentative decision as to whether some of your goals and programs might relate to areas such as: the search for personal identity, the basics of the Christian faith, the nature of your fellowship group, sexuality, family relationships, service to others, and the school situation.

The questionnaire that is given as an example is one that I have found useful with fellowship groups. You would probably want to alter it to some degree in order to include other basic needs that you think are a part of your group's profile.

The topical questionnaire. An example of a general topical interest finder is given in this handbook in the chapter entitled "The Sunday School." You may use this instrument as it is to determine topics that are of interest to your fellowship group, or you may wish to adapt it somewhat for the special situation of the fellowship setting. In most cases, whether you are using it for a Sunday school class, a fellowship group, or another type of youth group, you will probably find it advisable to alter the questionnaire by adding or deleting topics in order to make it more appropriate for your own group.

The activity questionnaire. The following is a sample questionnaire on programs and activities. Change the possible programs and activities to meet the needs of your group.

The rating column should be completed by numbers from 1-5 with 1 being low interest and 5 being high interest.

PROGRAMS AND ACTIVITIES QUESTIONNAIRE

POSSIBLE PROGRAMS AND ACTIVITIES	RATING	I WOULD PARTICIPATE IN (indicate by X)
A. Short-term Bible study		
B. Service projects		
C. Drama sessions (to do one or two plays)		
D. Music sessions (to rehearse and perform folk hymns and other music)		
E. Movie sessions (to attend and discuss films)		
F. Exchange programs (to visit other youth groups)		
G. Basketball team (coed)		
H. Softball team (coed)		
I. Question sessions (to explore the Christian faith with the pastor)		
J. Prayer and devotional sessions		

A final note on questionnaires. The use of the various types of questionnaires discussed above should give you a fairly accurate picture of the needs and interests of the young people. When setting goals and planning programs and activities, you should carefully consider the results of these and similar surveys. Remember, however, that the purpose of these instruments is to provide you with youth input regarding needs and interests. This input should be your starting point when you begin to set goals and plan programs and activities. You should also consider two other factors. First, the adult advisors should also have a say in determining the goals, programs, and activities of the group. Program planning is a joint effort by youth and adults. Second, you should be open to the possibility of adding other goals, programs, and activities in addition to those suggested by your survey results. In some cases, there may be additional areas that need consideration by your group. Use your own judgment and common sense. If you discover additional areas of this sort, don't hesitate to attempt some subtle education of the youth and adults in regard to other goals, programs, and activities that should be a part of their overall program.

Designing Your Programs

Your fellowship group can have interesting, relevant programs and activities. The key is to proceed in the right manner. The process that we suggest is one that involves determining the needs and interests of your group (through questionnaires such as those discussed above), setting goals to meet those needs and interests, and then designing your own programs and activities in view of the group's needs, interests, and goals. This procedure is not an easy one.

The easiest procedure is to use a standard fellowship group resource from your denominational publishing house or some other source. In many cases, because of factors such as time limitations, lack of available leadership, and limited budgets, relying solely on standard resources may be the only feasible approach. But, if you can find the time, the leadership, and the money, a custom-tailored program for your group is always the best alternative.

Annual Evaluation

A program evaluation questionnaire. In an ongoing group, it is possible to determine interests by having the youth themselves devise and respond to a questionnaire that is based on past programs and activities. The steps in producing and analyzing this survey are as follows:

1. Have the young people name all the programs and activities that they can recall from the past year. (You will immediately gain some insights based on what the youth are able to recall. The programs and activities named will usually be those that made an impact—either positive or negative. Those that are not named will generally be the ones that made no lasting impression on the youth.)

2. List the programs and activities on newsprint or a chalkboard in the order in which they are named.

3. Give each young person a pencil and a sheet of paper.

4. Have each person rate the listed programs and activities from 0 to 100 as if he or she were grading a school assignment.

5. Calculate the results by adding the figures for each program or activity and

165

dividing by the number of young people who responded.

Interpretation: You will have to use your own good judgment in interpreting the results. Generally speaking, however, it has been my experience that a group should seriously consider repeating those programs and activities that are rated 50 or higher.

A good procedure is to list in order of favorable ratings all the programs and activities considered and then have the group try to reach a consensus about which items should be repeated.

A program components survey. It may also be helpful to survey the youth concerning their ideas on (a) the amount of emphasis given to various program components during the past year and (b) the amount of emphasis that should be given to

these components during the coming year. The results should be tabulated in the manner suggested in the preceding program evaluation.

For More Help . . .

This chapter is an attempt to cover the basics of a youth fellowship group. There are many other resources available to help you. For more information (and some different perspectives), see other chapters entitled "What Groups Should We Offer?" "Planning With Young People," "Leading a Discussion and Maintaining Group Life," "Teaching Methods," "Looking at Your Group," "Raising Money," "Media," "Video," "Worship," and "Music! Music! Music!" For a listing of helpful resources, see the final chapter of this handbook.

In 1980 Sue Brownfield, Julie Seibert, and I wrote a book titled *Repairing Christian Lifestyles*. The book's primary purpose was to help youth examine their own lifestyles and to motivate them to lead lives of service to others. Some of our cynical friends predicted the book would have only limited appeal because it expected too much of young people. They were wrong! The book enjoyed high sales, and a new edition is being released by *faithQuest*.

Although we may occasionally expect too much from young people, we more often err in expecting too little. It is true that the current generation of teens is somewhat more inwardly directed than some past generations, but that is as much the fault of adults as of the teens. Young people can still be excited about service to others, and they generally find their own lives renewed in the process. There's significant truth to the Biblical teaching:

> *For those who want to save their life will lose it, and those who lose their life for my sake will find it.*
> Matthew 16:25

When we live selfishly, we often go through life frightened and anxious—with a sense that we are missing something significant. When we live in service to Christ and to others, willing to lose our own lives for the sake of others, our lives are transformed. Young people can begin to understand this concept as they have meaningful service opportunities through the life of the church.

The churches with the strongest, most successful youth programs always place considerable emphasis on service. As you examine your church's total youth program, be certain that significant opportunities to serve others are given to youth.

The fellowship group is the traditional youth organization for the implementation of service projects. In the chapter on "Fellowship Groups," we recommend balance among:

- Worship
- Service
- Education
- Recreation

As you plan with your youth group, be sure to provide service opportunities. The range can include as small a project as cleaning a room in the church and as large a project as starting a food pantry for the community. Youth groups often combine service work with a summer trip doing tutoring, painting, or other tasks at a mission site.

Sunday school and parochial school classes are primarily study settings and will understandably not do as much with service projects. That doesn't mean, however, that you should never do a service project with a class. Classes should be alert for service opportunities related to topics of study. A class discussing the need for world peace might want to write letters to congressional representatives and senators. A class discussing world hunger might want to collect canned food to donate to an area food pantry. A class studying a resource such as *Repairing Christian Lifestyles* may very well want to do several service projects because they flow naturally from the material being studied.

Youth choirs obviously give service to the church each time they sing. Be alert for other service opportunities appropriate for the choir. Many youth choirs enjoy making monthly or quarterly trips to perform at area nursing homes and visit with the residents. Some choirs have done concerts at children's homes and at state or federal prisons. While singing at the homes of shut-ins is most commonly done at Christmas, there's no reason why it can't be done throughout the year.

Special groups may actually be formed around a service project. Churches have formed youth groups to:

- perform clown ministry in hospitals and nursing homes.

- run a Saturday soup kitchen for the homeless (in a community where the regular soup kitchen was closed on Saturdays).

- make a video on local hunger needs.

- make a mission trip each summer.

- operate a teenage "HELP" line, with phones staffed by teenagers who will listen compassionately to other teens who have problems.

Service Project Guidelines

1. **Don't impose service projects on youth.** Help them be aware of the opportunities available, but let them make their own decisions. Other adults in the church will often try to recruit youth help. "Would the youth group help me solicit for the Cancer Society?" "Would the youth help serve our banquet?" Such suggestions are often worthwhile, but the decision to participate needs to be made by the young people themselves rather than by the adult advisors.

2. **Don't underestimate the cost or time required for a service project.** Projects can be more time-consuming and expensive than they first appear. Volunteering to paint the house of a low-income person is an excellent service project. Once youth have agreed to do it, however, it's critical to follow the project through to completion. That may mean more hours of work and more dollars for paint than anticipated. It's best to allocate more hours and money than you think will be necessary—build in a safety reserve! The same can be true of many other service projects. If the group's estimates are wrong, youth still need to complete the job. That's part of learning responsibility to others.

3. **Encourage responsibility,** but don't shame youth who avoid service projects. There will always be some youth group members who are conspicuously absent from service projects. It's tempting to shame or belittle them for failing to help, but that is almost always counterproductive. It's better to simply have those who did participate do lots of positive talking about how much fun they had; service projects usually are fun and produce a good feeling of accomplishment.

If you have difficulty completing service projects because not enough youth appear, have people sign up by name to help. Then you have specific commitments and are able to contact the young people who fail to appear. A pleasant but firm reminder is the proper approach in that situation.

4. **Use your church newsletter, bulletin, and Sunday announcements to let the congregation know about youth service projects.** Youth shouldn't do service projects for the purpose of receiving recognition, but the rest of the church does need to know about the good things young people do. That will help your church feel better about the youth, and it may motivate adults to do more service themselves.

5. **Always talk about service projects in positive terms.** Service projects are enjoyable

and satisfying. Your tone and attitude in talking with youth about service projects should always reflect that. If you sound like you don't think youth will want to do a service activity, they won't! If you project confidence and enthusiasm, they'll respond in the same way.

6. **When possible, let service projects grow out of study and other activities.** Study peace concerns, and then do service projects related to peace. Study local hunger needs, and then respond to those needs in meaningful ways. The "Resources" chapter shares several helpful materials.

Repairing Christian Lifestyles is an especially excellent resource for involving youth in study and service.

7. **Remember that there are many meaningful service projects.** In fact the rest of this chapter is devoted to service project ideas. As you read, you'll think of additional possibilities in your church and community.

8. **Check out the availability of volunteer service programs.** Develop a group program that explores what your denomination or other denominations are doing in training and placing national and international volunteers. Such programs are for post-high school young adults. During the high school years is a good time to think about volunteer programs.

Service to Your Church

1. **Paint a classroom or hallway in your church.** Work with your church trustees or property committee to be sure they approve of the color selected and agree on who will pay for the paint and supplies. Have an adult who is an experienced painter help with arrangements.

2. **Take responsibility for renovating a Sunday school or Christian education classroom.** Paint the walls and ceiling. Put new carpeting on the floor. Clean and straighten all shelves and cabinets. Buy or build more cabinets if needed. Make cushions for chairs. Put up a corkboard wall for display of posters, artwork, etc. (Of course, this could be a youth classroom—but it would be more meaningful to do something for another class.)

3. **Take responsibility for the church yard—on a one-time or regular basis.** Cut the grass, rake leaves, trim around sidewalks, trim bushes, plant flowers.

4. **Shovel the snow from church sidewalks and steps.** (Not a meaningful service project in San Diego, Phoenix, New Orleans, or Miami!)

5. **Refinish the sanctuary pews.** This can be a greatly appreciated project but is also lots of work. The youth need the guidance of people experienced in furniture refinishing.

6. **Build a wheelchair ramp for your church, or raise the money to pay a contractor for construction of the ramp.** This can be a very significant service.

7. **Accept the responsibility for the cleaning and maintenance of a particular part of the church** (two or three classrooms, for example).

8. **Have a team learn sign language and act as interpreters** for the deaf at worship services or in education classes.

9. **Make a video to help your church's annual financial campaign.** Show the various groups and services sponsored by the church. See the "Media" and "Video" chapters for more information.

169

10. **Provide child care at special events.** Churches generally have (or should have) child care arrangements during worship services. Many churches, however, do not provide child care for special events or some weekday activities. Youth can perform a significant service by making that care available without charge.

Service to the Poor

11. **Collect canned food for a food pantry operated by your church or by another community organization.** This can be done by encouraging people to bring canned food to morning worship or through home solicitation of church members.

12. **If your community or neighborhood does not have a food pantry for the poor, start one!** Involve other area churches in the collection of food. Generally the church office and some adult volunteers will also need to be involved to adequately handle requests and arrangements since youth are in school when many requests will be received. Youth can provide the push to form a pantry, help keep it stocked with food, and assist with deliveries.

13. **Help with a winter shelter for the homeless.** In many communities, churches rotate the responsibility of opening their doors in the evening as shelters for the homeless during the winter months. Volunteers are almost always needed to help set up cots, provide food, etc.

14. **If adequate shelters for the homeless are unavailable in your community, work to see that those facilities are provided.** This could be a project done within your church, with other churches, or with community organizations. Other groups in the church would need to be involved in such an effort,

but youth can be the driving force in getting something done.

15. **Help with a soup kitchen in your community.** Many soup kitchens for the poor need volunteers for evenings and weekends. These are good service opportunities for young people.

16. **Study the soup kitchen offerings in your community.** Sometimes these are only available for weekday lunches, leaving people without help on evenings and weekends. The youth can work with others in the church to provide evening or weekend meals.

17. **The youth group can adopt a low income family** by working with a social service agency in your community or acting on suggestions from your pastor. This can be a very ambitious project requiring a significant amount of fund raising. Fix up their home, be sure adequate food is available, and see what can be done about providing employment if that is needed. Adults in the church can help in locating job opportunities. It is very important to be sensitive to the feelings of the family. In some instances the "family" may be an elderly person living alone on a very limited income.

18. **Prepare a hunger meal for the church.** Serve a very simple, inexpensive (but good) meal like beans flavored with ham plus cornbread. Ask members to pay for the meal what they normally would for Sunday brunch at a restaurant. Donate the difference to a world hunger cause. After the meal, show a video or provide an informational program about world hunger. Distribute literature about denominational programs to help the hungry.

19. **Serve an early Thanksgiving meal or a Christmas meal in July for the homeless in your community.** Many organizations serve especially nice meals on Thanksgiving and Christmas, but normal soup kitchen meals are (of necessity) very simple. Provide an especially nice meal at a nontraditional time. Do so in cooperation with any existing soup kitchens in your community so that you aren't in competition with their efforts.

20. **Group members can cooperate with the national movement of people who choose to fast on the Thursday before Thanksgiving and donate the money saved to a world hunger cause.** Some send their contributions to Oxfam America, 115 Broadway, Dept. 4181, Boston, Massachusetts 02116, which is the major sponsor of the movement. You may prefer to send contributions to hunger programs sponsored by your own denomination. This will have the greatest impact if youth can involve not only their families but the whole church in the effort.

21. **Do a major study of poverty in your community.** Have youth interview city officials, social service agency leaders, and people who are homeless. Come up with recommendations to improve services to the poor, and share those ideas with church and community leaders.

22. **Initiate a letter-writing campaign for legislation that will improve services to the homeless and other poor people.** Do this on a city, state, or national level as appropriate. Newspapers can provide information about pending legislation and programs. Organizations such as Bread for the World and World Vision can also provide helpful information and suggestions (see "Resources").

23. **Undertake the renovation of a house to sell to a low-income family.** This will require that you work with your church's main governing board and perhaps with a financial institution in the community. Such projects have been very successful in many communities. A house badly in need of repair is purchased at a low price. Such a price, of course, still far exceeds any youth group treasury, so the church, as a whole, and a financial institution must normally be involved. The house is then renovated with volunteer work and donated materials, thus greatly increasing its value.

A financial institution (which wants to do so) can appraise the house at a much higher value than before the renovation. By selling it to a low-income family at the original price, it becomes affordable to them and available without any significant down payment. Some financial institutions will laugh at the idea and claim they "have to have" a large down payment. You can, however, find some public-spirited institutions that will cooperate. A financial institution that has had to repossess homes in bad repair may be especially open to this possibility! This plan makes a good house available for a family who could not normally afford one.

Environmental Projects

24. **Mount an attack on plastic!** During 1960, Americans threw away 200,000 tons of plastic. During 1989 the figure was 15 million tons. We are running out of places to put it! Have an educational campaign urging church families and community businesses to use biodegradable containers whenever possible.

25. **Collect papers and cans for recycling.** Many people have good intentions about recycling but just don't want to fool with the

171

mechanics of it. Encouragement from youth can make a difference. Put dumpsters on the church parking lot for papers and cans. This may be a convenient location for church members to bring items. Arrange periodic transportation of materials to a recycling center.

26. **Have a campaign urging people to walk more and drive less.** Environmental pollution from automobiles continues to be a major problem. Youth can influence their families and friends to avoid unnecessary driving.

27. **Have a letter-writing campaign concerning the environmental practices of industries in your geographical area.** News media will provide some information on environmental practices of local industry, but youth should also seek information from the companies. Send letters to the industries themselves and also to the media. Praise companies that follow good practices; encourage others to be better corporate citizens. Be sensitive to the fact that you may have church members who work at these companies.

28. **Select an endangered species and write letters to newspapers, legislators, and others urging steps to protect that species.** Learn all you can about the species selected, and try to identify other strategies to help.

29. **Study the problem of excessive consumerism, and develop strategies to influence the practices of church members.** We buy more than we need and throw away "old" clothing, furniture, and other articles that are still in good condition. Urge people to give discarded items (that are still in good condition) to agencies such as the Salvation Army. Remind people that less wasteful practices help preserve environmental resources.

30. **Make a video on a topic of environmental concern.** Present ways to avoid wasting paper; to lower consumption of plastics; to recycle paper, cans, and other products. See the "Media" and "Video" chapters for further information. Share the video with other church groups. You may also be able to show it on a local cable station.

Fund Raising

31. **Youth groups often do fund raising for a wide range of charitable causes.** The chapter on "Raising Money for Your Youth Group and Other Needy Causes" gives a detailed discussion of approaches to fund raising including guidelines for canvassing neighborhoods on behalf of charitable organizations such as the American Cancer Society.

Peace Concerns

32. **Have a series of programs to learn more about peace concerns.** Most of the projects suggested (33–39) require some knowledge of peace issues on the part of young people. Learning about peace concerns is itself a service project because it prepares youth to better interpret concerns to others. See "Resources" for several helpful study guides.

33. **Present a program on peace concerns for the families of group members.** Share practical ways to work for peace.

34. **Hold a "Peace Day" for children.** Do it on a Saturday, and invite all the children of the church. You can find excellent teaching/learning activities for children in the *Young Peacemakers Project Book* (see the

"Resources" chapter). Serve lunch at the church and include recreational peace activities as well as more serious study. Parents will love having a free day, teens will enjoy the interaction with the children, and the children will develop greater peace consciousness.

35. **Have group members develop their own brochure or flier on "Peacemaking."** Distribute it to members of the church. If you can get permission, distribute it at a large shopping mall on a weekend. Consider the possibility of putting up a "Peacemaking Booth" at a shopping mall. Share the flier or brochure and other information about peace.

36. **Make a video about peace.** See the "Media" and "Video" chapters for more information. Share the video with other church and community groups. Show it on a cable television station if possible. If you have a "Peacemaking Booth" at a mall (see suggestion 35), show the video there, too.

37. **Arrange your own exchange with another country.** Have your minister help contact churches in another country (your national denominational offices can probably help with this). Arrange a summer exchange. Send a member of your youth group to that country, and host a young person from that country in your community. It's a wonderful way to learn more about another culture and promote international understanding.

38. **Write letters to newspapers, congressional representatives, senators, and others expressing concern about world peace and international relationships.** Be sure to do suggestion 32 (on learning about peace) before undertaking this activity. Young people need to be well-informed before writing letters.

39. **If your pastor is open to the possibility, have a youth-directed worship service with an emphasis on peace.** See the "Worship" chapter for further guidance.

Justice Involvement

40. **Have youth select an instance of significant injustice in your community or state, and implement efforts to change that injustice.** An example: in 1989 an interracial youth group couldn't swim in a Saluda, South Carolina, pool that had racial segregation. The young people protested with letters and personal visits to leaders. The governor and a bishop got involved, and the pool was desegregated.

41. **Find an appropriate national or international issue which youth can help influence by writing letters to leaders and by educating family and friends.** An example: the Nestle Company for many years used what most people consider highly unethical marketing practices in Third World countries. The company convinced uneducated and impoverished mothers that purchased formula was better for infants than the mothers' own milk. The mothers (initially provided with "free" samples) began relying on the formula and then became dependent on it as they were unable to produce more milk themselves. They often went without essential food to purchase the formula. Because of contaminated water supplies and difficulty of the uneducated mothers in following instructions, the mixed formula was often hazardous to the infants. Malnutrition, diarrhea, and death resulted.

An international boycott of Nestle products and massive publicity forced the company to change their practices. The boycott ended in 1984. Recently, however, there have been reports that Nestle has renewed the unethical practices. This or another issue could be a good focus for group concern.

Drug and Alcohol Concerns

42. **Begin work in the area of drugs and alcohol with an educational emphasis.** Young people need to have the facts about drugs and alcohol before attempting to influence others. Gaining the facts will make them better interpreters to others whether you do further projects in this area or not. See "Resources" for suggested materials.

43. **Make posters and fliers about community resources for persons with drug and alcohol problems.** Distribute them around your community. Remember that you generally need to have permission before putting up a poster or distributing fliers on someone else's property.

44. **Make a video about drug and alcohol concerns.** You may want to focus especially on alcohol since so many people seem unaware that alcohol abuse is still a bigger problem than illicit drugs. See the "Media" and "Video" chapters for guidance. Show the video as many places as possible including a cable television channel. You may be able to get permission to share the video with public school classes.

Service to Children

45. **Develop a series of Bible stories or Bible studies on video to share with children's classes in your church.** See the "Media" and "Video" chapters for further guidance.

46. **Have youth help as teaching assistants at vacation Bible school or other** special study opportunities in your church. See suggestion 34 about a "Peace Day" for children. Also see suggestion 10 on helping with child care.

> NOTE: We do not recommend that youth be regular teachers of Christian education classes for children. The youth need to be in classes themselves, and children need adult leadership for regular classes.

Suicide Prevention

47. **Have a series of sessions for youth to teach them how to deal with depression themselves and how to help other young people who are troubled.** We especially recommend Sol Gordon's excellent book *When Living Hurts* and the accompanying guide (see "Resources"). This will equip youth to reach out in far more meaningful ways to other young people.

48. **Group members can help organize a HELP line for teens.** That's a telephone number that teens can call to talk about depression or other problems. Callers remain anonymous and, thus, feel more inclined to share their concerns. Phones are staffed by volunteers. This is a big project but also extremely worthwhile. The youth group will need the help and support of other church and community groups to make this a success. *Training is essential for all volunteers.*

Service to the Elderly

49. **Do yard work and cleaning for elderly people who belong to the church or who live near the church.** (Do it without charge, or it becomes fund raising rather than service!)

50. **Make monthly or bimonthly visits to an area nursing home.** Many youth groups visit nursing homes shortly before Christmas, and those visits are certainly good—but nursing home residents need contact the rest of the year, too. Group members can sing, bring refreshments, and visit with individual nursing home residents.

51. **Have an "Adopt-a-Grandparent" group.** Members individually or in pairs "adopt" church or community members who live alone and have limited mobility. Youth do volunteer yard and household work, visit informally, help with errands, and in other ways assist their adopted grandparents. Teens gain as much from this as the elderly. If you start such a program, it is important to continue it, or you will have some disappointed elderly persons.

52. **Serve a special meal for those in the church who are 65 years old or older.** This can be great near Thanksgiving or Christmas but may be even more appreciated at another time of the year.

53. **Share in a joint Bible study for a few weeks with a class of older people.** This provides an excellent exchange of ideas that will enrich both the youth and the older participants.

Clown Ministry Program

54. **Start a clown ministry program.** This can be done as part of a continuing youth group's activities, or it may provide the focus for a special interest group. Clowns can visit nursing homes, hospitals, and children's institutions. They can also share with church school classes and worship services. See "Resources" for materials that can help you organize a clown ministry.

Youth Mission Projects

55. **Have youth perform a service project at a mission site.** Projects can include tutoring, painting a building, helping construct a building, renovating low-income housing, and more. Your minister can help you obtain names and addresses of mission sites. Be advised that mission sites which accept local church work groups often must be reserved a year or more in advance. For more information on mission trips, see "Overnight and Longer," which contains detailed planning advice. When youth return, they should share their experiences with the whole church.

While youth group mission projects are traditionally carried out at locations a few hundred miles away, remember that you may also have deserving mission programs very close to your church. The adventure of a trip to a more distant mission program is part of the appeal, but don't exclude service to mission agencies close to your church.

56. **Select a small number of youth to work an entire summer at a mission site.** This provides a far different experience than an entire group spending one or two weeks on a mission work project. You will still need to make contact with mission sites about a year in advance. Mission sites that have extensive summer programming for children are the most likely to appreciate a teenage volunteer for the summer. You should seek mission sites in the United States or Canada. We do not recommend sending youth to other areas for this kind of work. Volunteers to countries with radically different cultures need to be older and more experienced than youth group members.

The mission site will need to provide food and lodging but should not be asked to pay a salary. Your youth group or the church may wish to make available a small salary or a scholarship for young people who participate in this way, but there is also merit to the work being done without any compensation. A small payment to help with out-of-pocket expenses may make it possible for youth to participate who could otherwise not afford to do so. Your church definitely should pay for the round trip transportation of each young person.

Unless your church is very large, you will not have more than three or four young people who can devote a whole summer to mission work. The program seems to work best when the young people selected will be going the summer between their junior and senior years of high school. This kind of activity requires a great deal of maturity and is not recommended for younger teens. If your church establishes a tradition of sending youth at the end of their junior year of high school, interested youth and their families will be able to plan ahead for the experience.

When the young people return from the summer's service, they should be invited to give programs for church organizations and to speak briefly at worship services. Generally, each young person will end up going to a different mission site. Most mission sites will not want more than one all-summer volunteer. While this makes it a little harder on the young people, it means

your youth group and church will have the benefit of exposure to several different mission programs.

Some additional cautions on youth mission work: There is always the danger of youth (or adults) who do one or two weeks of volunteer work at a mission site feeling they have accomplished more than they actually have. The mission site must always devote significant staff time to work with the youth group, and that reality often means the financial gain to the mission, as a result of the volunteer work, is rather limited.

Mission sites encourage work groups because such groups are an excellent way for churches to learn about missions. This caution is not intended to minimize the importance of what the young people do, but it is important to keep things in perspective. It's very important for youth to interpret the work of the mission site to the whole congregation. *That interpretation to others and the personal knowledge gained by the youth may advance mission more than the specific work done by the youth.*

If the mission site provides meals for your work group, you should expect to pay for those meals. (This is not the case for youth who work for an entire summer at a mission site.) You should also plan to pay for paint and other building supplies. Those should be considered part of your youth group's donation to the mission site.

This chapter contains several exercises which you may find helpful to do with your group. While they are especially good for use with fellowship groups, they can be used with Sunday school classes, Bible study groups, and in many other settings. You are free to reproduce these exercises for use in your own local church. Please contact *faithQuest* if you want to use them in any other settings.

What's the Difference?

Many high school people are active in a fellowship group and in a church school class. While some overlap of purpose and similarity of activity is unavoidable, a fellowship group and a church school class function better if their purposes are distinct and their activities different.

It is important that your group not be too much like church school classes in your church. When those groups are too much alike, they will often become competitive with one another. Few young people want to do the same thing twice a week, so they will often choose one group over the other.

Even with clear differences between the fellowship group and the church school class, some young people will still choose one and not the other. That kind of selection, however, works to the advantage of the church. If a young person dislikes study and both the fellowship group and church school class have a study focus, that young person will be lost. If a young person wants serious Bible study and talk about the faith, a church school class that tries to act like a fellowship group will be neither helpful or appealing.

A SENSE OF BELONGING

This exercise is especially helpful if done about midway through the year. You will need to make enough copies of items 1-32 for each member of your group. Ask the young people not to put their names on the exercise. Explain that the papers will be mixed up later so that each person will be looking at someone else's paper for discussion.

Emphasize that this exercise will not be helpful unless each person responds as he or she really feels. Since no one will know whose paper he or she has during tabulation and discussion, people should feel free to respond honestly to the 32 statements.

Collect the papers when everyone has finished. Mix up the papers thoroughly so that they are no longer in the order in which you collected them. Then pass the papers back to the group members.

Tabulate the results of this exercise by asking for a hand count on each statement and recording the totals. Each person will participate in the hand count on the basis of the paper which he or she is holding rather than on the basis of the way in which he or she personally responded. "How many have a paper with a yes for statement 1? How many have no? How many responded in another way (by leaving the item blank or by writing in a response such as sometimes)?"

Yes or No?

_____ 1.   I felt comfortable upon entering the room tonight.

_____ 2.   Everyone already present greeted me when I arrived.

_____ 3.   I feel that everyone here is a personal friend.

_____ 4.   I feel that I am as well-liked as anyone else in this group.

_____ 5.   I feel that I am not as popular as some members of this group.

_____ 6.   I feel that my opinions are respected in this group.

_____ 7.   I have opinions that I would like to share in the group but keep them to myself.

_____ 8.   I can remember when someone in this group affirmed my opinion or statement.

_____ 9.   I can remember a time when someone in this group made me feel foolish or stupid.

_____ 10. I can remember a time in this group when I expressed appreciation for an opinion or statement made by another member of the group.

_____ 11. I can remember a time in this group when I criticized or embarrassed someone for an opinion or statement made to the group.

_____ 12. There is at least one person in the group whose comments are very hard for me to take seriously.

_____ 13. At least one member of the group never takes my comments seriously.

_____ 14. I can remember a time in this group when someone asked my opinion about an issue or decision.

_____ 15. I can remember a time in this group when I asked someone for his or her opinion about an issue or decision.

_____ 16. If I miss a group meeting, another group member will let me know that I was missed and help me feel that my presence is important.

_____ 17. If someone else misses a group meeting, I will let that person know that I missed him or her and will help that person feel that his or her presence is important.

_____ 18. I have shared an event, feeling, or opinion with this group which I would have been afraid to share with most people.

_____ 19. Others have shared events, feelings, or opinions with this group which they would not have shared with most people.

_____ 20. I can remember a time when I have betrayed the confidence of a group member.

_____ 21. I can remember a time when a group member betrayed my confidence.

_____ 22. I come to this group because my parents want me to come.

_____ 23. I come to this group because it meets many of my own needs.

_____ 24. I come to this group because of the other members of the group.

_____ 25. This group helps me relate my Christian faith to daily life.

_____ 26. This group helps me better understand God.

_____ 27. This group helps me feel more like part of the church.

_____ 28. This group has done a project which benefited the church.

_____ 29. I do my share on work and service projects of the church.

_____ 30. Others do their share on group work and service projects.

_____ 31. I come to the group more for parties and social activities than for any other reason.

_____ 32. Some other group members come primarily for parties and social activities.

You may not have time to discuss all 32 statements, but you should discuss at least one or two statements from each of the following categories. Spend the greatest amount of time on those statements which reflect a high need for improvement. Carry out this discussion in groups of six or less if your total group is larger than ten.

Category 1. Items 1-5 measure the extent to which people feel liked and accepted in the group. You should consider the size of the group as you examine these responses. For example, if there are only six group members, then you should be concerned about even one person responding that he or she was not greeted on arrival. If your total youth group has sixty people (even though your discussion or caring/sharing groups are smaller), you should not expect every person to be greeted by every other person. **For discussion:** What factors determine "comfort" in a group? (Possible responses would include knowing other people, a physically attractive room, a good advisor.) Which factors are most important? Is it reasonable to want to be more popular than others in a group? Why, or why not? Is it reasonable to want to feel as popular as others in a group? Why, or why not? How can your group improve the level of acceptance felt by members?

Category 2. Items 6–15 concern the extent to which members feel free to express their opinions and needs to the group. Obviously, time does not permit everyone to share every thought with the whole group. It is very important, however, that people feel free to share what they wish; number 7 is a good measure of this. **For discussion:** Why does the group suffer when members do not share opinions and needs? What changes would help people be more willing to share opinions with your group? To what extent is each person responsible for sharing his or her opinions with the group? Why? To what extent is each person responsible for encouraging other group members to share their opinions? Why?

Category 3. Items 16 and 17 concern the readiness of group members to follow up when people are absent. **For discussion:** How would you feel if you missed three or four group meetings and no one checked to see why you had missed? Should your group have an intentional plan to insure that there is communication with people who are absent? Why, or why not?

Category 4. Items 18-21 assess the extent to which group members are willing to share personal problems and the extent to which the group keeps the confidence of people who do share such problems. **For discussion:** If you discovered that someone violated your confidence by talking about your personal problems outside of the group, would you be willing to share those problems with the group again? Why, or why not? Do people intentionally gossip and break confidences, or do those things happen by accident or by not thinking? Why, or why not? In what way could your group help members feel free to share personal problems? Why is it beneficial to have a group with which one can share family problems, school problems, problems in dating relationships and in spiritual life?

Category 5. Items 22-24 are concerned with why members come to meetings. Note that none of these asked whether or not the reason given is the primary reason. **For discussion:** What do you think are the best reasons for coming to a youth group? Which reasons can your group influence?

Category 6. Items 25-28 concern the kinds of help the group gives to its members and the church. You should be concerned if most members do not feel that the group helps them in all these areas. **For discussion:** Does your group have enough balance in caring/sharing times, study, recreation, and service projects? Why, or why not? What changes, if any, should be made?

Category 7. Items 29-32 measure the extent to which members feel that they, as individuals, and the group, as a whole, share in responsibility for work and service. Do not be surprised if several people have responded as though they work hard and others do not. **For discussion:** How do you feel when you think someone else does not do his or her share of group work? Should parties and social events only be for those who share in work and study opportunities? Why, or why not? In what ways can parties and social events be used to gain new members for the group? How can everyone be encouraged to share in work and service projects?

WORKING TOGETHER EXERCISE

Make copies of these statements, and use the exercise with your group. Ask members to indicate the extent to which the following characterize your group, using a scale from 1 to 5. One (1) indicates that the item is not very characteristic of your group. Five (5) indicates that the item is extremely characteristic of your group.

_____ 1. Everyone has a clear understanding of the purposes of this group.

_____ 2. Everyone is committed to the purposes of this group.

_____ 3. The leader (president, etc.) of our business or decision-making meetings clearly has control of the group.

_____ 4. Everyone understands the role of the officers of the group.

_____ 5. Everyone understands the role of the advisor(s) or teacher(s) of the group.

_____ 6. Major events and projects are planned far enough ahead to allow adequate preparation.

_____ 7. When an event is planned, the responsibility for carrying out that event is clearly assigned to one or more people.

_____ 8. If someone misses a group meeting, we have a clear plan to follow up on that person.

_____ 9. We have a clear plan to regain inactive members.

_____ 10. People are free to express their opinions and feelings in this group.

_____ 11. Decisions made by this group relate to the interests and needs of all group members rather than those of just a few people.

_____ 12. Our group has a clear budget and a plan to raise that budget.

_____ 13. All members understand the rules or expectations for conduct at group meetings.

_____ 14. All members follow and respect the rules or expectations for conduct at group meetings.

_____ 15. Our group offers a balance of experiences in worship, study, service projects, and social or recreational events.

_____ 16. All members work hard at creating an atmosphere of trust and concern.

_____ 17. All members of the group accept their share of responsibility for projects of the group.

After members have had time to complete the exercise, quickly go through it, item by item, and take a hand count of the number who gave a 1 or 2 rating to that item. Those items receiving the most 1's and 2's are areas that especially merit attention.

Discuss: Which of the areas most need improvement? How can those improvements be accomplished? In what additional areas are improvements needed to help us work together as Christians?

Building Up and Tearing Down

Each of the following behaviors or events could happen in your group. Consider the extent to which the behavior or event builds up or tears down the group. What response should be made to these situations by the group? To what extent does the response of the group determine whether the behavior or event strengthens or damages the group? Why?

1. A group member continuously dominates conversation and presumes that everyone agrees with him or her.

2. A member confides with the group that he or she has had suicidal thoughts.

3. The group learns that a member has unsuccessfully attempted suicide.

4. A group member shares that he or she is in danger of flunking a course.

5. A group member says that everyone else in the group will be excluded from heaven because they are not "born again."

6. A group member is excited because he or she has just been given a new car.

7. A group member continuously looks for and points out evidence that the group does not like him or her.

8. A person who has just moved into the community comes to the group for the first time.

9. A parent of a group member dies.

10. A group member is hospitalized following a serious automobile accident.

11. A group member shares that he or she has been physically abused by a parent.

12. A group member shares disappointment over not having a date for a major school dance.

13. A group member shares that he or she is having serious trouble deciding on a career.

14. A group member shares that he or she is having serious trouble spending enough time on homework.

15. A group member quits coming and seems to have developed a serious drinking problem.

16. A group member smokes marijuana at the church just before a group meeting.

17. A group member comes whenever there is a party or social event but rarely comes at other times.

18. A group member consistently fails to show up for work or service projects.

19. A group member is quiet and almost never shares his or her opinion with the group.

20. A group member is going to move to another community.

Finger Painting

Have each group member do a finger painting which shows how he or she wants to

181

feel about the group. Then let each person show his or her painting to the group and briefly explain it. You may wish to show a painting of your own to the group. People may give explanations like these: "I used lots of blue because I want this group to be gentle and smooth like a smooth lake." "I used yellow in the center and dark colors around the outside. I want this group to be my light in a dark and difficult world." "I used lots of reds and oranges because those are fun colors, and I want this group to be an enjoyable one."

If time or resources do not permit finger painting, ask each person to describe the color that best represents the way he or she would like to feel about the group and why. Explanations may be very similar to those given for finger painting.

Form a circle for prayer. Have people join hands in the circle. Explain that you will start by saying: "God, help our group to be . . . . " Then each person, moving around the circle to your left, should add a word or phrase, for example: kind, loving, caring, blue, honest, building up, warm like the sun, a refuge in times of trouble, a source of strength. If someone does not wish to share a word or phrase, that person can decline by squeezing the hand of the next person.

RAISING MONEY
FOR YOUR YOUTH GROUP
AND OTHER NEEDY CAUSES

The Hidden Purpose

No youth group would say that its primary purpose was to raise money. Yet groups often spend their time and energy as though fund raising were a high priority. They raise money to help their own program expenses, local church needs, and various charitable causes. A single year can include car washes, slave days, spaghetti dinners, chili suppers, ice cream socials and innumerable selling projects. I've been with youth groups that sold cheap jewelry, pictures of Jesus, stale candy, poor light bulbs, dead plants, and harsh toilet paper! The young people end up pressured to sell items or render services they would rather not; church members are subtly coerced into buying junk or unwanted services; and adult advisors get headaches sorting out change, billings, reorders, refunds, and returns.

Many Sunday school classes escape the necessity of fund raising because the Sunday school or church budget pays for curriculum materials and other class expenses. Students have no obligation to raise funds beyond placing a token offering in the collection plate.

Most informal youth groups, however, are not so fortunate as Sunday school classes. Some fund raising may be unavoidable and even potentially beneficial for a youth group. No youth group, however, exists for the primary purpose of raising money; and allowing this to become a hidden purpose may drain time and energy from more important goals. To protect the health of the group, the young people, and the adult advisors, the reasons for fund raising need to be clearly stated; and a conscious decision should be made about the amount of effort to be allocated to fund raising.

Funding Program Expenses

Every youth group will have expenses. These may include curriculum materials, devotional booklets, magazines, refreshments, films, parties, admission fees (to movies, parks, bowling alleys, etc.), retreats, camps, and trips. There are at least seven common sources of money for these needs. Although some groups rely on one single source, most use a combination.

1. **Youth groups may charge dues to members on a weekly, monthly, or yearly basis.** This may take the form of an annual amount or may be a monthly "pass the plate" approach. Young people are accustomed to paying dues in scouting, 4-H, and many school organizations. Dues that are not overly high may be an acceptable method to many young people, and the paying of dues may increase loyalty to the group.

Dues become detrimental to a youth group when they are excessive and so emphasized that they are a barrier to those with limited resources.

2. **A weekly collection or offering with no set requirement may avoid putting pressure on any single individual.** Such collections, however, do not normally yield much money. A few people object to an "offering" being used primarily for the benefit of the people giving the offering.

3. **The church budget may include an amount for youth group expenses.** Curriculum materials and film rentals are

then charged to the church and the bills paid by the church treasurer. Expenses incurred by advisors or young people for refreshments can be submitted for reimbursement. Retreat, camp, and trip expenses may even be paid from the church budget.

When the church budget actually covers almost all the youth programming expenses, both the young people and the congregation as a whole are made aware that youth programming is part of the ministry of the church. Young people are not asked to pay for their own group expenses but are encouraged to pledge or donate to the total budget of the church. Such an approach is a strong affirmation both of the importance of young people to the church and of their responsibility for the needs of the whole church.

If all youth expenses are paid from the church budget, however, the total may be frightening. Most congregations are reluctant to include a large amount for youth programming when the men's and women's groups are almost always self-supporting.

4. **In fact, the men's and women's organizations constitute another source of money for many youth groups.** These organizations are especially responsive to providing scholarships for retreats, camps, and trips. If these gifts are at least occasionally accompanied by reporting from the young people to the adult organization, the result may be dialogue that is healthy for all concerned.

5. **The adult advisors become the primary support for many youth groups.** They provide free transportation and refreshments, pay retreat expenses for young people with limited resources, and buy books and magazines for discussion and activity suggestions.

This approach is quite common but also hazardous. Even though a particular advisor or advisors may have adequate personal finances to assume these expenses, they may still end up feeling imposed upon and may set a standard for programming that the next advisors can't afford.

Advisors naturally want to do some special things for the young people in their group, and they should be free to do so. They should not, however, permit themselves to become a major funding source for group expenses.

6. **Donations from the young people don't always take the form of dues.** Group members may gladly take turns bringing refreshments and paying their own expenses for bowling, movies, and retreats. This approach is a common one. The chief difficulty is that some group projects may be too expensive for some members. A weekend retreat can easily cost twenty to fifty dollars a person. Even providing refreshments for a group of 25 can cost five to ten dollars—or more. Dues, offerings, and donations may come from money young people have earned but, more often, it comes from parents. Even an affluent family may have difficulty if two or three family members are teenagers and participate in several organizations.

Churches that rely heavily on this approach need to provide a "help fund," which adult advisors can use as necessary to aid particular young people. Unfortunately, it is sometimes difficult to know when a teenager needs financial assistance.

7. **Groups very frequently use some fund-raising strategy to pay for all or part of their expenses.** The multitude of approaches to raising money will be evaluated in more detail later in this chapter.

How Much Is Needed?

The chapter "Planning with Young People" discusses the budgeting process. In considering the best means of funding a youth program, it is important not to underestimate the expenses involved.

Depending on the kind of programming done, the financial needs of a youth group can be extremely high.

A group of 21 young people with four adult advisors developed the following list of projected expenses for the year:

Refreshments for regular weekly meetings:
$15.00 a week for 50 weeks
$750.00

Resource books and curriculum materials
$210.00

Film and video rental
425.00

Winter retreat: $45.00 each for 25 people
1125.00

Postage and printing
150.00

Bowling party: $3.50 each for 25 people
87.50

District workshop for adult advisors (fees, meals, travel)
120.00

Pizza party: $5.00 each for 25 people
125.00

Summer camp: $95.00 each for 25 people
2375.00

Three lock-ins (food and materials): $2.50 each for 25 people on 3 occasions
187.50

Miscellaneous/Contingency
150.00

TOTAL: $5705.00

Of course, the preceding budget could be reduced in several ways. The group could choose to use only films that are available rent-free from denominational or public audio-visual libraries. The young people could choose less expensive refreshments or could even decide not to have refreshments. The bowling party could be eliminated, and the retreat, lock-ins, and summer camps are not essential. However, no group wants to eliminate everything! A youth group must be realistic about the amount of money available, but youth activities are not necessarily cheap. The preceding budget is not atypical, though most youth groups do not identify expenses so carefully.

There are, of course, many other options. In making program and budget decisions, it is important for the young people and adult advisors to recognize that someone will be paying for all the activities.

Who Should Pay for Youth Ministry?

Ministers, adult advisors, young people, parents, and church boards hold a variety of opinions about how the expenses of youth ministry should be met. The best way may differ from church to church depending on the resources of the congregation and the families. These guidelines are not applicable in every situation but may be helpful.

1. **The basic expenses of youth ministry should be covered by the church budget.** The fact that informal groups meet at times other than Sunday morning and pursue more recreational activities does not make them less vital parts of the educational and evangelistic ministry of the church. Such groups are doomed to frustration if most of their time must be spent in raising money for their own programming.

The church budget should include funds for curriculum materials, books, educational and religious film rentals, craft materials, postage and printing expense, money to reimburse advisors and teachers for expenses incurred, leadership training for advisors and teachers, and a discretionary fund to help less fortunate young people with retreat and camp expenses.

The young people should be strongly encouraged to make individual contributions to the church budget. Youth representatives should be on the church board and should be involved in planning the budget. This approach reinforces the relationship between youth ministry and the total ministry of the church.

2. **If almost all group members have reasonable financial resources, the cost of bowling, attending a movie, going on a retreat, and similar activities should be paid on an individual basis.** Adult church members could understandably be displeased if their donations to the church were used on a regular basis to pay for parties. The church should, of course, pay for an occasional interest-building party and offer help to those needing assistance with party, retreat, or camp expense. Young people should be cautioned against planning too many expensive activities.

Young people may also help with expenses by taking turns providing refreshments for meetings. Most can afford to do this a few times a year. This not only helps the budget but also deepens the identity of the young people with the group.

3. **Dues should not be charged unless this can be done in a very low pressure way.**

4. **The adult advisors should not make a practice of paying expenses for the youth group.** If the advisors want to host an occasional party, GREAT! However, they should not pay for refreshments every week or subsidize postage, paper, films, and resource materials.

5. **Scholarship offers from men's and women's clubs should be gratefully accepted.**

6. **Fund raising by the group should normally be for one of two purposes.** First, money should be raised for worthy benevolent causes in the church and community. Second, money may be raised for a summer trip or a similar project. In this way, the purpose of money raising is always very clear and such projects have definite "beginning" and "ending" times.

Community Collections and Youth Groups

Almost every community has several massive fund-raising efforts each year. The causes are familiar ones, and most are extremely deserving: cancer, heart disease, muscular dystrophy, birth defects, world hunger, overseas medical care, etc. The efforts sometimes take the form of a house-to-house canvass and sometimes take the form of a walk or swim with participants recruiting "sponsors" for X-cents a mile or lap.

The organizations responsible for these drives generally have difficulty recruiting enough people for the neighborhood canvasses, and church youth organizations are frequently approached for assistance. The primary difficulty posed for your group is that there are too many worthy causes, and you probably cannot respond as a group to every one. Your annual group planning meeting (you SHOULD have one!) may be the best time to evaluate the various charities in your community and to decide which one (or ones) should become group projects. Never assume the liability as an advisor, teacher, or leader of responding to a last-minute phone call for help with: "Of course, my group would be glad to canvass ten square blocks." Always let the group make the decision; and try to avoid letting it be a last-minute decision by anticipating the campaigns that are normal for your community.

These guidelines may be helpful to you in planning involvement in house-to-house canvasses:

1. **Communicate with the congregation about your group's involvement and indicate what geographical area will be covered by the church's young people.** Those in your congregation who live within that area will respond more warmly (and generously) to the callers, knowing they are from their church. You can share this information through the church newsletter, the bulletin, and by Sunday morning announcement (if your pastor is willing).

2. **Do the canvass as a group.** Meet at a common place at the start of the canvass, and agree on a place and time to meet when finished. Young people enjoy this kind of effort much more when working with others than when going out alone.

3. **For the same reason, assign the young people to specific streets by pairs rather than individuals.** This makes the project more enjoyable and is also a good safety precaution.

4. **Photocopy for each person maps of the area being covered.** Then color on the map the specific street(s) and/or block(s) assigned to each pair. Just giving the assignments verbally is not enough—most young people (and adults!) will become confused without a map. Also write on the map an emergency phone number where a responsible adult can be reached if any trouble or accident occurs.

5. **If any of the canvassing will be done at dusk or after dark, encourage the young people to wear bright colored clothing.** You may want to consider bright arm bands for each person.

6. **When the group reassembles at the end of the canvass, make provision for refreshments and possibly some kind of entertainment.** The group will be ready for refreshments after several hours of walking. Group life can be enhanced by this kind of experience.

7. **Report the results of the canvass to the group and the congregation:** both the total results for the community and the specific results of your group's work.

Walks and swims for benevolent causes are organized in ways fairly similar to neighborhood canvasses. Consider these guidelines in addition to the ones that will no doubt be provided by the organization sponsoring the walk or swim:

1. **Make the involvement of your young people a group project, as suggested for the neighborhood canvass.** Have a common starting point, participate in pairs if appropriate, and gather for refreshments and sharing at the conclusion.

2. **Have the young people begin obtaining sponsors at an early date.** Use the newsletter, bulletin, and announcements to inform the congregation of the group's participation. That will increase their receptivity when asked to sponsor a young person. Suggest to your group that it is not fair for everyone to ask the pastor to be a sponsor!

3. **Be certain that those participating take reasonable precautions for health and safety:** bright clothing if the event is outside

and continuing into the evening; time to dry off properly after a swim; appropriate shoes for jogging; an emergency phone number in case of problems.

On some occasions, your group may wish to raise money for a community cause by some other means: a bake sale, a chili supper, a selling project, etc. All these approaches are fine if agreeable to your group.

Local Church and Denominational Causes

You may want to exercise some caution that your group does not become so involved in community drives that they have no time, energy, or enthusiasm for local church or denominational needs. There are many church-related causes that your group may wish to consider supporting. Raising money for these needs can help your group become more aware of the nature of the church and better embody the kind of concern Christ has taught us to have.

1. **Most local churches will occasionally seek nonbudgetary assistance with a specific building-improvement project.** This might be new pews for the sanctuary, a stove for the kitchen, an organ, new furniture for the youth room(!), new paraments for the altar, a new educational wing, etc. Your group may want to have a special project to raise money for such a cause. If your young people identify a specific need in the church such as a VCR or new furniture for some church school rooms, they may wish to ask the board for permission to raise money for that need if no churchwide response is underway.

2. **Churches sometimes need extra help with specific programs.** These could include funding for a senior citizens' group, scholarships for a church-sponsored nursery school or day care center, materials for vacation church school, or funding for a choir director. Any of these could be an appropriate project for your group.

3. **The world hunger cause has gained widespread attention in most of our churches.** Almost every Protestant and Roman Catholic church has made some response through appropriate denominational channels. You can involve your young people in this kind of cause at several levels: through education about the problem and why the church should be involved; through the actual raising of funds; and through consideration of changes in lifestyle that may help increase the available food supply. Your group could offer a "Third World Meal" to the congregation as an educational and fund-raising strategy. That might be a meal consisting primarily of rice, beans, or another inexpensive product used as a primary source of nutrition in undeveloped countries of the world.

Show a film about world hunger, and ask those attending to donate what they would normally pay for a meal in a restaurant. Since the cost of the meal to those preparing it will be extremely low, the difference can be donated to a world hunger project.

Most denominations have suggestions available for specific world hunger projects and strategies for raising money for world hunger. Your pastor can help you find more information.

4. **Virtually every denomination has missionaries, health and welfare institutions (homes for the elderly, homes for disturbed children and young people, hospitals, retirement centers), and colleges and**

universities deserving of support. When your group decides to raise money for such causes, be sure to obtain adequate educational information through your pastor or denominational offices so that your young people can be informed of the reasons for the fund-raising effort.

Always let the young people themselves select the specific project which they wish to fund. Those projects are always more meaningful to them than projects proposed by you or other adults in the church.

If your youth group takes a summer trip, you may wish to consider visiting some church-related institutions. After firsthand exposure to them, your young people will be more enthusiastic about doing something to help.

5. **Many denominations have a benevolence fund that specifically supports projects chosen by a regional or national committee of young people.** Your minister will have further information about these or can direct you to other sources of information.

6. **Whenever you are raising money for a church or denominational cause, be sure to communicate to the congregation the reason for the fund-raising effort and the specific goal the group has established.** Give periodic progress reports on ticket sales, donations, etc. The congregation appreciates this kind of information and will respond better to a specific cause and goal, regardless of the means being used to meet the goals.

Hot Dogs, Eggs, Pancakes, and Soup

Serving a meal (breakfast, brunch, lunch, supper, or dinner) is a time-honored and generally successful way of raising money in a local church. Most churches have well-equipped kitchens (even if the Sunday school classrooms and the youth area are in horrible repair!), and those kitchens often receive inadequate use in relation to the money that has been invested in them.

1. **A planning committee needs to begin well in advance,** whether you are thinking about a chili or spaghetti supper, a Mother's Day brunch, a pancake breakfast, or a ham dinner. Most organizations fail to adequately recognize the amount of planning and work that goes into a successful money-making meal.

2. **Involve the parents of group members in this kind of project.** You will need substantial help in supervising the preparation and serving of food. Parents who may be unwilling to assume ongoing leadership for a group will often respond enthusiastically when asked to help on a one-time event. Most adult advisors are swamped by this kind of project unless they have other adult help. Be sure to have a few parents in the kitchen, and involve them in the preliminary planning if possible. Most youth groups can identify a few parents who have had considerable experience in serving large dinners. Be alert to the fact that, while women most frequently prepare and serve dinners in the church, some men may be professional chefs or managers of restaurants.

3. **Check the church calendar well in advance and reserve the date of your choice.** It may also be a wise precaution to check with the pastor or an older member of the church to be certain that a traditional meal or event not yet on the calendar will not conflict with your group's project. In many churches, you need to reserve the date three to six months in advance. In some very large churches, you may need to select a date as much as a year ahead.

189

You should also clear with the minister or church office whether you need the permission of the church board or any other group before publicizing and holding the meal.

4. **Use every possible means of publicity:** posters in the church and neighborhood, announcements from the pulpit, the church newsletter, Sunday morning bulletins, community newspaper announcements, etc. Begin your publicity at least six weeks before the event.

5. **Print tickets in advance and urge group members to sell them.** Also make tickets available to the church office and to parents who wish to help. Without advance ticket sales, you will have considerable difficulty determining how many people for whom to buy food, how much help is needed on the day of the meal, and how many tables should be set up. Advance sales almost always boost attendance and profits. You may want to allow for some last-minute customers, but plan to sell most tickets well in advance.

6. **Set the price after you have determined the per person cost of groceries that must be purchased.** Also remember that you will incur some expense with posters, newspaper ads, and printing tickets. While too high a price may keep customers away, most groups err by making their price too low and thereby doing a tremendous amount of work for very little profit. If you and the group members are uncertain how to calculate this kind of cost, seek the help of a parent or some other church member who has had experience in such projects.

7. **Sign up group members (and parental supervisors) for all the important stages:** ticket sales, publicity, food purchase, food preparation, dining hall setup, serving, cleanup.

If your group is small, you may need to have each person involved with every stage. It may also be good to have someone telephone group members the day before the meal to remind them of their job assignment and the need to be present on time.

8. **A GOLDEN RULE WHICH MUST NOT BE VIOLATED:** *Leave the kitchen as clean or cleaner than you found it!* If you do otherwise, you and your group may be ostracized permanently by those responsible for the kitchen.

9. **If your church has an employed janitor, attempt to cooperate with that person in your arrangements.** You may want to consider a small gift to the janitor, recognizing that your group's project will cause some added inconvenience, no matter how thorough a job of cleaning may be done.

Light Bulbs, Bushes, Toilet Paper, Jewelry

Selling projects are popular with most youth groups. A great deal of care is needed if a selling project is to be successful without causing a nervous breakdown for the advisor! The profit margin in selling projects is often a substantial one, and young people are accustomed to participating in them through Scouts, 4-H, school, and other organizations.

1. **Never begin a selling project without carefully checking out the company from which you are obtaining the merchandise.** Obtain the names, addresses, and phone numbers of other group leaders who have worked with the company. If the company

will not cheerfully give you that information, do not have anything more to do with them. Find out how cooperative the company is, how good their products are, and how willingly they accept unsold merchandise.

There are so many companies that offer selling projects and the management of them changes so frequently that any attempt at a summary listing in this book would be misleading. Beware, however, of the painful reality that many of these companies are not reputable. *Group* magazine tries not to accept advertising from unreliable companies, so their advertisements may provide a good starting point (see the "Resources" chapter for information on *Group*).

2. **Carefully evaluate the product itself.** Ask for samples. Is the product of good quality? Would you like to have it, eat it, use it, or whatever one normally does with it? Have similar products been sold in your community or church neighborhood in recent months? Is the company willing to guarantee that they will not supply another group with the same product if that group is going to be in chronological or geographical competition with you?

3. **Communicate carefully to the congregation what you are selling, the purpose for the money raising, and the financial goal.** Keep the congregation informed of your progress.

4. **Have one person responsible for dispensing the merchandise and collecting the money.**

5. **If the product is a perishable one, such as candy, be certain that it is properly stored;** and remind the young people of the need to store it carefully in their homes.

6. **Have a training session before the selling campaign begins.** In the agenda for that session, include such activities as:

● reminding group members to always introduce themselves and explain their purpose;

● showing ways to present the product without being obnoxious or pushy;

● discussing a printed calendar of the dates for the campaign; and

● role playing some selling situations for the benefit of the group.

7. If you anticipate that most of the selling will be on a house-to-house basis, **assign group members specific blocks or streets to avoid duplication at the same homes.**

8. **Set clear and realistic goals for sales.** Don't order more merchandise than you can reasonably expect to sell. If the company has provided you with "goals," you can normally reduce those goals by 25 percent. Remember that it is always better to run out of candy, candles, jewelry, etc., and have to reorder than to be left with an enormous quantity of items to return.

Some companies offer plans in which group members simply take orders the first time out; a single person then collects those orders and sends one order to the company; and then a second trip is made to deliver the orders. Such plans avoid the necessity of returning unneeded items. The primary difficulty is that this approach is more time consuming for the young people, who must make two trips to each house instead of one.

9. **Have a person or persons designated to call group members once or twice during the sales campaign to check on their**

progress and encourage them to be finished by the agreed date.

10. **Provide some kind of identification badges for your young people,** so they are readily accepted as representing the church. Many people are reluctant to buy if it is not obvious that the money is being used for a benevolent purpose rather than personal gain.

11. **If any purchasers are unhappy with the product, refund their money promptly, even if you fear the company will not accept the product back.** Unhappy customers, especially when they are members of the church, always cost you and the church more in good will and future cooperation than the cost of cheerfully returning their money.

12. **There are, unfortunately, no good guidelines as to what products sell best.** The answer depends on where you live, on what other products are sold by other fund-raising organizations, and on the time of the year in which the campaign is conducted. In general, Christmas cards and gifts are not a good idea unless you begin extremely early or have a tradition of selling a particular item for that season.

Car Washes

Car washes are thoroughly enjoyed by most young people; they provide a service that most adults purchase anyway and involve relatively little overhead expense.

1. **Use careful publicity arrangements,** as in any fund-raising effort, including the bulletin, newsletter, pulpit announcement, community newspapers, and posters. You should also encourage group members to tell people in their neighborhoods about the car wash and perhaps to sell tickets in advance.

2. **Explicitly designate the person or persons who will be permitted to drive cars that day.** This should be a person with a license (NOT a learner's permit) and a good driving record. Check with them to be sure they have current insurance coverage and that their parents do not mind their driving someone else's car for the purposes of the car wash. If no one in your group is of legal age to drive, you will need to recruit some adult help in moving cars.

3. **Choose a place for the wash that has an adequate water supply and good drainage.** Occasionally a filling station or garage will let a youth group hold a wash on their premises.

4. **Though most young people (and adults) are convinced that they know how to wash cars, assume nothing.** Have a training or orientation session before the car wash. You may want to seek the advice of a car dealer, garage manager, or service station manager as to what cleaning products are best to use and what procedures should be followed and avoided. Cars can be seriously damaged by the use of abrasive cleaning products or the failure to adequately rinse off soap. Do not use anything except water and a vacuum cleaner on a car's interior unless you have professional advice readily available.

Service Days

Most communities are familiar with "Service Days" on which young people do yard work, housecleaning, and odd jobs in exchange for a financial donation. These can be enjoyable ways of earning money and may also be a useful service.

1. **Follow the same publicity guidelines that have been given previously.** Have a

single phone number that people can call to request assistance in advance or on the slave day itself. But don't depend on people to call. Have group members actively recruit business in advance of the day by checking with friends and neighbors about assistance they may need.

2. **Rather than setting a flat hourly rate, simply ask people to donate whatever they feel is appropriate.** This enables you to do a genuine service for those on limited incomes, and those with adequate resources will generally give you more than you would have requested.

3. **Always assign youth in pairs if you know nothing about the people who have requested their services.**

A Smattering of Other Ideas

1. Have young people provide the vacation replacement for the church janitor.

2. Sell an assortment of Christian books.

3. Offer children's books and toys prior to the Christmas holidays.

4. Have a film festival of topical or popular movies. Be careful about laws on charging admission to such showings. It may be best to request a specific "donation."

5. Sponsor a church talent show with a small admission charge.

6. If your church does not disapprove, have a dance.

7. Bake sales are trite but also good money-makers, as long as group members (and advisors!) don't eat up the profits in advance. Group members can also enjoy making peanut brittle and other candy.

8. Have a marathon Bible reading or Bible study by group members, and recruit sponsors.

9. Offer Halloween insurance, and clean up windows and yards that have been vandalized. But make very clear what the limits of liability are that you will assume!

10. Print and sell a calendar with the birthdays and anniversaries of all church members.

11. The *IDEAS* series, published by Youth Specialties, contains many excellent fund-raising suggestions (address in the "Resources" chapter).

Ideas

Here are some ideas for games, parties, and other recreational activities. Most are familiar ideas, but sometimes a reminder of the familiar is helpful. The "Resources" chapter lists many other publications which have excellent recreation suggestions. As you look through the list of resources, note especially the helpful *Ideas* books from Youth Specialties and also *Group* magazine which are continuing sources of suggestions for recreation.

You'll notice a large number of suggestions here are related to food! That reflects the importance of food both to young people and to the authors of this book.

1. **Progressive Supper.** You need several parents to host this activity which brings young people into one another's homes. Group members travel by car between homes for the various courses of a meal, usually: appetizer, salad, main course, dessert.

The number of homes needed depends on the size of your group. As a general rule, you don't want one household to host more than two carloads of young people (8–12 youth). If there are ten youth in your group, four homes are all you need. You may have a family that can accommodate a much larger group for dessert. The appetizer and salad courses are sometimes combined. Most youth groups who try this rate it a "favorite activity," and parents generally enjoy their role as hosts.

2. **Supper by Numbers.** In my part of the country, this traditional youth group activity used to be called a "Mystery Meal." Teens now use "mystery meal" and "mystery meat" so often in reference to school lunches that the connotation is no longer a positive one! This meal can be served by a task force of teens and an advisor or by a group of parents or other adult volunteers. It usually works best with at least a few teens as part of the preparing and serving crew. You assign a number to everything! For example:

1-spoon	2-drink
3-pickles	4-knife
5-salad	6-mustard
7-fork	8-hamburger bun
9-french fries	10-salt
11-hamburger	12-baked beans
13-pepper	14-catsup
15-brownie	

Serve the meal in three "courses." For each course, each young person orders by number what he or she wants. The mystery is that the menu isn't posted! Youth only know that the numbers 1—15, for example, are available. Asked to select five numbers for the first course, a surprised young person may get a spoon, pickles, salad, hamburger bun, and catsup. Most young people have a good time with this meal and the necessary trading of food items.

3. **Make-Your-Own-Sandwich.** This suggestion isn't an evening's program but is a good approach to providing a snack or meal to go with other games and activities. The planning team assembles a large number of sandwich materials, sets them up buffet style, and lets group members put together their own sandwiches. Include three or more kinds of bread (or large sandwich buns), several kinds of lunchmeat, two or more kinds of cheese, lettuce, sliced tomatoes, sliced pickles (sweet and dill), sliced onions, and a variety of condiments (catsup, regular mustard, "hot" mustard, mayonnaise).

4. **Pizza Party.** Pizza parties never go out of style with young people and are

always a great favorite. You can have the party at your church with young people making the pizzas or have it at a local pizza parlor (ideally in a separate room or at least in a reserved area). If you have it at the church, remember that only a portion of the youth will be able to actively participate in making the pizza—you need games or other activities for most of the group while the pizza is being prepared. If you go out for pizza, have the youth group budget or church budget pay the bill. It's fine to collect a contribution from each young person ($1, $3, or simply a voluntary amount), but you don't want a table of ten youth trying to decide who owes what on the bill for that table!

5. **Blindfolded Meal.** This is a simulation experience which is a lot of fun but also helps young people identify better with the handicapped. Divide the group into pairs. One member of each pair blindfolds the other before entering the room for the meal. The person who can see shouldn't do anything for the blindfolded person except give directions: "You'll find the fork about three inches to the left of your left hand. If your plate were a clock, the corn would be at the position of the number four." Take time to talk about the experience after the meal; don't remove blindfolds until the discussion is finished.

6. **Love Feast.** This draws on a tradition of the early church in which communion was generally celebrated as part of a full meal. This activity is a meaningful one that could well be considered a worship experience or educational program. It's included here because it's such an enjoyable experience that it can also be considered recreation (and has lots of food involved!). A love feast combines a full meal, communion, and sharing of affirmation for one another.

Proceed like this:

● Open with prayer.

● Read about the Last Supper in Scripture.

● Share a full meal together.

● Go around the group, focusing on one person at a time, and have others share two or three reasons why they especially love and appreciate that person.

● Share in communion.

7. **Hunger Meal.** There are many variations on this strategy for helping young people better understand the reality of world hunger.

One option involves randomly dividing the group into thirds for a meal: one-third receive a meal of steak or chicken; one-third receive a simpler meal of sandwiches and fries; and one-third receive a meal of rice or beans. Then the group discusses the experience and the recognition that the world's resources are not equally divided.

A second option involves every person eating a simpler meal than usual—generally beans or rice. My own preference is to be sure the meal is appealingly served. The difference in price between this meal and a fuller meal at a restaurant is generally donated to world hunger by the group.

Obviously both strategies are intended to stimulate discussion about world hunger and to help youth identify somewhat with people who have little to eat. Unless being done as part of a retreat or lock-in, which provides substantial time for reflection and sharing, I strongly recommend the second option in

195

which all youth receive the same food. With the first option, some of those receiving the meal of rice or beans have real feelings of resentment about the experience. Those feelings can provide an excellent basis for discussion and result in much better understanding of the disadvantaged of the world, but you may not be able to work through those feelings in an evening's program.

The second option provides an experience that is enjoyable enough to have a recreational dimension, but the accompanying discussion and donation of money to world hunger will increase awareness of hunger issues.

Some youth groups make the mistake of having the "simple meal" an unappetizing meal. That does no good! Eating bad- tasting food doesn't make youth better identify with the hungry; it just upsets them. It would be better to have a hunger fast than to serve bad-tasting food. (Hunger fasts can be a good strategy, but that discussion definitely doesn't belong in a chapter on "Recreation"!)

8. **Youth Thanksgiving Dinner.** Have a special Thanksgiving dinner for the youth class or group a couple of weeks before Thanksgiving. The young people should be involved in the planning and food preparation—including baking the turkey. Many groups have at first resisted the idea ("We have turkey at school and at home.") only to make it a tradition after the first time. You can also combine this with the love feast described earlier in this chapter.

9. **Make-Your-Own Ice Cream Sundae.** For a great event as part of an evening's activities, have a wide range of toppings available for the sundaes. This can be even better with homemade ice cream if enough

mixers are available from the families of group members.

10. **Chocolate Tasting Party.** Here's a wonderful event! Instead of a "wine tasting party" (not a good idea for a youth group!), have a chocolate tasting party. Members volunteer to bring enough of their favorite chocolate treats for everyone to sample, and additional items can be purchased from the youth group or church budget. A little of each will be sufficient if most members bring something.

Diet pop and skim milk are the recommended drinks to go with this high calorie program! One group's treats included five varieties of brownies, two kinds of fudge, three kinds of chocolate pastry, four kinds of chocolate cake, eight kinds of homemade chocolate candy, Godiva chocolates, Hershey kisses, Mars bars, Snickers bars, and a variety of other purchased chocolates. Obviously, servings were very small—bite size! (Consider having a few nonchocolate goodies available in case any members or guests are allergic to chocolate.)

11. **Alternative Foods Party.** This idea is as high in nutrition as the last idea is high in sugar and calories! Have a party with snacks chosen for high nutritional value and as alternatives to junk food. Fresh pineapple, sliced apples, sliced oranges, sunflower seeds, a variety of nuts, and other goodies make a nice change of pace. It's also an excellent way to remind teens that more nutritious foods are delicious, too. You could combine these refreshments with a program about health, nutrition, or the Bible and the body. (See suggestions in the "Resources" chapter.)

12. **Guess the Food!** How much of our ability to identify food and drink is based on seeing what we are about to consume? In

this game, blindfolded members try to guess different kinds of foods they are served. Before doing this, find out if any members have food allergies. You don't want someone to have an asthmatic attack caused by milk, mushrooms, or chocolate! You can structure the game in several ways: (a) have a small number of draftees or volunteers to do the tasting; (b) divide into teams and have one person at a time from each team taste items; or (c) do it without competition but let every person, probably in groups of two to eight at a time, share in the tasting.

You'll have to change the order if the same substances are used more than once, or else those who taste later in the game will have an unfair advantage (and thus not have as much fun). You can use a broad range of foods and drinks, for example: Pepsi, Coca-Cola, R.C., Dr. Pepper, Sprite, 7-Up, lettuce, cabbage, tomato, hamburger, catsup, mustard, cheddar cheese, Swiss cheese, cottage cheese, mushroom, squash, cucumber, bread, donut, angel food cake, radish, celery, carrot, mayonnaise, apple, cherry, date, fig, orange, grapefruit, kiwi, sardine, tuna fish, bologna, ham, asparagus, spinach, milk, coconut milk.

You'll need to have a good supply of small cups or glasses, spoons, etc., for this event. If you wish, you can stimulate interesting discussion about how we perceive flavor and about the capabilities and limitations of our senses. You can also talk about the advertising claims of various food products. Primarily, however, this is a fun activity. Be sure to eat all the leftovers!

For an interesting variation, include Chinese, Korean, Mexican, and Japanese foods in your samples.

13. **Picnics and Cookouts.** These are almost always successful youth activities, and the mechanics of the events are familiar to all of us. You may want to combine a softball game or group hike with the picnic or cookout. Be sure you do have enough recreational activities scheduled or available at the location.

14. **Pancake Night or Waffle Night.** Pancakes and waffles are delicious, but we usually don't think of them as youth group foods. Young people will respond well to a pancake or waffle evening and can have fun helping in the preparation. If you want to have waffles, you'll need to borrow waffle irons from several families unless your group is very small.

15. **Plastic Bubble.** Make a large plastic bubble that your group can inflate with a fan and use as a focus of interest. These are made out of clear plastic drop cloths (the kind used to protect furniture and floors from enthusiastic painters!) and electrical tape. Tape the plastic sheets together to create a long tube, which the fan will later inflate.

You need two openings. One opening is a small one where the fan is to be inserted. Bunch the plastic around the fan cage and tape it in place, being careful not to let the plastic extend inside the cage where the fan will shred it.

The other opening is a flap where people enter the bubble. You need to let one plastic cloth overlap another by about four feet; the overlap will help keep the bubble inflated even though you will not tape the plastic together at your "doorway," which should be four to five feet high (it won't hurt people to stoop as they enter!).

Lay out the plastic sheets so the bubble is at least six feet high and eight feet wide. The length depends on the size of your group and available space. I've seen bubbles that were ten feet high, twelve feet wide, and eighty feet long. The larger your bubble, the longer it will take the fan to inflate it, but the more stable the bubble will be once inflated.

People should remove their shoes before entering the bubble since the soles can rip holes in the plastic. With that precaution, the bubble is surprisingly durable and can be used many times. (You don't want to buy the cheapest plastic drop cloths available—look for some of modest thickness; the price differential isn't significant. The number you need depends on the cloth dimensions and the size of the bubble you want to make.)

Most youth groups have a lot of fun with the bubble and enjoy meeting in it. You can put pillows on the floor, project lights and films on the sides, and use it as a discussion setting or a futuristic space simulation. Your group will come up with other imaginative ways to use the bubble.

16. **Car Rally.** Youth groups always enjoy a car rally. The person or team planning the rally makes up a very specific route and seals instructions in envelopes for each car. A picnic or refreshments generally come at the end of the course.

Speed limits are always observed; the goal is to smoothly and accurately follow the instructions—not to set a new speed record. You do need someone who has participated in successful car rallies to help establish the route.

17. **Scavenger Hunt.** Scavenger hunts are always fun. Sharing in the process brings young people closer together and generally tests their ingenuity. Always give the lists to pairs or groups rather than to individuals. Use as much creativity as possible in developing lists for the hunt. For an interesting alternative try . . .

18. **Polaroid Scavenger Hunt.** Provide a Polaroid camera for each team. You can generally borrow enough cameras from church members. Teams can be two to six people. The event is often done by automobile, though the necessity for that depends on the kind of list you develop. Some possibilities include taking pictures of the following:

- your team standing (fully clothed!) in a bath tub (someone else will have to take the picture!)

- a person who knows what the word *koinonia* means

- an armed forces object from World War II

- a baby born within the past six months

- a building scheduled for demolition

- a gasoline station pump

- a cross

- a family eating supper

- a pink toilet

- a person with red hair

- a person who served in the Vietnam War

- a person with a shopping cart

- a person with shaving cream on his or her face

- a 1957 Chevrolet

- a Volkswagon bug

- a BMW convertible

- a fresh tomato

- a Bible that is at least one hundred years old

- a person wearing a lampshade for a hat

19. **Going to the Movies.** The "Media" and "Video" chapters of this book contain many suggestions for viewing and discussing motion pictures. You'll probably do most of your work with movies using VCRs at the church or in a home. At times, however, you may enjoy going as a group to a current motion picture at a theater. If possible, you will want to preview the motion picture in advance. Newspaper, magazine, and television reviews and advertisements may give you helpful information but will not always tell you everything you want to know about the film. Motion picture ratings can be very misleading—causing some movies to sound appropriate for a youth group when they are not and also saddling some excellent films for youth work with R ratings. Trust your own judgment rather than that of other people. The advantage of viewing the film in advance is that you can do a better job leading discussion afterwards. There's nothing wrong with seeing a movie for recreation only, but you'll still have opportunity to discuss it informally with youth group members.

20. **Valentine Party.** Have a Valentine Party! It's a classic youth event well enjoyed. Dancing can be part of the party if appropriate for your denominational tradition.

Play a variation of "Spin the Bottle." Instead of kissing the person the bottle lands on, have that person share an opinion with the group on something related to love, dating, or marriage. After sharing an opinion, that person poses the next opinion question and then spins the bottle to select the person who responds. Questions can include: What is the most important characteristic in a marriage partner? Would you like a date who was more like a spaniel or more like a poodle? Why? What movie star would you most like to go out with and why?

The crossword puzzle about love in the Scriptures (found at the end of this chapter, p. 202) is an appropriate exercise for a Valentine Party.

21. **Have a party with a youth group from another church.** You can choose a nearby church of the same denomination, or you can intentionally choose a youth group likely to be different from your own. A Catholic group might consider inviting a Protestant group. A suburban youth group might invite an inner-city group. Be sure to include several games as mixers at the start of the event.

22. **Fifties Party.** Have a party with dress and music from the 1950s.

23. **Relay/Race Night.** Hold a variety of races. You can use the same teams for all the races, or change them along the way. Race examples include:

- Wheelbarrow race: one person holding the feet of another.

- Water-filled balloon race: teams stand in lines. Pass the water-filled balloons from person-to-person without using hands. The balloon has to be held between the chin and neck, under the armpit, or between the knees.

- Lifesaver and toothpick relay: team members hold toothpicks in their mouths and use them to pass Lifesavers.

- Three-legged race: tie ankles or legs together.

- Balloon-break race: race to break balloons by sitting down on them.

24. **Birthday Parties.** Some groups have birthday parties for each member. I once had a small group that liked birthday parties so well that we celebrated not only the birthdays of group members but also those of Martin Luther, John Calvin, John Wesley, Thomas Merton, Martin Luther King Jr., Mother Theresa, and the President! A very large youth group may decide to celebrate several birthdays on the same night. Develop a list of those celebrating birthdays and a list of helpers: name, birthday, date, plans food, plans games, plans worship. Those people who sign up to plan food, games, and worship for a person's birthday should give special consideration to the preferences of that person.

25. **Swimming Parties.** These are a great summer event. Two cautions: (a) Be sure a lifeguard is available. (b) Try to reserve a pool or beach section so that outsiders don't interfere with your party. If you want to build a Bible study out of this experience, you can have an interesting discussion about the role water plays in Scripture. Use a concordance to look up passages. See especially: Genesis 1:1–19; Psalm 42:1–11; and Matthew 3:11–12.

26. **Halloween Party.** Some Christians are uncomfortable celebrating Halloween because it is a "pagan holiday." It's also part of our culture, and youth don't take seriously the "evil" dimension of the day. A party can actually be an occasion to talk about claims of spiritualism from the standpoint of the Christian faith. You can have a haunted house in the church basement, apple bobbing, and a hot dog/marshmallow roast. For further information, see the junior high lock-in schedule in the chapter "Overnight and Longer."

27. **Ice Skating.** Youth groups almost always enjoy ice skating. Remember, however, that you'll have some members who haven't gone ice skating before. You'll need to arrange skate rental as well as instruction for those who are first-timers. Have hot chocolate or cider afterwards.

28. **Christmas Caroling.** While caroling for nursing homes, shut-ins, and church families is truly a form of service, it's also so much fun that it belongs under recreation, too. Have hot chocolate and cider afterwards.

Remember that you can have your group go singing any time of the year. The weeks prior to Christmas don't have to be the only time we do this enjoyable and worthwhile activity.

29. **Roller Skating.** Roller skating goes in and out of style with youth—but it never stays out of style for long. It's a lot of fun and easier to learn than ice skating. A few large churches have roller skating rinks. Assuming that your church isn't that fortunate, find a rink that you can rent exclusively or that won't be too crowded at the time you go.

30. **Bowling.** This is another traditional youth group activity that is almost always enjoyed. You need to have lanes reserved, however, or you'll find your group spread too far around the bowling alley or waiting too long for lanes. Advance arrangements are important.

You also want a bowling alley where you aren't likely to have inebriated people in other lanes heckling your teens. The amount of alcoholic beverages served at some bowling alleys can make that a problem.

31. **Name That Tune.** This game is based on an old radio and television show and is still greatly enjoyed. The person or team in charge plays selections from songs, and contestants or teams try to identify the songs in as short a time as possible. Try a mix of rock, country, classic, jazz, and hymns!

32. **Come-As-You-Are Party.** This is another old favorite that is still a great way to draw members into the group or to reactivate those who have stopped coming. The party is often held at a different time than the regular youth meeting. Parents are contacted in advance so that they know their offspring will be picked up at a particular time. One normally hopes for parental cooperation in keeping the son or daughter at home and also in not warning the son or daughter about the party. Those coordinating the party then pick up teens and bring them to the church. The surprise element makes it fun and also makes it hard to say no.

33. **Peanuts Night.** This evening is focused on the cartoon strip "Peanuts" and on the food of the same name. Consider the following activities:

- Divide people into groups on the basis of these Peanuts characters: Lucy, Linus, Snoopy, Charlie Brown . . .

- Use Peanuts posters to decorate the meeting area.

- Rolling Peanut Race: roll peanuts with your nose.

- Shelling Peanuts Race: peanut shelling. (For a real challenge, have members try it barefoot—though they may not want to eat the peanuts shelled in that way!)

- Game: find the Great Pumpkin.
- Make up Peanuts cartoons.

- Have peanut butter and jelly sandwiches with milk or soft drinks.

- Make peanut brittle (if you have good adult guidance). You may wish to share the candy with shut-ins.

34. **Carnival Night.** A carnival is a lot of work but also a lot of fun. Your group can do it for another youth group; adults can do it for the youth of the church; or it can be done as a fund raiser. Booth possibilities include: refreshment booth, dunking booth, guess-someone's-weight booth, strength-test booth, kissing booth (chocolate kisses!), fishing-for-prizes booth, throwing booth (balls at objects).

Your group will come up with additional ideas. Some groups have done very elaborate carnivals in which the whole church has enjoyed participating. Some churches have found this an enjoyable way to host youth from several churches in the area, sharing refreshments and visiting together following the carnival activities.

VALENTINE'S DAY CROSSWORD PUZZLE

Across:

1. This prophet compared a woman who was unfaithful in her love for a man to the Hebrew people's unfaithfulness to God.

3. The Good Samaritan parable was told to answer a question about who the_____ is that we are to love. (See Luke 10.)

4. The Old Testament book_____tells us to love others as we love ourselves.

7. Jesus turned water into wine to bless the marriage at_____.

8. Jesus tells us we should even love our _____. (See Matthew 5:43.)

Down:

2. Though a great leader, David sinned in sleeping with _____, who was the wife of another man; and then David plotted the death of that man. (See 2 Samuel 11.)

5. According to this famous love poem, love never ends but _____ will come to an end. (See 1 Corinthians 13.)

6. 1 John warns us to love God more than the _____. (1 John 2)

7. God's love has been made known to us through _____.

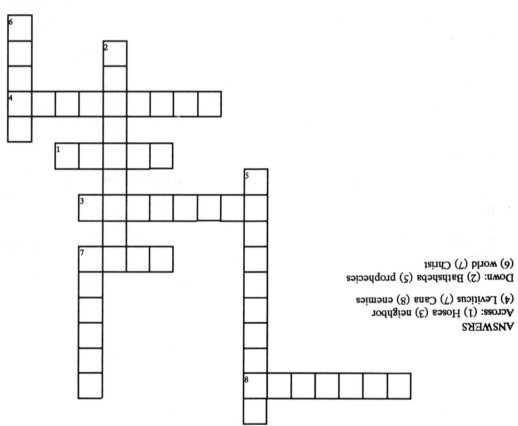

ANSWERS
Across: (1) Hosea (3) neighbor (4) Leviticus (7) Cana (8) enemies
Down: (2) Bathsheba (5) prophecies (6) world (7) Christ

202

"Music! Music! Music!" So went a hit song of the 1950s! Were you around then? Whether you were or weren't, you are probably quite aware that whatever music was or wasn't in the '50s—it is certainly the center of the universe for many teenagers today. Today's youth are bombarded by sounds of their music! It reverberates from millions of high-powered stereo systems! And millions of teenagers resonate to its beat! Although there may be a few exceptions, it is reasonably safe to say that if you want to have a successful ministry with youth, you must be able to connect at some point with their music!

Getting to Know Their Music

If you are convinced from the start that all this teenage music is a bunch of junky noise, you are mistaken! So, if you're absolutely down on rock-and-roll and all the current pop music and you feel that you can successfully do youth ministry without relating to the musical interests of teenagers, fine! Good luck! Skip the first half of this chapter! But if you feel a little (or very!) insecure in this area and you would like to have some help, then read on. We'll try to help you out!

Actually, the fact is: Some of the music of the current rock scene is just "a bunch of junky noise"! There is good and bad in every kind of music. And also, in every kind of music, there are some artists and styles that are going to appeal to you as an individual more than others will.

All of which brings us to **Guideline One** about relating to the teenage music world: **Listen openly and without prejudice, but feel free to have your own preferences and dislikes.** You may develop a fanatical devotion to U2, have no use for Madonna, and feel that Guns N' Roses is just a bunch of formless noise. Don't hesitate to express your preferences, but allow the same freedom of choice for the teenager who may be into heavy metal or southern rock.

To the uninitiated, teenage music sounds like one big undifferentiated din like the noise of thousands of "clanging cymbals" or groaning guitars! To those who take the time to listen to it and to evaluate what they hear, however, it soon becomes evident that the world of teenage music is diverse, encompassing a wide variety of styles from the easy-listening sounds of soft rock to the agitated beat of the heavier rock idioms.

In any youth group, you will probably find people whose tastes and primary interests will be centered on many different categories and types of music. What you need to do as a youth worker is: (1) discover the point in this musical spectrum at which you feel most comfortable; (2) dig in and get to know something about youth music in general (and your area in particular); and then (3) listen openly and freely to the music preferred by those whose tastes are different from yours. As you listen more and more, you may find yourself opening up to values and attractions you had not previously discovered in such types as heavy rock, soul music, disco, southern rock, or whatever styles you had not been able to develop an interest in.

Guideline Two: Read about pop music and the people who produce it. We especially recommend the magazine *Rolling Stone,* which provides reviews of pop music albums, articles about pop music stars, information on concert tours, and general material on the youth and pop-music scenes. Record reviews and articles on pop music also appear regularly in most of the audio magazines. My own favorite among these is *Stereo Review,* which has several very competent reviewers of pop music albums.

Group magazine and *Sojourners* provide helpful reviews of current music from a distinctly Christian perspective. *Group* provides discussion suggestions which can be very helpful. *Sojourners* looks at the values communicated through music and will help you gain new perspectives on many artists and their work. *Cultural Information Service* provides many good reviews of current albums. While the *Cultural Information Service* perspective is not as clearly Christian as *Sojourners* or *Group*, it has a sensitivity to values not found in some other music reviews.

Check your bookstores and libraries regularly for new books about pop music. They constantly roll off the presses, and, although some are just pulp and trash, many are not only informative but also quite interesting.

Guideline Three: Spend some time each week listening to various kinds of teenage music on the radio. As you begin to get involved with the pop-music scene, you will discover right away that, although some stations play a variety of different kinds of pop music, most tend to specialize in only one type of music. Some of the most common of these are soft rock, heavy rock, Top-40, disco, soul, country-and-western, and golden oldies. Try to get a feel for the stations that the youth you work with are listening to. Although generalities are risky in this respect, you will probably discover that younger teens tend to listen more to Top-40 and disco, high-schoolers seem to favor heavier rock and some soft rock, and students near or at college age tend toward soft rock and oldies. But you don't have to depend on generalities! Ask the youth! And then do some listening on your own!

MTV is carried by most cable companies, and almost all young people watch it. Some teens seem addicted to it. The music videos can seem very strange to adults because the visual images and the musical lyrics often don't seem to fit together. There's an intentional dreamlike quality to many of the visual images. As you watch several videos, you'll begin to get a better feel for them and can better understand their meaning. You'll find sensitive, beautiful videos, humorous videos, sexually suggestive videos, and some violent videos. You can also see broadcasts of music concerts and interviews with music stars. MTV has so much influence on youth that it's important for you to be exposed to it.

Another good way to get into the music of your own group is to have several listening parties during your youth group meetings. Have the youth bring their own records. Serve popcorn and soda. And let the young people share their musical preferences with one another and with you! A word of caution: Be sure to have a "round-robin" rule—each person gets to play only one selection in turn; and all get to have an opportunity to share! By operating in this manner, you can avoid a catastrophe such as I encountered one Sunday when the whole group got treated to (or mistreated by!) a full hour of Jethro Tull, which was the favorite of one of our group's more vocal members!

As an added bonus for you and the group, ask each person to tell something about the background(s) of the recording artist(s) and the ideas in the song(s) selected. With such a procedure, you may be able to delve into various ways in which this music is related to the Christian faith (more on this later!).

Guideline Four: Don't fake it and don't worry about it! Most young people can spot a phony a mile away! So don't try to appear to know more about their music than you really do. They don't expect you to have an encyclopedic knowledge of the history of rock from Haley to Halen. What they do expect from you is a sympathetic ear and an interest in what interests them. When it comes to pop music, no one can know it all. So don't try to "show off"! And don't worry about the possibility that your knowledge may be only a fraction of that of most of the youth with whom you work. Just be natural and follow your own interests! And be open to theirs!

Using Pop Music in Youth Ministry

The music that the majority of teenagers—those in the church and those outside it—are listening to is not the music of the church! It is music produced by people and groups with names such as Madonna, U2, R.E.M., Bruce Springsteen, Guns N' Roses, Michael Jackson, Jon Bon Jovi, Def Leppard, Debbie Gibson, Jody Watley, Paula Abdul, and Cher. And regardless of the glory and beauty of much of our standard church music repertoire, the fact remains that most youth are not going to relate to it as well as they relate to the music of the secular pop music scene! Conclusion? A wise youth worker will attempt to utilize some of pop music's good tunes—and many good song lyrics—as tools for enriching the church's ministry to youth!

But how shall we use pop music? What message does it have for the Christian? Does it say anything of value for the Christian faith? Well, the possibilities for using pop music in youth ministry are almost endless—limited only by the limits of our own creativity and imagination! For starters, here are a few ideas:

1. **Discuss the lyrics of pop songs—their meaning and their implications for the Christian faith.** Although some pop songs have words that are hopelessly inane, many of them have words that express, often very poetically, some important ideas about life as we encounter it. Sometimes these words reflect a viewpoint that is in agreement with the teachings of the Christian faith.

Sometimes the words promote values that run counter to the gospel message. In both cases, however, the words are worth exploring. Regardless of whether a song expresses Christian ideas or not, it can still be a good starting point for helping youth relate the faith to their world.

The possibilities for subject matter are enormous. Today's pop music deals with life, death, love, hate, sex, jealousy, morals, ethics, the church, war, peace, politics, joy, sadness—to name just a few topics. You may start with the songs themselves and just discuss topics as they arise. Or you may start with a topical emphasis and look for songs that relate to your choice for discussion. Regardless of which approach you choose, don't hesitate to ask the youth themselves for suggestions of songs. They will probably have plenty of ideas. And their input will greatly improve the chances of having a successful discussion.

Here are a few suggestions that should make your discussions more meaningful:

● If possible, play the records or tapes on a good stereo system. Young people are used to hearing good music reproduction, and if you use a cheap, tinny-sounding record player or a small, inadequate cassette player, you are beginning with two strikes against you. The music and lyrics should always be presented with as much audio fidelity as possible. Many churches do not have a

205

good stereo system. See if members of your group will bring their equipment for class or group sessions. If you do borrow equipment, see that it is handled by the owner or by people familiar with it.

● In most cases, your discussions will be enhanced if you prepare in advance a wall chart (or chalkboard) on which you or the youth have written out the words to the songs to be discussed. Even with recording artists who sing and enunciate very clearly, the use of a lyric chart of this sort will help to focus your group's attention on key words and phrases.

● Start your discussion with specific questions and then move to more general questions. Begin by asking about particular words and phrases, rather than by asking a general question such as "What does this song mean?"

● Whenever possible, select in advance some scripture passages that relate to the discussion. Use a concordance or a topical index to help you track down relevant passages. Or consult with your pastor. He or she should have many ideas on how to use Scripture in your discussions and also some thoughts on how to present the main teachings of the Christian faith.

● Don't be judgmental! Feel free to give your witness and your ideas, but let the youth themselves discover which values in their music are positive and which are not. Remember: The best learning experiences occur when we make most of the discoveries ourselves!

2. **Organize a concert special.** Have your youth group or class attend a concert and then participate in a discussion afterward!

Rock concerts provide super material for discussion! In addition to discussing the music itself, you and the youth can gain many insights by evaluating other aspects of the concert—the lifestyles of the musicians, the price of the tickets, the behavior and attitudes of the audience, and so forth.

A key decision in planning a concert special is the choice of concert to attend. In most youth groups, the musical tastes are so diverse that you may have difficulty in deciding on a concert that will appeal to all, or even most, of the youth. For this reason, if the youth can afford it, it is usually a good idea to have two or three concert specials during a given period, thus, allowing for a fairly wide variety of music to be experienced by the group. An important criterion for your choices should be the question of meaning and relevance. It is best to choose concerts featuring musicians whose songs say something meaningful and relevant to the needs and interests of your group.

If recordings of the concert musicians' material are available, these should be used in the discussions following the concerts. If many of the youth are not very well-acquainted with the artists and their music, it would also be a good idea to play recordings of some of the artists' songs prior to the concerts as well. An additional resource that will provide useful information for your discussions is Dennis Benson's book *The Rock Generation*.

The use of concert specials will not only help you and the youth to understand more about what pop music and the pop music world are all about; it will also produce some very good by-products. Special "field trips" of this sort tend to build a better group feeling. And they help to make the faith more relevant to an important aspect of the average teenager's experience!

3. **Use pop music in your young people's worship services!** As you become more familiar with the music that youth are listening to, you will discover that many pop songs can be used in worship experiences. Be on the lookout for songs that relate to worship. Listen with the youth in your group. They will probably have a lot of suggestions. And their ideas will make your worship all the more meaningful!

How should pop music be used in worship? There are many methods. You can play the recordings and have the youth sing along or just listen to the songs. If you have musicians in your group, the songs can be done "live," either by using the printed music or by having someone with musical expertise listen to the recordings and determine the keys and the chords. Another good way to use pop music in worship and in other settings is to have your group produce and present slide-and-tape shows using the songs as the audio element. For more information on this method, see the chapter entitled "Media."

4. **Write new words for pop music melodies!** Since many of the pop music songs, particularly the soft rock variety, have good, singable melodies, they are often adapted for use with new words that express elements of the Christian faith. If you and/or any of your youth have a talent for writing song lyrics, you may find this approach a very exciting one!

To get a feel for this type of endeavor, you may want to check out some of the better known attempts at this type of adaptation. Some are very simple, such as substituting the name "Jesus" for the name "Vincent" and changing the phrase "took your life" to "gave your life" in Don McLean's song "Vincent" (from his album *American Pie*, United Artists). Others can be more involved, such as the song "Jesus Christ" sung to the tune of "Edelweiss" from the Broadway musical *The Sound of Music*. A particularly imaginative adaptation is the use of the words to John Ylvisaker's folk hymn "Thanks Be to God" (No. 6 in *Songbook for Saints and Sinners*) with the tune from the song "Windy," recorded several years ago by the group known as The Association.

But you don't have to be limited by the type of work already done in this area! The possibilities are endless! Why don't you give it a try? Listen to a pop song that you like. Get the melody firmly in your mind. Then brainstorm about some ideas for a Christian song. Once you've got the ideas, try putting them in a verse form to match the music. It's easier than you may think. And you will be pleasantly surprised at the results!

Sample Discussion Starters

Here are some sample discussion ideas based on currently popular music and artists. These are provided in part as discussion starters but primarily to give you ideas for approaches to discussion about popular music.

1. Pepsi used a commercial featuring **Madonna** which included a burning cross and other images that offended many Christians. Pepsi withdrew the commercial and their sponsorship of a tour Madonna was conducting at the time.

Madonna has aggressively sought publicity throughout her career, and she effectively used the cancellation to her advantage. She often wears crosses but gives little evidence of actively embracing the Christian faith. In a 1991 *Rolling Stone* interview, she acknowledged believing in God but not in traditional Christian terms.

She was also a center of controversy a few years ago when nude photographs of her were published. She had permitted the photographs at a much earlier point in her career when she was not well-known, and she claimed to be angry when they were released again to capitalize on her fame.

For discussion: Was Pepsi right to withdraw its sponsorship? Why, or why not? How do you feel about Madonna's use of Christian symbols when she doesn't seem to thoroughly embrace the faith? Should the owner(s) of the nude photographs have released them again to capitalize on her fame? Why, or why not? What prices do performers often pay for success?

2. *Rolling Stone* once called **R.E.M.** "America's best rock and roll band." Band members Michael Stipe, Bill Berry, Peter Buck, and Mike Mills have consistently taken anti-alcohol and anti-drug positions. They've also been very concerned about the impact of their music on youth.

Get their album *Green* which focuses on environmental issues. The song "Orange Crush" about the use of the herbicide Agent Orange in Vietnam is especially thought-provoking. Talk about the album and about R.E.M.'s obvious concern with social issues. Look at the creation narrative in Genesis 1—3. Discuss our responsibility for the world in which we have been placed.

3. Talented performer **Debbie Gibson** started her career while still a high school student. She is considered relatively "unspoiled" and still retains strong friendships from the days before her spectacular success. Fame at such an early age would represent a "dream come true" for many young people. Have group members develop lists of the advantages and disadvantages of so much success at such an

early age. What "normal" experiences would become difficult if one were a major success while still in high school?

4. Lead **U2** singer, Bono Vox, is a dedicated Christian as are two of the other members of this four-man band. While they have not "preached" their Christianity like some religious musical groups, there can be no doubt about U2's concern for advocating the way of Christ. There are few commercially successful rock groups that have a distinctly Christian emphasis. U2 stands out almost alone in this respect.

Some good U2 albums to play and discuss are *The Unforgettable Fire; Boy, War,* and *Under a Blood Red Sky."*

The *Unforgettable Fire* has two songs about Martin Luther King, Jr., and his struggle for civil rights. The song "Pride" speaks of "three men" who "came in the name of love." One obviously is Martin Luther King, Jr. Who are the other two men? Is this also a song about Jesus? The song "MLK" has a hymn-like quality, and it even contains a prayer that can be used in relationship to Jesus. Have your group use these two songs in a devotional way, and then talk about them.

5. Listen to some songs by **Emily Saliers** and **Amy Ray**. *The Indigo Girls* offers music rooted in faith and related to the struggles of life. The song "Closer to Fire" describes a faith journey: "Darkness has a hunger that's insatiable, And lightness has a call that's hard to hear." Relate those words to the Prologue to the Gospel of John (John 1:1-14). Talk about the images of light and darkness as they relate to Christ and the world.

The same album includes "Prince of Darkness" (about drugs and the destructive power of nations); "Secure Yourself" (a beautiful song that can be used in worship); and "Kid Fears" (about barriers to happiness and accomplishment).

6. Christian musician **Ken Medema** has a growing following. His music definitely is not rock, but young people respond very well to it. Medema's talent has special significance because he is blind. As a college student, he was discouraged from studying music because of his blindness, but he has persevered. Probably no Christian musician has songs with such compelling messages as Medema. Sometimes he presents a direct Christian witness in a song; sometimes he lends a Christian perspective to an important issue but without using any Christian vocabulary.

He can be controversial and doesn't hesitate to challenge us about our faith. His album *Kingdom in the Streets* includes a song "Corner Store Jesus" which asks: "Do you want a corner drugstore Jesus passing out happiness pills?" The song is a great introduction to a discussion about what we seek from Christ. Do we seek "happiness" and an easy life from Christ? Or do we follow him in service, wherever that may lead us?

The song "Tomorrow's a Mystery" talks about Christ seeming to be out of sight when we look in front for him. Medema offers reassurance: "But I know that you [Christ] have been there. 'Cause I see the rocks and flowers shine." The song is an excellent introduction to discussion about the ways we discern God's presence in our lives.

7. **Amy Grant** is a Christian musician who has been gaining a much broader secular following. Youth groups almost always respond positively to any of her albums.

Amy is married and interrupted her career to give birth to a child and spend substantial time at home. She felt that it was her responsibility to give the child the best possible beginning in life, and she was willing to risk her career to do that. That shows a set of values not often found in the popular music community. Use her situation as an introduction to a discussion about the tension between career success and family life. We like to promote the concept that parents can have very successful careers and give good nurture to children. Yet parents can be faced with difficult choices. Help your young people explore the responsibilities that are part of giving birth to a child.

8. **Sting's** album *The Dream of the Blue Turtles* has some very thought-provoking songs. The opening number "If You Love Somebody, Set Them Free" is ready-made for discussion of the necessity for mutual support of individual growth in a love relationship. Discuss the ways in which the approach suggested in his song is a reflection of the kind of loving concern for other people that is taught by Jesus Christ.

On the same album, "Love Is the Seventh Wave" is an intense song dealing with the need for humanity to turn back from the path of nuclear self-destruction that it is following. This song calls us to look for a "deeper wave" that may be rising among humanity—the "seventh wave" of love.

Use the Vast Storehouse of Christian Folk Music!

In the '60s, many progressive church musicians began writing what seemed to be a new kind of music—Christian folk music! Actually, this particular musical endeavor, though it had new aspects, was in many ways quite traditional! Throughout the centuries, the church has often used folk tunes and folk-type tunes as the basis for hymns. What was new was the prolific outpouring of material that has continued right on through a couple of decades! And, even though the folk-music craze of the '60s has passed, many of the Christian folk hymns continue to be very popular, primarily because they provide melodic, rhythmic alternatives to the standard hymns of the church!

The market is absolutely flooded (perhaps even glutted!) with this type of music! There are folk songs and hymns to suit just about every taste. If you are just getting into Christian folk music, the biggest problem that you will encounter will be deciding what to buy and what to use! As a first step, probably the best approach is to purchase one or two of the best songbooks available and then slowly to enlarge your collection by spending a lot of time looking around in stores that specialize in church materials and resources.

Three of the best collections of Christian folk hymns (and some of the more usable pop songs) have been compiled by a musical whirlwind named Carlton ("Sam") Young. They are (in order of publication): *Songbook for Saints and Sinners*, *The Genesis Songbook*, and *The Exodus Songbook*. All three of these collections are available both in small pocket-size editions containing words, melodies, and chord markings, and also in larger piano-accompaniment editions. Although all three contain an abundance of Christian folk hymns, the proportion of pop music to folk-style music increases from the first book to the third. My own favorite is *Saints and Sinners,* but it is my impression that youth generally prefer *Genesis.* The third book, *Exodus,* has not had the popularity of the two earlier ones; but all three are excellent resources and, in my

opinion, all of these collections should be in the library of anyone working with youth in the church!

Another superb collection is *The Young Life Songbook.* This book, sponsored by the Young Life group, contains a balanced collection which includes gospel-type folk hymns, other types of folk hymns, many spirituals, and some more standard numbers. This collection is available in a large, piano-accompaniment version and also in a small, pocket-size edition that contains words and chord markings, but no melody lines. One word of caution: Some of the musical notations and chord markings are incorrect! This problem, though regrettable, should not deter you from buying the book. A competent musician will readily recognize the errors and can easily make the necessary corrections.

Another notable collection is *The Avery and Marsh Songbook.* This book contains a wealth of good material, much of it keyed to the Christian year and worship services. It is the result of the musical output of two very prolific writers, and it is quite good. This collection does not have the variety of musical styles contained in the resources discussed above, but it does offer enough very good, easily singable songs to merit its purchase by anyone wishing to expand his or her library of Christian folk music. It is available both in a large, piano-accompaniment version and in a smaller version containing words, melodies, and chord markings.

You may find that the best course of action for you and your youth group is to compile your own folk hymnal. By so doing, you can make sure that you have readily available in one collection the songs that your group likes best. Such a hymnal can be duplicated by mimeographing or photocopying or, if you want to go "big time," by utilizing the offset-press method offered by many commercial copying firms. Warning: If you do compile your own hymnal, be sure to get permission from each publisher for the use of each song, and be sure to state the appropriate copyright information on the title page of each song! To secure permission, write publishers and tell them: (1) which songs you wish to use; (2) whether you want to use words and music or just words alone; (3) the nature of your publication (for example: "a youth hymnal to be used in the Anytown Community Church youth fellowship group"); and (4) the number of copies that you would like to make. Most publishers will grant permission for this type of usage for a nominal fee. In some instances, you may be able to secure permission to use the music in this way without charge!

Have Your Youth Perform Musicals!

Many groups have had great success with this type of activity. There are plenty of youth musicals on the market. As a rule, these consist of collections of ten to twenty or so musical numbers dealing with a central theme. Most are scored for chorus and soloists, with accompaniment by piano, guitars, and a rhythm section. Some of the better known of these are: *Tell It Like It Is*; *Natural High*; *New Wine*; *Step into the Sunshine*; *Truth of Truths*; and *I'm Here, God's Here, Now We Can Start.*

Generally speaking, musicals of this sort are theologically conservative but are not objectionable for a middle-of-the-road, mainline church group. The music usually consists of a combination of styles, ranging from folk rock to Broadway musical sounds!

In churches where there is an interest in this type of musical activity, using these musicals can be a strong positive influence for youth! If you plan to get into this type of music, make sure that you can muster a good core group of youth who will work at learning the music (usually a minimum of a dozen or so teenagers) and some competent musicians who can select, lead, and accompany the music!

Use the Old, Standard, Campfire-Variety Folk Material

In our attempts to be "with it" in terms of pop music and the new wave of Christian folk music, many of us overlook the tried-and-true youth group songs that have been used for the last forty years or so—the old standards that many of us sang when we were members of church youth groups! Don't underestimate the potential of the old fellowship songs! Youth who have been raised on the likes of U2, Debbie Gibson, and Bruce Springsteen will often respond very positively—and with the excitement of new discovery—when they are first exposed to such songs as "Lonesome Valley," "Shalom Chaverim," "Tell Me Why," and "Dona Nobis Pacem."

Look around in your church library and local Christian bookstores. Consult the catalogues from your denominational publishing house. See what you can find. Such old collections as *Lift Every Voice*, *Sing It Again*, and *We Sing* offer a wealth of youth musical material that many of us have bypassed in our attempts to be ultra-contemporary! Remember: Many of the old folk songs have a lasting charm and vitality that have withstood the test of time!

Write Your Own!

In my days as a national youth staff person with the United Methodist Church, I

211

was constantly astounded by the abundance and the high quality of Christian songs written by ordinary lay people throughout the country! And now, I still keep my eyes and ears open for such material—and I continue to find it in abundance! A lot of people are writing good Christian folk music!

Most people who are not professional songwriters tend to keep their musical gems under wraps; they seem to feel that somehow what they produce can't possibly measure up to what is composed by people who do this sort of thing day in and day out on a professional basis! In many, many cases, however, this simply is not true! While having great respect for professional Christian folk song writers, I have to say that I have been amazed and delighted by the kinds of songs that nonprofessional people, youth and adults alike, turn out as expressions of their faith in God and Jesus Christ!

So, don't be bashful! If you or the youth you work with have any musical ability at all, give it a try! Take a standard church music text—a hymn, the doxology, the Lord's Prayer, or whatever—and write a new tune for it! Or, express your faith in your own words! Write down your own ideas and then put them into verse form. The rhyme pattern is up to you. In most instances, the second and fourth lines of each four-line section (technically called a quatrain) should rhyme. But there are no hard-and-fast rules. The rhyme and the rhythm are up to you. As long as it fits your music, it's right!

If you don't know how to "notate" (that is, to put the music down in notes), don't worry! Just play and/or sing the song for your choir director or some other person with musical expertise, and ask him or her to help you put the song down in musical notation.

Remember: A key factor in writing Christian music (or other types of music!) is inspiration, what I choose to call the inspiration of the Holy Spirit! Many songwriters—Paul Stookey, Billy Joel, for example—have had the experience of being a "vehicle" through which something beyond us speaks to other people! Open yourself up to the Spirit! God may have a song to give to the world through you and the youth with whom you work!

Use the Hymnal!

It is true that many teenagers are turned off by most of the standard hymns in our hymnals! But there are some interesting possibilities for imaginative use of standard church hymns. Here are a few ideas to get you started.

1. **Sing hymns to alternate tunes!** In the back of most hymnals, there is a section called the "metrical index." Most of us ignore this apparatus. But it offers all sorts of possibilities for using the hymnal differently. The important fact to note is that all hymn tunes with the same metrical markings can be interchanged!

Let's look at how this metrical scheme works. Hymns are grouped in the metrical index according to the number of syllables in each line. A hymn listed as "8787," for example, contains eight syllables in the first line, seven syllables in line two, eight syllables in line three, and seven syllables in line four. On the basis of this system, you can easily interchange hymn tunes. For example, the hymn "Savior, like a Shepherd Lead Us" (generally sung to the tune "Bradbury") can also be sung to the tune of "God of Grace and God of Glory" (usually the tune "Cwm Rhonda") and vice versa.

Obviously, the possibilities are almost unlimited! The most apparent advantage of this metrical scheme is that it makes it possible for us to sing to a familiar tune words that had originally been set to an unfamiliar tune. But beyond that, the use of the metrical index can result in a lot of fun activities as you and the youth experiment with singing hymns to different tunes!

Of particular value for those wanting to alter hymns in this manner are the more frequently used meters: SM (Short Meter: 6686); LM (Long Meter: 8888); CM (Common Meter: 8686); and CMD (Common Meter Double: 8686.8686). In most standard hymnals, these four meters alone include about one hundred hymns.

2. **Sing some of the pentatonic hymns as rounds!** Most hymnals contain several folk-type hymns that utilize what is called the pentatonic (five-note) scale. In the key of C, for example, the notes involved would be C, D, E, G, and A. Such pentatonic tunes may be sung as rounds without any harmonic clashes.

To sing a pentatonic hymn as a round, have one group start at the beginning of the first phrase of the hymn, then have the second group start the first phrase as the first group begins the second phrase. If you use a third group, this group would begin the first phrase as the first group begins the third phrase. For example, if you use the pentatonic hymn "Amazing Grace," have the first group begin the hymn at the beginning; then have the second group begin the hymn as the first group begins the phrase "That saved a wretch . . . "; then have the third group begin the hymn as the first group begins the phrase "I once was lost . . . . "

In addition to "Amazing Grace," two other common pentatonic hymns are "How Firm a Foundation" and "What Wondrous Love Is This." Many nonpentatonic hymns may also be sung as rounds, although round-singing is usually more difficult with hymns that employ more than the basic five notes of the pentatonic scale. But it's fun to try! Work with your choir director or some other competent musician to ferret out other hymns that may be sung this way. Even with the more difficult hymns, round-singing can be a lot of fun for your group.

3. **Rewrite the words to some of the traditional hymns.** Many of the hymns in our standard hymnals have very good tunes but somewhat irrelevant, often outdated words. The world view of many of our hymns is not particularly relevant to modern people; and this irrelevancy is especially obvious in regard to youth. The fact is: Our world, and notably our American society, does not relate well to such terms as *shepherd*, *lamb*, *king*, *throne*, *slaves*, and *sheaves*.

So, what can we do? We can write new words, words that express 20th-century concepts, words that are meaningful to modern American youth.

A good example of what can be done in this regard can be found in the words that R. G. Jones wrote to be used with the traditional tune "Dix" (usually used as the tune for the hymn "For the Beauty of the Earth"). The hymn is called "God of Concrete, God of Steel."

There can be no doubt that these modern words for the tune "Dix" are relevant! They use concepts that are an integral part of the 20th-century world. And, with a little effort, you and the youth with whom you work can produce the same kind of new and relevant musical statements for today's church. Just choose a standard hymn tune. Get the melody fixed in your mind. Or, better still, do a metrical analysis by counting the syllables in each line of the hymn's text.

213

And then write your own words. You can do it!

And, while you're at it, why don't you try your hand at using inclusive language in the hymns? A few years ago, some friends of mine made a listing of inclusive hymns—you know, those hymns that don't refer to "man" and "mankind" and those that don't dwell on the idea of God the *Father!* Well, in many respects, the results were commendable! The problem is, however, that many of the hymns that could be called inclusive are, in most other regards, among the worst hymns that we have! And many of the hymns that were left out of this nonsexist hymn list are, except for their sexism, among the *best* hymns that we have!

The solution? People who are interested in having hymns that are more inclusive need to rewrite some of our sexist hymns. Such an attempt can be either very easy or very difficult, depending on the complexity of the problems involved. Nevertheless, there are multitudinous instances in which "men" or "man" could be changed to "all" and other similar changes could be made.

4. **Sing the doxology to various tunes—an activity that can provide you with some interesting musical settings for the blessing prior to your group's fellowship meals.** The standard doxology ("Praise God from Whom All Blessings Flow") can be sung to many tunes. It is a Long Meter song (LM:8888)—one of the most common types of church music meters. Most hymnals contain several dozen LM settings in addition to the standard tune "Old 100th."

5. **Go through the hymnal with the aid of a skilled musician, and sing some of the hymns that are rarely used in your church services.** Hymnals contain several hundred hymns and most churches use only a fraction of that total during any given year. Some of the best and most interesting hymns are still quite unfamiliar.

Conclusion

Be open to the values in all kinds of music. Martin Luther is reputed to have said: "Why should the devil have all the good tunes?" The history of the church has shown this adage to be true. Throughout the centuries, all kinds of music have been used by the church. Christianity has borrowed from the classics (such as the works of Bach, Beethoven, Hayden, and others). It has adapted folk music; it has picked up nationalistic words and tunes; and it has even borrowed barroom tunes.

The Christian faith can be expressed musically by traditional hymns, by Christian folk hymns, by classical anthems, by pop music. Just keep your eyes and ears open. The world of music is wide and diverse. And it is an unlimited and fertile resource for people involved in youth ministry—and Christian ministry, in general.

214

Many young people find the typical church worship service to be an enormous turn-off! And many adults probably feel the same way! The fact is, although some people find meaning or, at least, comfort in the traditional worship services offered in most churches, a great many others consider the typical worship service somewhat less than satisfactory, whether they admit it or not.

Because of the lack of vibrant, meaningful worship experiences in our churches, we thus face a multi-faceted problem when we approach the question of worship and youth ministry. We have to deal with the education problem—the lack of understanding of what worship is all about: its purpose, its meaning, its components. We have to deal with the tradition problem—the fact that most people, whether they like what happens in worship or not, still have a strong, emotional relationship with what they have experienced in countless church services. And we have to deal with the innovation problem: the question of how to change things, how to determine what is good in the new approaches, and how to mix the new and the old.

So what do we do about worship, this highly technical area that in so many ways has been and continues to be the special province of ministers and other professionals trained in this area? How do we discover what worship is all about? And how do we make worship more meaningful—particularly to youth?

This chapter is an attempt to deal with some of these problems and questions. It is not an exhaustive attempt. Volumes have been written on worship without exhausting the subject, and a single chapter cannot be expected to cover the material completely. But this chapter is an attempt at a good, solid introduction! It will help you learn more about the basics of worship theology, and it will also help you discover ways to make worship more meaningful for youth!

A Basic Theology of Worship

Many attempts at worship innovation fail because the innovators do not have an adequate understanding of what worship is all about! In a lot of cases, ministers and others try something new in worship simply because they believe that the new is better than the old. What often happens, unfortunately, is that an old, inadequate way of doing things is replaced by a new method or approach that is just as inadequate—or even more inadequate! In most cases, this pitfall can be avoided if one makes an attempt to understand the meaning of traditional modes of worship before trying to replace present procedures with new ones!

The Meaning and Purpose of Worship. People have many and varying ideas as to what worship is all about. Some people feel that the purpose of a worship service is to give the worshiper a good feeling, a feeling of comfort and reassurance about life. Others feel that a worship service should inspire the worshiper; they believe that one should come away from worship with a "high," an exalted feeling resulting from some "mountaintop experience" in which the worshiper is transported spiritually to a plane of existence above and beyond our everyday mundane experiences. Still others feel that the purpose of worship is to help people become more conscious of their responsibility to live Christlike lives of service to other people.

While all these ideas about worship are certainly commendable, they do not focus on the central purpose and meaning of worship. In fact, *they misplace the emphasis of worship by focusing on the worshiper rather than on God*. Whatever happens to the worshiper in a service is a by-product. The main purpose of worship is not to produce a particular feeling or experience for the worshiper, regardless of how important such a result may be for the worshiper's own personal life. *The main purpose of worship is to praise and glorify God!* And true worship occurs when our attention and our efforts are focused on this goal. Ironically, all the good things that happen to us in worship occur most dramatically and most forcibly when we participate in a service that is directed toward proclaiming God's glory and greatness!

The word *worship* itself is an interesting word! And its history tells us a lot about the meaning and purpose of worship. According to the dictionary, the word *worship* comes from the Old English word *weorthscipe,* which we may translate into modern English as "worth-ship." In a properly focused worship service, what we do is to affirm God's "worth-ship" for our lives. We declare the value and meaning that God has for us!

In any worship service, there is, of course, a time for examining our own lives, for discovering how our lives could be changed and improved. But this worshiper-oriented aspect is secondary. And in order for it to occur in ways that are deep and lasting, it must happen in the context of an experience that focuses on the centrality of God in our lives!

The Components of a Worship Service.

Let's look at what happens in a typical worship service. Although most worship services have a dozen or so parts, there are five basic categories for describing the actions that occur in a typical service. It's easy to remember these five basic components of worship because they form an acronym A-C-T-E-D.

A—Adoration and praise of God.

Worship is first and primarily adoration and praise of God. Regardless of whatever personal agendas we may bring to worship, the main purpose of worship is to praise God. For this reason, we should always open a worship service by glorifying God. Usually, we begin with the minister or some other person calling the people to direct their attention to the value of God for their lives. Strictly speaking, this "call to worship" is not a part of the worship service itself, but rather a prologue to worship. In some churches, the musical prelude and the call to worship are listed separately at the beginning under a heading such as "The Service of Gathering."

The actual worship service itself really begins with the first statement of praise, usually a hymn, sometimes designated as "The Hymn of Praise." To emphasize the primary purpose of worship at the beginning of the service, we generally use a hymn such as "Holy! Holy! Holy!" or "Praise to the Living God," rather than hymns such as "Are Ye Able?" or "Onward, Christian Soldiers," which do not strongly emphasize the praise motif.

Figuratively speaking, worship has two primary focuses: the *vertical* and the *horizontal.* And we begin worship with the *vertical* focus, by symbolically looking upward to God and affirming the value of God for our lives.

How out of place it would be to begin worship with the sermon or a baptism or the offering! The mind balks at such suggestions—and rightly so! Somehow we realize that it would not be the thing to do! The first act in the drama of worship must be vertically oriented.

So we sing a song of praise. Then we perform other actions that affirm our

216

relationship to God. These actions may include an affirmation of faith, the responsive reading of a praise-oriented Psalm, or the singing of traditional canticles of praise, such as a doxology or the Gloria Patri. The important thing to remember about the opening actions of a worship service is that they should focus our minds on the adoration and praise of God!

C—Confession. Once we have declared our praise of God, we are ready for step two— confession. As we affirm God's value for our lives, we become conscious of our failure to keep our part of the covenant relationship that God has established with us. We realize that in many ways we have failed to do God's will and that we have done some things that are contrary to God's will. So we make a confession of our failures, and we ask for God's forgiveness.

Some Protestants are not comfortable with an act of confession. The act of confession is not to be seen as a personal put down, an act of groveling in the dust. Confession is not designed to produce guilt. On the contrary, confession is designed to remove guilt. Confession should be a liberating action that frees people from guilt by informing them that they are forgiven and accepted by God. For this reason, the words of forgiveness and pardon are very important; these words assure us that our confession is heard by God and that we are freed from guilt and enabled to lead new lives in Christ!

T—Thanksgiving. Having confessed our sins and failures and having realized that we are forgiven and accepted by God, we come naturally to the third part of the drama of worship—Thanksgiving. Whereas the first two categories were primarily vertically oriented, here the horizontal element is introduced. In the main act of thanksgiving,

for example, we bring our offering of money to the altar of God (a vertical focus), but we do so with the full realization that much of our offering will be used to help people in need (a horizontal focus).

Many parts of the service can be seen as acts of thanksgiving. Choral anthems and solos, for example, can be viewed as offerings of thanksgiving to God. This category can also include hymns of thanksgiving (like "Now Thank We All Our God") and musical offerings such as the doxology and the Gloria Patri. Also related to this category are announcements of opportunities for service and fellowship, since these activities constitute one of the main ways in which we do the work of the church—one of our offerings to God.

E—Education. A fourth category of worship actions is the category that includes our discussion of the ways in which the word of God relates to our lives. I refer to this category as Education. But it may also be designated by several other "E words": Enlightenment, Edification, Elucidation. This category is often called "The Service of the Word," since it includes worship actions that help us relate the Bible to our lives.

In most churches, the main actions under this category are the Scripture readings, a hymn of preparation, and the sermon. For many congregations, another important element in this category is the stating of concerns and celebrations, those aspects of people's lives that need to be looked at by the worshiping community.

Much of the focus of this category is horizontal, since the focus here is on how the word of God relates to people's lives. Nevertheless, the vertical aspect is still present, since the concerns of the worshipers are viewed in regard to the worshipers' relationships with God. This category could best be diagrammed as a triangle, since the people's relations with one another are always discussed in regard to their relation to God and the biblical word!

D—Dedication. The final category of worship actions is dedication. No worship service is complete without a response by the people. This response may take many forms. In some churches, it centers on an "altar call," by which the people are invited to come to the altar and renew their lives. In other traditions, it may consist of simply a hymn of dedication. In some congregations, there is also a responsive "act of dedication" by which the worship leader and the people affirm their renewed dedication. Also included in this category is the benediction or blessing, a prayer in which the worship leader and/or the people pray for God's blessing as they go forth to live their lives in the light of their renewed dedication. In this final category, the *horizontal* and *vertical* focuses of worship are both present, as the worship leader and the people dedicate themselves as a community to renewed emphasis of a particular aspect of their relationship with God.

These five categories often occur in the order in which they are found in the acronym: Adoration—Confession—Thanksgiving—Education—Dedication. I personally prefer to design worship services in this order—so as to keep the focuses of the worship actions clear-cut and easily recognizable. It is not necessary, however, to have the elements flow in this manner. These five types of components can be interspersed throughout the service in various combinations. Just be sure that whatever order you choose makes sense. The service should have an orderly, logical flow to it; and people should be aware of what they are doing and what their actions signify!

Liturgy. To conclude our discussion of the theology of worship, let's look at another important worship word. The word *liturgy* is usually used today as a general term designating the readings, prayers, hymns, and so forth, that constitute a particular worship service. But the word *liturgy*, like the word *worship*, has an interesting history that can teach us something very important about worship.

The word *liturgy* comes from the Greek word *litourgia*, which literally means "the work or service of the people." The term was originally used to refer to military service. Then it was broadened to refer to government service of any kind. Later, it was used to refer to the worship services of the church.

The basic meaning of the word *litourgia* gives us a hint as to how a worship service should be put together. In our modern world, because of all the time demands that people have, most worship services are designed by the clergy, people whose daily work includes planning worship. Whenever possible, however, it is a good idea to try to get back to the original process—to have worship designed and led by the people themselves. Worship is usually most meaningful when it is "the work of the people," when it expresses the concerns and celebrations that are a part of the people's everyday lives. As a worker with youth, you are in a unique position to plan worship services of this sort. You can work with the youth in your church to make sure that their own worship services grow out of their needs, interests, and ideas!

Learning About Worship

Many young people, like many adults, have very little knowledge of what worship is all about! The lack of knowledge was amply demonstrated to me in my first parish. On my first Sunday there, I attended the youth fellowship meeting, which was planned and led by a group of senior high youth and their adult advisors. Most of the evening's activities went quite well. There was a fellowship supper, followed by an interesting discussion session, a business meeting, and some recreation. When the time came for the closing worship service, we all trekked into the cold and dimly lit sanctuary where some of the youth and adults led us in a hymn, a scripture reading, a selection from the devotional magazine *The Upper Room*, and a benediction.

What was wrong with this service? It was not bad! It was just dull and unimaginative! And it had very little relationship to the youth and their everyday experiences. The youth squirmed and looked about nervously throughout this brief service. When it was over, they quickly exited, obviously glad to be through with what had been essentially a meaningless ritual!

But worship can be meaningful and exciting! It can have a magnetic force, drawing the worshipers into an experience that is related to their needs and interests. In order for such an event to occur, however, there must be diligent planning and thoughtful consideration of how the service will be put together. And before that planning process can occur, there must be some understanding of what worship is all about!

You may find it helpful to have the young people spend some time learning about worship. A three- or four-session seminar on the meaning of worship can be an excellent way to prepare the youth for the very involved process of planning and leading worship services. The following are some suggestions for activities that will deepen the young people's understanding of worship:

1. **Use a questionnaire** to help you discover how much the youth know about worship and how they feel about your church's (and your youth group's) worship services. Here is a sample questionnaire:

(1) The part(s) of our worship services that I like most is (are)_____
_____
_____
_____

(2) During our worship services, I personally feel_____
_____
_____
_____

(3) In my opinion, the purpose of worship is_____
_____
_____
_____

(4) The part(s) of our worship services that I dislike most is (are)_____
_____
_____
_____

(5) In my opinion, the music in our worship service is_____
_____
_____
_____

(6) I attend worship because_____
_____
_____
_____

(7) I think that our worship services could be improved by _____
_____
_____
_____

(8) In my opinion, the sermons that are preached in our worship service are ___
_____
_____
_____

(9) Our worship services are (are not) relevant to my everyday life because ___
_____
_____
_____

2. **Secure several copies of a worship bulletin used in a recent service in your church.** Discuss with the youth the main ideas in the above section "A Basic Theology of Worship." Then, using the acronym A-C-T-E-D discussed in that section, have the youth go through the worship bulletin and identify elements that may be classified as Adoration, Confession, Thanksgiving, Education, and Dedication. Try to reach a group consensus on the categories to which the various parts of the service belong.

3. **Have the youth write their own prayers for use in worship.** Explain the elements that are often included in prayers: praise of God; confession of sins and failures; thanksgiving to God for personal and/or group blessings; concern for one's own needs (petition); concern for the needs of others (intercession); requests for God's guidance; requests for renewed dedication to the Christian life. Then have the youth work as individuals or in small groups (2-9 people) to write prayers in their own words.

It may be helpful to have the youth examine several published prayers in order to get further ideas. Several collections of prayers for personal devotionals and public worship are suggested in the final chapter of this handbook.

4. **Have the youth write their own creeds.** Begin by discussing what the youth themselves believe about these subjects (and others that you may wish to add): God, Jesus, the Holy Spirit, the church, heaven, hell, sin, salvation, the Christian life, the Christian's responsibility toward other people. Then have the youth work in small groups (2-9 people) to write their own statements of belief.

If additional help is needed, have the youth read through some of the traditional creeds of the church. Make it clear that such an activity is being done to give them a feel for how creeds are put together. Your ultimate goal should be to have the youth express their own beliefs in words that they feel comfortable with!

5. **Have the youth select some standard hymns from your church's hymnal for use with each of the five categories discussed above.** For help with this activity, use your hymnal's topical index, a handy reference tool found in most standard hymnals.

6. **Have the youth select folk hymns for use with each of the five categories.** Many excellent songs of this type can be found in the following collections: *Songbook for Saints and Sinners, The Genesis Songbook, The Young Life Songbook,* and *The Avery and Marsh Songbook.* Be sure to check these collections for topical indexes, which will help you in this activity. For more information on folk hymnals, see the chapter "Music! Music! Music!"

7. **Have the youth write new words to some of the standard hymn tunes in your**

church's hymnal; and/or have them choose a song that is currently popular and write new words that could be used in a worship service. For more information on this type of activity, see our chapter entitled "Music! Music! Music!"

8. **Have the youth paraphrase one or more of the Psalms in their own words.** Encourage them to use modern words and images and to relate the Psalms to their own everyday experiences. Good choices for this activity are Psalms 1, 8, 14, 23, 27, 51, 90, 100, 121, 133, 149, and 150.

9. **Have the youth select and read scripture passages from some of the more readable versions of the Bible.** I especially recommend the translation entitled *Good News for Modern Man* (also called *Today's English Version*) and Clarence Jordan's very imaginative paraphrases in the *Cotton Patch Version*.

10. **Have several young people prepare and deliver brief sermons on subjects that interest them.** Use a concordance or a topical index to the Bible to help the youth select scripture passages that relate to their ideas.

11. **Have the youth make banners for worship.** Banners may be made from felt, burlap, or other kinds of heavy cloth. Lettering and symbols can be cut from cloth and either sewed or glued to the banners. For many imaginative ideas on banner making, consult Betty Wolfe's work *The Banner Book.*

12. **Have the youth make slides and use them as the visual part of a slide-and-music presentation expressing aspects of the Christian faith.** Information on slide making and slide-and-music presentations may be found in the chapter on "Media" in this handbook and in many of the resources listed under the media section in our final chapter.

13. **Have the youth spend some time getting better acquainted with your church's hymnal.** Several suggestions for activities of this type are given in our chapter entitled "Music! Music! Music!"

14. **Help your young people learn more about the Christian year.** Even if your denomination does not observe the liturgical year, there is much to be gained by learning how the church has traditionally organized its worship around the various church seasons. Youth and adults should have a basic knowledge of such seasons as Advent, Christmastide, Lent, Eastertide, and Pentecost and some understanding of why different colors are used during the various seasons. If you need help with this activity, consult a reference book from your church or local library, or ask your minister to help you with your preparation.

Preparing and Leading Worship Services

In my own denomination, and in many other denominations, youth are considered full laity! With all the forward strides that have been made in the area of youth rights, many churches no longer view youth as junior members; instead, young people are increasingly being recognized as full members of churches, with the right to serve on church committees and have a voice in church affairs. Unfortunately, one area in which youth and even adult lay people often do not have the right of full participation is the area of worship!

Even in the matter of worship, however, there is much more openness than there used to be in regard to youth participation.

And I believe that, as youth workers, it is our responsibility to push for even greater involvement of youth in planning and leading the worship of the church!

Youth can assume many roles in the week-to-week worship life of the church. They can serve as lay readers and as ushers. They can serve as liturgists, actually leading the worship services. And at times they can be responsible for giving sermons. On some occasions during each year, the youth should also be given the privilege and responsibility of planning and leading entire services! I firmly believe that if you work with your youth by using some of the suggestions given above, the youth of your church can do a very creditable job of leading not only your youth group but also the congregation at large, in meaningful worship experiences!

Where do you start? Well, you start by choosing a time slot for your youth-led service. And then you negotiate with the powers-that-be in your church in order to secure permission for the youth to be in charge of a service. Getting such permission is usually not a difficult matter. Most churches and pastors will readily consent to having a "Youth Sunday," during which the entire service is led by the youth. You may also discover, as I have, that your church is open to having the youth lead the worship on special occasions. I have had especially good luck at lining up youth-led services on such occasions as Wednesday evening services during Lent, an evening service on Good Friday, an Easter sunrise service, special services during Advent, and Sunday morning services during slack periods (that usually means the summer months). Try some of these suggestions for starters, and then ask for permission to lead some regular Sunday morning services during the main part of the church year!

Once you have lined up an occasion for a youth-led service, you are ready to get to work! Review with the youth the main parts of a worship service. Then work with the youth to choose a theme for the service. Next, choose music and other service elements that relate to your theme. If possible, have the youth write some parts of the liturgy themselves. Then arrange the elements of the service in such a way as to insure a logical, meaningful order of service. Finally, *practice!* Go over the service several times, preferably in the sanctuary of the church. Be sure that you and some of the youth spend time sitting in the pews and listening so that you may advise the worship leaders concerning diction, pacing, gestures, projection, and so forth.

You may want to make the service entirely innovative. But I suspect that you will discover, as I have, that the best approach is one that combines the old with the new. Whatever approach you take, the service should feel natural to the youth; it should utilize prayers, music, and readings with which they are comfortable!

As an example of a youth-led, multi-media service—a service that combines the old with the new by using such varied forms as standard hymns, pop music, folk hymns, movies, slide-and-music presentations, and modern dance—here is the outline for a service that a youth group prepared for a Good Friday worship experience.

222

THE CRUCIFIXION: THEN AND NOW
*A Multi-Media Worship Experience
for Good Friday*

Prelude
"Kyrie Eleison" from *Mass in F Minor* by the Electric Prunes
(recorded music with modern dance interpretation)

Hymn: "Were You There?"

Scripture: Matthew 26:36-46 *(New English Bible)*

Slide-and-Music Presentation
"Gethsemane" from *Jesus Christ Superstar* (slides showing examples of oppression in modern society)

The Trial of Jesus—an excerpt from the play *Christ in the Concrete City*

Scenes from Then and Now
A simultaneous projection of two movies without sound: one showing stills of great paintings depicting the life of Jesus; one showing scenes of violence in today's world. Background music: "Silent Night/Seven O'Clock News" by Simon and Garfunkel

The Crucifixion
A live reading of Mark 15:16-39 from *Today's English Version*. Background music: "The Carriage of the Cross" from the soundtrack to the movie *The Robe*. Visual:

a slide of Jesus on the cross projected onto the cross at the front of the sanctuary.

The Prayer of Confession and the Words of Forgiveness and Pardon
(words written by the youth, with the prayer of confession containing references to ways in which people are oppressed in today's society)

Hymn: "What Wondrous Love Is This?"

The Prayer for New Life
(words written by the youth)

The Litany of Silence: A Period of Individual Meditation

The Dance of Silence
(recorded music: "The Sounds of Silence" by Simon and Garfunkel with modern dance interpretation)

Hymn: "The Lord of the Dance"

The Going Forth
(a responsive act of dedication with words written by the youth. Recorded music for going forth: "Fantasia on a Theme of Thomas Tallis," by Ralph Vaughan-Williams)

As you can see from the above outline, this service does not follow all the rules for designing worship services. For one thing, the service does not start with a hymn of praise. The praise element occurs at various points in the service—most noticeably in the final hymn. Also, there is no act of thanksgiving in the usual sense. But these changes from usual worship practices were made intentionally and, more importantly, *they were made with the full knowledge of how things are ordinarily done!* Rules are fine! But there is some truth to the adage that rules are sometimes made to be broken!

223

This service, which is a special service of penitence and self-examination, omits the hymn of praise at the beginning, because the youth preparing the service wanted to establish the vertical relationship in a different way—by affirming at the outset the sacrificial nature of God's relationship with us! Also, the mood of the service is meant to be more somber than that of a typical service, which would ordinarily start with a joyous hymn of praise!

You should feel the same kind of freedom in planning your services! The important thing is to know what the traditional worship practices are in order to be able to change the traditional on the basis of good, well-thought out reasons! Innovation based on knowledge and good, sound reasoning—this is the key to creating new and meaningful worship experiences!

A Final Word

Don't assume, on the basis of an example such as the service outlined above, that every youth-led service has to be a big production! You can make your service as simple or as complicated as you wish! There is room for innovative thinking even when one is planning a ten-minute devotional service for a Sunday evening youth fellowship meeting. Just give careful consideration to what you are doing. Give some thought to the purpose of worship. And give a lot of thought to the purpose of each part of your service. Choose words, music, media, and so forth, that will present the theme of your service in an interesting and meaningful way.

And remember: as we said at the beginning of this chapter, the main purpose of worship is to glorify God! In order for our worship to be innovative rather than just gimmicky, in order for our worship to be an in-depth experience rather than just a happening, we must always plan and act in such a way as to make ourselves more aware of the value that God has for our lives!

Increasing numbers of youth groups have one or more overnight events each year. Overnights that are held in the local church with young people bringing sleeping bags (or not sleeping at all!) are generally called lock-ins or mini-retreats. Retreats at lodge or camp facilities involve more elaborate preparation and may be one, two, or even three nights in length. Camps are usually held in the summer, are five or more days in length, and are often sponsored cooperatively by several churches. Some churches sponsor trips that are even longer than a camp experience.

All these events involve more expense, time commitment, adult help, and planning than most youth activities. However, these longer blocks of time offer several important benefits:

1. **Spending extended periods of time together improves relationships in a group.** This kind of experience may be especially valuable near the beginning of a group's life. If your youth activities run parallel to the school year, a fall retreat will build a sense of community that will continue through the year. Short term, special interest groups will develop a sense of community much earlier if members share in a lock-in or retreat.

2. **Longer blocks of time make some activities possible that Sunday morning church school and regular evening meetings do not permit.** Many simulation games, elaborate art or media projects, and extended consideration of some themes can best be done in a lock-in, retreat, or camp setting.

3. **The passage of time (at least a week) between regular meetings of classes or groups causes loss of impact and continuity.** Most young people and many advisors have difficulty remembering the content of the previous week's discussion. Longer blocks of time together greatly increase the sense of continuity and the impact of experiences.

4. **If previously inactive young people can be encouraged to attend a lock-in or retreat, they will have enough time to gain some acceptance into the group and are more likely to return to subsequent activities.**

5. **The change in setting opens people to new possibilities.** Free time provides opportunities for personal reflection, interpersonal sharing, and private meditation which most young people and adults miss in the rush of daily life. Concentration on a particular theme encourages intensive thinking and personal reflection. Perhaps most important, the total experience encourages an openness to the presence of God that is deeper and more intentional than normally experienced.

Purpose, Theme, and Planning

In planning overnight experiences, youth classes or groups can easily fall into the trap of simply filling blocks of time with games, videos, worship, or study. While such overnights will still produce an improved sense of community, the experience can be greatly improved by a unifying theme and clear goals. The activities selected and time blocks used should grow out of the theme and goals for the event.

The planning committee for an overnight event does not have to be large but should include at least two young people and an adult. It may be helpful to check off the following questions as you plan:

_____ 1.   What are the purposes of the event? Possibilities include building community, learning more about a topic of interest to the group, introducing a short-term group to a theme, doing a work or service project, planning the year's activities, preparing a multi-media presentation.

____ 2. What theme is both attention getting and an honest expression of your purpose?

____ 3. Who is to come? Are guests to be invited?

____ 4. Who will be responsible for recruiting an adequate number of chaperons?

____ 5. Where will the event be held? What are the charges for the facilities? Who will reserve the facilities? If it is to be at a retreat or camp setting, you may need to make reservations several months in advance. Even if you are just having an overnight in the church, you should check with your minister or church office to reserve the church and to be sure you will not be in conflict with anyone else. Some churches are reluctant to permit a lock-in on Friday night if a wedding or other major event requiring an unusually clean church is scheduled on Saturday.

____ 6. What are the exact dates and times for the event? These need to be determined almost simultaneously with the selection of the location. If you are traveling to a retreat or camp site, when will you need to leave and when will you be back?

____ 7. What will you have for meals and snacks? Who will purchase the food? Who will prepare it? If you are going to a lodge, there may be a staff there who will prepare meals and snacks, but you will still need to communicate with them about choices available (if any). Some facilities will insist on providing all food, including snacks; others would prefer that you bring your own snacks. What will the cost of meals and snacks be? If you will be purchasing groceries, an experienced parent may be able to help you estimate the cost. Are meal and snack times fixed, or can you be flexible?

____ 8. What activities will help accomplish your purposes and theme? Is there a resource book or curriculum unit that relates to your theme and from which you could select activities? You may want to consider such activities as: Bible study, values clarification, role playing, artistic expression, simulation games, sensitivity exercises, slide making, videos, and discussion groups.

As you think about possible activities, begin to develop a tentative schedule for those experiences. Remember that a group may willingly spend a long amount of time on activities such as simulation games, slide making, and artistic expression because these involve change of pace and opportunity to move about. Most groups will not profitably work more than 60-75 minutes on heavy discussion or study. Who will be responsible for leading these activities?

226

____ 9. What kind(s) of worship experience(s) do you want to provide? At a lock-in, you will probably want only one major worship service, but at a retreat or camp, you may want several. You will want to consider worship activities that represent a change from traditional Sunday morning services. You may want to use folk hymns rather than more traditional ones, and your worship will probably be very informal. You may also want to substitute a media experience (slides made by the participants or a short video) or a discussion for the sermon. Who will provide leadership for worship? Who will provide the music? If you want to share communion, can a minister be present to consecrate and serve the elements (most denominations permit only the minister to serve communion)? Will any guests from other denominations be present who might be unable to share in communion? How can worship be related to your theme?

____ 10. In what recreational/social activities would you like the entire group to participate? Possibilities could include: volleyball, a haunted house, dancing, swimming. Who will be responsible for these? What activities are most appropriate in terms of your theme?

____ 11. What options are available to people during free time? You do not want to structure every minute of the overnight. Considerable value comes in providing time for personal meditation, informal discussion, and recreation. Be certain that music, table games, or other options are available. If you fail to provide any options for the use of this time, you can be sure that enterprising individuals will find something to do. Unfortunately, you may not approve of it.

____ 12. What will be the time schedule for the event? You were asked to think about a tentative schedule as you selected activities. Now put together meals, snacks, learning/study activities, worship, recreational/social activities, free time, breaks, and sleeping hours into a careful schedule. You may have to change some activities and eliminate others to stay within the available time.

____ 13. Who will order or obtain the needed materials such as curriculum books, films or videos, projection equipment, stereo, records, table games?

____ 14. What will be the total cost of the retreat including lodging, food, curriculum, film or video rental, recreational equipment or fees? Is the church helping any with this expense? How much will you need to charge each person coming?

____ 15. What optional/alternative activities should you have in case changing weather or the failure of some materials to arrive upsets your plans?

227

____16. What kinds of publicity will you use? You can use phone calls, letters, group announcements, newspaper or radio advertising, and other means. Are your publicity plans clear about the cost of the event, what people should bring, how transportation will be handled, what will happen at the overnight, when reservations are needed and to whom to send them, dates and times of the experience? Does your publicity adequately communicate any restrictions on who may come?

____17. If you are going to a retreat or camp setting, do you want to pool rides?

____18. What can be done to help a group member or interested person attend who does not have enough money? Can your group treasury or the church help? Your minister may be able to give you the names of adults who would help.

____19. What rules or expectations are necessary for the event? Who will be responsible for sharing them? for enforcing them? Do any of these rules or expectations need to be communicated before the overnight?

____20. If the experience will be at some distance from your local church, do you need emergency medical treatment permission from parents? Many states require that retreat or camp directors have such an authorization in writing, or medical officials may not be permitted (or willing) to provide emergency treatment. Check with an attorney if you are in doubt. A form such as this may be adequate.

PERMISSION FOR MEDICAL TREATMENT

I give permission for my son/daughter to attend the retreat. I further grant permission for a licensed physician, chosen by the retreat director, to perform emergency medical treatment including X-rays, the prescription of drugs, or surgery for my son/ daughter. I will assume liability for any resulting expense not covered by insurance.

_____   _____
(date)   (parent or guardian)

Lock-ins or Mini-Retreats

Lock-ins or mini-retreats have grown in popularity in many parts of the country. They are generally held in a local church, begin between 6 p.m. and 10 p.m. in the evening, and end between 7 a.m. and 10 a.m.

the following morning. Young people sleep on the floor in sleeping bags. Since lock-ins are held in the church itself and food is purchased and prepared by the young people (with some adult guidance or help), the cost is much lower than a retreat held at a lodge setting. Since activities may begin late at night and finish early in the morning, they are not in conflict with many school, community, or work activities. They are primarily in conflict with sleep! Several special factors are important for a successful lock-in:

1. **Don't be overly concerned about the sleep young people are missing.** Some sleeping time should be scheduled and enforced for junior highs, since they do tire more quickly than senior highs and become irritable and unpleasant when exhausted. However, a few hours of sleep is adequate for most junior highs; and you will have greater success enforcing a sleeping period if it is not overly long and begins after several hours of activity.

Most senior highs will not be harmed by staying up one night. If sleeping time is scheduled and enforced at a senior high lock-in, you will often encounter massive resistance if not outright refusal. If you make sleep optional and simply enforce quiet in two sleeping areas (fellows and gals in separate areas!), those who have busy days coming will be able to slip away from the group and sleep.

You need to be gentle but firm about the requirement of sleep for junior highs and the requirement of quiet sleeping areas (for those who want to sleep) for senior highs. If you find that your junior highs simply refuse to sleep no matter what you do or if parents demand that all senior highs sleep some, forget the preceding advice and live with the realities of your situation.

Some local churches have males and females sleep in the same room. While there is nothing wrong with this (if properly supervised), many parents are uncomfortable with the practice. I recommend using separate rooms.

2. **Be very clear about the rules or expectations governing the lock-in.** These should be developed by the planning committee or the youth group as a whole, but there are some areas that must be covered:

- What time will the doors be locked? Under what circumstances if any, can people enter or leave the church after that time? If this is not clearly understood, some young people may be tempted to stay out extremely late on a date while their parents assume they are in the church.

- Who can come to the lock-in? In a small rural community, you may be willing to accept any young people who want to come even if they are not specifically guests of someone in your group. In most urban areas, you will need to require that no one come unless invited by a group member. You should also be clear about the age of guests and the number of guests that any single person may bring. Do not permit senior highs to attend a junior high lock-in or junior highs to attend a senior high lock-in, unless your class or group normally combines those ages. People out of high school should not be permitted unless they are present as invited chaperons.

- What areas of the church are "off limits"? Many church buildings are too large for it to be advisable to let people roam anywhere they wish. The sanctuary should be off limits unless you are having a worship service there or unless it has been designed for multipurpose use. Congregations react badly to orange soda spots on the carpet, potato chips in the pews, and misplaced hymnals. If you are using the church school classrooms for activity groups, discussion groups, or sleeping areas, be sure that ongoing projects and displays are not disturbed.

• Where are the sleeping areas?

• In what areas is food permitted?

• Will smoking be permitted in any area? If so, where? A personal comment: I dislike letting junior or senior highs smoke. I avoid giving permission to smoke to junior highs since many have not established the habit yet. I don't want them to learn it at a church event. If several senior highs have already established the habit, it may be better to designate a smoking area than to play police officer in the restrooms all evening. You will need to visit with your minister about this. Obviously, drugs and alcohol are prohibited.

• What will be the consequences of serious misbehavior? The most natural ones are refusing permission to attend future lock-ins or calling the parents of the offender. Do not threaten such action unless you are willing to carry it out.

If someone does push too far too often, calling that person's parents and having them take their son or daughter home is very effective. Most parents, if awakened at 2 a.m. or 3 a.m., will be sufficiently angry that young people do not want to risk that fate.

3. **Overplan the evening!** Do not take a chance on running out of activities and having free time with nothing to do. Bored young people can invent many activities which you and other adults will not appreciate. You should provide free time, but always have games or other activities available during those times.

4. **Allow adequate time and people-power for good cleanup of the church.** You not only want to leave the church as clean and orderly as you found it—you want to leave it cleaner, if possible! Dust, straighten, sweep the floor, mop any area where food or drink has been spilled, replace paper towels and toilet paper in the restrooms, wash all kitchen counters and tables where food has been prepared or served. A committee should be designated for this purpose, but everyone should help by not being unnecessarily messy.

Even if your church has an employed custodian, you should be sure the young people do most of the work so that the custodian does not resent their presence and so that they learn responsible stewardship of church property. Since the custodian inevitably has to do a little extra straightening following a lock-in, consider giving him or her a small donation.

A couple of sample schedules may be helpful to you in planning lock-ins of your own. The following schedule is for a junior high lock-in on the theme "Halloween, the Occult, and the Bible." It was done on the Friday evening of the weekend before Halloween, and those who wished were encouraged to wear masks.

JUNIOR HIGH LOCK-IN

7:30 p.m.-8:00 p.m.	**Arrival and Registration** Put sleeping bags in designated areas Informal games
8:00 p.m.-9:00 p.m.	**1st Session** Share rules/expectations for the evening Introduction to the theme Values clarification exercise on heaven, hell, the devil, and spiritualism Directed Bible study on the above terms
9:00 p.m.-9:15 p.m.	**Short Break** Munchables (popcorn, chips) and cider
9:15 p.m.-10:15 p.m.	**2nd Session** Do telepathy and other ESP experiments Look at horoscopes Discuss the difference between prediction and prophecy

10:15 p.m.-11:30 p.m.	**Break**
	Late night supper:
	    Make-your-own sandwiches
	    Chips and dip
	    Cookies
	    Soft drinks
	Trips through a spook house
	Informal games

11:30 p.m.-12:30 a.m.	**3rd Session** Artistic expression on the heavens and hells of this life Sharing of projects and discussion
12:30 a.m.-1:00 a.m.	**Break** Apple-bobbing Informal games
1:00 a.m.-1:30 a.m.	**Devotions**
1:30 a.m.-7:30 a.m.	**Sleep!**

7:30 a.m.-8:30 a.m.	**Rise and Shine** Donuts, juice, and milk Cleanup
8:30 a.m.-9:00 a.m.	**Evaluation and Morning Devotions**

If you are interested in having a lock-in on a similar theme, you may want to consult Elinor Horwitz's *The Soothsayer's Handbook—A Guide to Bad Signs and Good Vibrations.* It includes ESP experiments, astrology background, and other helpful information. You can find good articles on many areas of the occult and on prophecy in *The Interpreter's Dictionary of the Bible.* Most denominations have one or more curriculum units on prophecy.

The "spook house" was set up in a basement area. People were taken through in small groups after being "taken prisoner" by witches. They were blindfolded and had their hands loosely tied before entering the house. The witches told an appropriately gruesome story and let people feel the remains of past victims (peeled grapes, raw liver, cow brains, and the joint of a cow leg—all available from the local grocer). Rattling chains and chilling moans were played over a tape recorder. Before leaving the spook house, each group was required to answer questions about Biblical prophets. They did not do well with the questions but did enjoy the spook house.

The next schedule was developed for a senior high lock-in on the theme "Death and Dying in Christian Perspective."

SENIOR HIGH LOCK-IN

8:00 p.m.-8:30 p.m.	**Arrival and Registration** Music Informal games
8:30 p.m.-9:30 p.m.	**1st Session** Share rules/expectations for the evening Values clarification exercise on death Small-group discussion of the exercise
9:30 p.m.-9:45 p.m.	**Short Break** Munchables (popcorn, chips) and soft drinks
9:45 p.m.-10:45 p.m.	**2nd Session** Film: "Though I Walk Through the Valley" Small group discussion of the film

10:45 p.m.-11:45 p.m.	**Break**
	Make pizzas and salad
	Late night supper:
	pizza
	salad
	soft drinks
	Music
	Informal games

| 11:45 p.m.-12:30 a.m. | **Small Group Bible Study of 2 Corinthians 15** |
| | Sharing of other concerns |

| 12:30 a.m.-12:45 a.m. | **Short Break** |

12:45 a.m.-1:30 a.m.	**Worship**
	Singing
	Shared prayer
	Brief meditation
	Communion

| 1:30 a.m.- 3:30 a.m. | **Choose:** Feature film or sleep |

3:30 a.m.-7:30 a.m.	**Choose:**
	Sleep
	Continue discussion on death
	Music area
	Table game area
	Artistic expression area

7:30 a.m.-8:30 a.m.	**Everyone Up!**
	Breakfast: pancakes, juice, milk
	Cleanup

| 8:30 a.m.-9:00 a.m. | **Evaluation and Morning Devotions** |

Some churches that have experienced serious conflicts with many youth activities have begun using a monthly lock-in to pull together all the young people connected with the church. With good adult guidance and careful planning, lock-ins can be extremely effective. Other lock-in themes could include:

- New Year's Eve Party and Covenant Service
- Program Planning for the Year
- Film Festival

- Work Night: Painting a Room in the Church
- Group Building
- World Hunger (Have a planned famine; see the "Resources" chapter)
- Focus on a Biblical Theme

Retreats

Retreats differ from lock-ins or mini-retreats in length and location. They are, by nature, more expensive because of transportation, rental expense, and length. The change in setting and longer period of time provide some advantages over lock-ins. Some additional factors should be considered in planning a retreat:

1. **In most areas, you will find it necessary to reserve a retreat facility several months in advance.** Before doing so, consult the church, school, and community calendars. You don't want your attendance to be low because of predictable conflicts.

Do not plan a retreat in conflict with a major youth choir event or a school basketball tournament.

2. **Be sure that you understand the rules and costs of the facilities you will be using.** You will want to make the site rules and any additional rules of the planning committee clear to everyone. Cover such concerns as to how far people may wander and explore outdoors, whether smoking will be permitted, and when sleep is required. At a retreat, it is important that everyone sleep well so that getting up and staying awake the next day is not difficult. People need more sleep during a 48-hour retreat than a 12-hour lock-in.

3. **Arrange car pools for transportation to the site to save expense and inconvenience.**

4. **In your budget, include reimbursement to chaperons for their lodging, food, and transportation expenses.**

CONFIRMATION RETREAT

The following schedule was developed for a confirmation class retreat near the beginning of the year's instruction. The retreat was intended to help the young people grow closer as a group and learn more about the Bible. The biblical background and exercises come from my

books *Major Issues and the Bible* and *The Bible Game Collection*. The minister was present for all the retreat except Sunday morning. The young people were all junior highs. Each "small group" consisted of one adult and four or five young people.

FRIDAY EVENING

8:00 p.m.–8:30 p.m.	**Arrival and Registration** Put belongings in sleeping areas
8:30 p.m.–9:45 p.m.	**1st Session** Ground rules for the weekend Read 1 Corinthians 12 Brief input on goals for the weekend Small groups complete and discuss the "Biblical Overview" puzzle from *The Bible Game Collection* (*BGC*).
9:45 p.m.–10:30 p.m.	**Free Time** Snacks: popcorn, apples, cider
10:30 p.m.–11:15 p.m.	**2nd Session** Two adults give brief (5 minutes each) input on how the Bible has helped them in their daily lives. Small groups make posters or collages about the Bible and daily life
11:15 p.m.–11:45 p.m.	**Evening Devotions**
11:45 p.m.–12:00 a.m.	**Break**
12:00 a.m.	**Bed? Lights Out!**

SATURDAY

7:00 a.m.–8:00 a.m.	**Everyone Up!** Showers, etc.
8:00 a.m.–8:30 a.m.	**Breakfast**
8:30 a.m.–9:00 a.m.	**Free Time**
9:00 a.m.–9:45 a.m.	**Third Session** "The Mighty Carnack" on the Bible, based on "An Overview of the Bible" in *Major Issues and the Bible*. Information presented to the group about the major divisions of the Bible.

9:45 a.m.–10:00 a.m.	**Break**
10:00 a.m.–10:45 a.m.	**4th Session** Small groups complete and discuss "The Old Testament" puzzle from *BGC.*
10:45 a.m.–11:00 a.m.	**Break**
11:00 a.m.–12:00 p.m.	**5th Session** Small-group members take a trust walk in pairs: each person experiences being led while blindfolded. Discussion on the need for trust in the class and in life; our ability to trust God. Look at Psalm 37:3–6 and Luke 8:22–25.
12:00 a.m.–12:30 p.m.	**Lunch**
12:30 p.m.–3 p.m.	**Free Time** Activities available: Music Informal visiting Planned games Do school work Hiking Nap Personal meditation
3 p.m.–4:30 p.m.	**6th Session** Ministerial input on the early church and 1 Corinthians 12. Small groups make posters or collages based on 1 Corinthians 12 and discuss their work.
4:30 p.m.–5:30 p.m.	**Free Time**
5:30 p.m.–6:30 p.m.	**Supper** Singing
6:30 p.m.–7:30 p.m.	**Organized Games**
7:30 p.m.–8:15 p.m.	**7th Session** Small groups complete and discuss "The New Testament" puzzle from *BGC.*

8:15 p.m.–8:30 p.m.	**Break**
8:30 p.m.–10:30 p.m.	**Feature Film** (*E.T.* video) Popcorn and soft drinks
10:30 p.m.–10:45 p.m.	**Break**
10:45 p.m.–11:45 p.m.	**Worship** Singing 1 Corinthians 13 Sharing of appreciation for one another Communion
11:45 p.m.–12:00 a.m.	**Break**
12:00 a.m.	**Bed! Lights Out!**

SUNDAY

7:00 a.m.–8:00 a.m.	**Everyone Up!** Showers, etc.
8:00 a.m.–8:30 a.m.	**Breakfast**
8:30 a.m.–9:00 a.m.	**Free Time**
9:00 a.m.–10:00 a.m.	**8th Session** Small groups play "The Bible Game" from *BGC*
10:00 a.m.–10:30 a.m.	**Free Time**
10:30 a.m.–11:30 a.m.	**Break**
12:00 p.m.–12:30 p.m.	**Lunch**
12:30 p.m.–2:00 p.m.	**Free Time** Activities available as on Saturday
2:00 p.m.–2:30 p.m.	**9th Session** Small groups evaluate the retreat experience
2:30 p.m.–3:15 p.m.	**Closing** (cleanup and load cars)

3:15 p.m.–3:30 p.m.   **Closing devotions**

3:30 p.m.   **Homeward bound!**

Camps

Some people would define a camp as a "long retreat." Camps are commonly five days or longer, are held at a location away from the local church, and are generally in the summer season. Most church camps are offered on a denominational basis and may involve young people and counselors from many local churches. You can, however, reserve facilities for a local church camp. This extended time has some exciting possibilities for a youth group.

Many senior high groups take summer trips to places of religious or historical significance as an alternative to a traditional summer camp. Such trips may involve significant work at a mission site. Since most groups will have to choose between taking a trip and having or attending a camp, it is important to note some of the differences between these experiences.

1. **Most trips are more expensive than residential camps because of the added expense of transportation.** The transportation itself may be difficult to arrange since you need drivers and cars for several days or the use of a bus or van. Unless you do your own cooking, meals purchased en route will be more expensive than those at a residential camp.

2. **Trips are heavily focused on seeing places of interest or on doing work projects.** Camps are more focused on relationship building and personal growth. Trip experiences always result in improved relationships and personal growth, but those are by-products rather than the main experience. You and the youth group need to determine your primary purpose for a week-long summer activity: giving service through work on a mission project; providing an enrichment and learning experience in another part of the country; or having opportunity for personal growth and study.

3. **While most summer trips are made by a single youth group or by two neighboring groups, many denominational camps involve interaction by young people from many local churches.** The interaction with new friends has value that is often overlooked. Denominational camps may also be offered throughout the summer so that your young people do not have to be free the same week in order to attend.

If you are planning a camp at a residential site, you will find the information previously in this chapter under "Purpose, Theme, and Planning" and "Retreats" of significant help. There are some additional considerations in planning an event as lengthy as a camp.

1. **Unless you have extremely creative leaders working with you, the selection of a resource book or study book may be crucial to the success of the camp.** Providing meaningful and worthwhile experiences for the number of hours involved at a camp is difficult unless good guidance is available.

2. **It is critical that adults who will be serving as counselors for the camp spend adequate time in planning and sharing *before* the camp begins.** Most good denominational camps require a weekend of

238

intensive orientation for all counselors. If those who will be counseling at your camp live in close proximity or belong to your church, you may be able to provide much of this preparation during the winter months.

3. **All counselors should become familiar with the camp site itself.** What areas may be explored? What wildlife can be observed? What evidence is there of erosion or other environmental problems? In what ways can campers learn through their environment?

4. **Counselors should be chosen with particular care.** There is no "free time" for a counselor at camp. You need people who are mature enough to make a total commitment of themselves for the week and who like young people well enough to enjoy the experience.

5. **A good night's sleep becomes very important in an experience as long as a camp.** Many young people enjoy "raids" between cabins in the middle of the night. Raids consist of running through another group's cabin while shouting, screaming, or singing. This may involve stealing underwear (if any is lying around) and throwing water on people who are sleeping. Raids are fun—but they are also dangerous since people can easily be hurt running in the dark, and scuffles may develop between the "raiders" and the "raidees." Protect everyone's rest and safety by discouraging raids. If they become a problem, visit with the young people about the potential danger involved.

6. **In most climates, study and work experiences should be concentrated in the morning and evening, with swimming, rest, and related activities during the afternoon hours.** Strenuous games should not be done during the hottest period of the day.

7. **Most study activities should be done in small groups for maximum sharing.** Ideally, these groups should include a counselor and five or six young people.

8. **Be sure to provide snacks each evening.** Young people burn up a lot of calories at camp, and the time between supper and breakfast is too long without a snack.

9. **Plan a wide variety of total-camp worship and recreational experiences.** While maximum learning comes in small groups, campers need the interaction and stimulation of total camp activities.

10. **As with any experience, rules and expectations should be carefully explained.** Be certain the young people know the geographical boundaries of the camp and any rules that are particular to that site.

11. **If you are having camp at a location that expects you to do your own cooking, you should recruit some adults specifically for that purpose.** Expecting the same people to serve as counselors and cooks is presumptuous. You can't watch the stove and the campers at the same time!

12. **You may want to do one or more cookouts during the week.** If the setting is an especially rustic one, you may do all your meals in this way. Be sure to have at least one adult present who has had experience in campfire cooking, and provide time *before* the camp begins for that individual to give orientation to other adults. The bibliography suggests some books that give good instructions and tested recipes for outdoor cooking.

13. **Have as many evening campfires as possible!** Young people love the informality of worship around a campfire, and this may

be part of the magic of camp. Always be sure the fire is properly extinguished or isolated from combustible materials before going to bed, or the magic of the evening may become the destruction of the camp.

14. **If you are planning a camp cooperatively with one or more local churches, involve adults and young people from those churches in the planning process from the beginning.** Do not make detailed plans and then expect them to become excited about your plans.

15. **Your involvement as an adult may be as director, dean, or counselor for a camp planned at the denominational level rather than by your own youth group.** If this is the case and some from your youth group are attending, be careful to involve them in interaction with those from other churches. Many new friendships are made at this kind of camp, and young people may be more open to visiting with people they do not interact with on a daily basis during the year.

JUNIOR HIGH CHURCH CAMP

The following plans were for a local church camp for 22 junior highs on the theme "Creative Expression of Yourself and Your Faith." Sixteen of the junior highs were from that church and six were guests. Four adults served as counselors. One was a college student majoring in art who helped the other counselors with some technical matters. All the projects were relatively simple. The Bible study time focused on John M. Winn's *The Rhythm of Renewal: The Bible in the Life of Devotion. Sing and Celebrate* was used as a song book. We had the use of six cabins at a large campsite. Four cabins were used for sleeping, and two were rearranged for projects. Another camp was in progress the same week; except for cookouts, we ate meals at the same time in the camp dining hall. Since the other campers were elementary level, we did not attempt any shared activities with them except meals.

The basic rules of the week were:

1. All scheduled activities, both small group and total group, are required.

2. Do not interfere with activities of the other camp.

3. Respect the lights-out time so that we all get enough rest.

4. Since the elementary campers are neighbors and will be going to bed earlier than our camp, noise should be kept low after 9 p.m.

5. Site regulations require that everyone wear shoes (except in the shower and the swimming pool!). Swimming suits cannot be worn in the dining room.

6. We hope you will explore in the woods, but be sure to take another person with you for protection against getting lost or hurt. If you are injured in the woods, you might be unable to get help yourself.

The small groups had both fellows and gals, though the cabins, of course, were sexually segregated. The supplies for the art projects were kept in the project cabins, but as much as possible was done out-of-doors.

MONDAY

9:00 a.m.–10:00 a.m.   Meet at the church and load cars

10:00 a.m.–12:00 p.m.   Drive to the campsite

12:00 p.m.–1:00 p.m.   Lunch at the camp. (Parents who had driven had lunch with us before unloading cars and returning home.)

1:00 p.m.–2:00 p.m.   Receive cabin assignments and move in

2:00 p.m.–3:00 p.m.   Sharing of mutual expectations and finalizing of plans for the week. Sharing of possible activities for free time.

3:00 p.m.–4:30 p.m.   Swimming

4:30 p.m.–5:00 p.m.   Free time

5:00 p.m.–5:45 p.m.   Small groups:
Bible study—Session 1 ("Waiting Is the Beginning of the Christian Experience")

5:45 p.m.–6:00 p.m.   Break

6:00 p.m.–6:30 p.m.   Supper

6:30 p.m.–7:30 p.m.   Free time

7:30 p.m.–9:00 p.m.   Small groups:
Finger painting to express a feeling or emotion from the Bible study, such as anger, love, disappointment. (Some made paint from berries, which worked well except for stained fingers!)

9:00 p.m.–9:30 p.m.   Free time
Snacks: Watermelon

9:30 p.m.–10:30 p.m.   Worship around the campfire

10:30 p.m.–11:00 p.m.   Free time

11:00 p.m.   Lights out! Bed!

TUESDAY

7:00 a.m.–8:00 a.m.	Rise and shine! Showers, etc.
8:00 a.m.–8:30 a.m.	Breakfast
8:30 a.m.–9:00 a.m.	Free time
9:00 a.m.–12:00 p.m.	Small groups: Bible Study—Session 2 ("Waiting Is the Beginning of the Christian Experience"). Work with clay sculpture, using clay from the campsite. (People take breaks as they wish and need.)
12:00 p.m.–12:30 p.m.	Lunch
12:30 p.m.–1:30 p.m.	Free time (especially for rest and personal meditation)
1:30 p.m.–3:30 p.m.	Swimming
3:30 p.m.–5:00 p.m.	Small groups: Finish work with clay. Bible Study—Session 3 ("Receiving Is the Blessing of the Christian Experience")
5:00 p.m.–6:00 p.m.	Free time
6:00 p.m.–6:30 p.m.	Supper
6:30 p.m.–7:00 p.m.	Free time
7:00 p.m.–8:30 p.m.	Scavenger hunt for nature objects
8:30 p.m.–9:30 p.m.	Free time Snacks: popcorn (made over the fire) and lemonade
9:30 p.m.–10:30 p.m.	Worship around the campfire
10:30 p.m.–11:00 p.m.	Free time

WEDNESDAY

7:00 a.m.–8:00 a.m.	Rise and shine!
8:00 a.m.–8:30 a.m.	Breakfast
8:30 a.m.–9:00 a.m.	Free time
9:00 a.m.–12:00 p.m.	Small groups: Bible Study—Session 4 ("Receiving Is the Blessing of the Christian Experience"). Experiment with personal, devotional writing, prayers, or poetry. Those who wish may do more with painting and sculpturing.
12:00 p.m.–12:30 p.m.	Lunch
12:30 p.m.–1:30 p.m.	Free time
1:30 p.m.–3:30 p.m.	Swimming
3:30 p.m.–4:15 p.m.	Small groups: Bible Study—Session 5 ("Sharing Is the Response of the Christian Experience")
4:15 p.m.–7:30 p.m.	Cookout: Foil-wrapped dinner (hamburger, potatoes, carrots, and onions wrapped in foil and cooked on hot coals); bread. Campers mix and crank ice cream.
7:30 p.m.–8:30 p.m.	Free time
8:30 p.m.–9:30 p.m.	Organized games Homemade ice cream
9:30 p.m.–10:30 p.m.	Worship: Close with a "benedicting silence." By mutual agreement, campers and counselors agree not to talk until breakfast and to use the silent time for personal devotion and thought.
10:30 p.m.–11:00 p.m.	Free time
11:00 p.m.	Lights out! Bed!

THURSDAY

7:00 a.m.–8:00 a.m.	Rise and shine! Showers, etc.
8:00 a.m.–8:30 a.m.	Breakfast Silence ended with the blessing before eating
8:30 a.m.–9:00 a.m.	Free time
9:00 a.m.–12:00 p.m.	Small groups: Bible study—Session 6 ("Sharing Is the Response of the Christian Experience"). Slide making to express an aspect of sharing in response to the Bible study.
12:00 p.m.–12:30 p.m.	Lunch
12:30 p.m.–1:30 p.m.	Free time
1:30 p.m.–3:30 p.m.	Swimming
3:30 p.m.–5:00 p.m.	Small groups: Continue with slide-making Bible study—Session 7 ("Dying Is the Question of the Christian Experience")
5:00 p.m.–6:00 p.m.	Free time
6:00 p.m.–6:30 p.m.	Supper
6:30 p.m.–7:30 p.m.	Free time
7:30 p.m.–9:00 p.m.	Camp talent show and slide show
9:00 p.m.–9:30 p.m.	Free time Snacks: Toasted marshmallows, *somemores*, hot chocolate
9:30 p.m.–10:30 p.m.	Worship around the campfire. Communion service.
10:30 p.m.–11:00 p.m.	Free time
11:00 p.m.	Lights out! Bed!

FRIDAY

7:00 a.m.–8:00 a.m.	Rise and shine! Showers, etc.
8:00 a.m.–8:30 a.m.	Breakfast
8:30 a.m.–9:00 a.m.	Free time
9:00 a.m.–12:00 p.m.	Small groups: Bible study—Session 8 ("Dying Is the Question of the Christian Experience") Using the medium of your choice, express something about death in response to the Bible study.
12:00 p.m.–12:30 p.m.	Lunch
12:30 p.m.–1:30 p.m.	Free time
1:30 p.m.–3:30 p.m.	Swimming
3:30 p.m.–4:15 p.m.	Small groups: Bible study—Session 9 ("Rising Is the Answer of the Christian Experience")
4:15 p.m.–7:30 p.m.	Cookout: Beef stew, hot applesauce, celery and carrot sticks, lemonade
7:30 p.m.–9:00 p.m.	Camp dance
9:00 p.m.–10:00 p.m.	Free time Snacks: cheese, crackers, apples, cider
10:00 p.m.–11:30 p.m.	Closing worship service including expressions of love and appreciation for each other
11:30 p.m.–12:00 a.m.	Free time
12:00 a.m.	Lights out! Bed!

SATURDAY

7:00 a.m.–8:00 a.m.	Rise and shine! Showers, etc.
8:00 a.m.–8:30 a.m.	Breakfast
8:30 a.m.–9:30 a.m.	Cleanup
9:30 a.m.–10:00 a.m.	Transportation arrives. Load cars.
10:00 a.m.–10:15 a.m.	Prayer circle before returning home

Youth Trips

Trips with young people are a tremendous amount of fun. They also create significant memories which stay with youth for the rest of their lives. You should certainly be open to this kind of activity for the youth of your church. You must also be careful not to underestimate the amount of effort and expense involved.

The churches I've pastored have all been in the Midwest which has made possible a large number of directions for travel. I've taken groups of young people:

● to John's Islands, South Carolina, to tutor in an ecumenical reading camp for underprivileged children,

● to Washington D.C., to visit the Smithsonian,

● to Manhattan to study the many creative forms of ministry practiced there, including Metropolitan Church in Harlem, Riverside Church, and St. John's Cathedral

● to Nashville, Tennessee, to visit denominational agencies and a church-owned ethnic minority college,

● to Wisconsin in the winter to ski and enjoy other winter sports,

● to North Dakota to do a service project on an American Indian reservation through a mission center,

● to Cape Cod to enjoy the ocean and to study the changing natural world,

● to New Orleans to learn about unique ministries in the French Quarter and to visit other mission agencies in the area,

● to Oklahoma City to attend a national youth meeting of my own denomination,

● to San Antonio to attend a nondenominational youth meeting,

● to Phoenix, Arizona, to attend a nondenominational youth meeting,

● to Colorado for a back-packing trip.

There are numerous possibilities for travel. Some local churches even take young people on trips to Europe. I've never personally taken a youth group to Europe because the fund-raising task required for

246

such a trip has always looked a little too overwhelming. The idea of such a trip, however, is exciting and I may well do it with a youth group at a future time.

Wherever you decide to go, here are some guidelines to help you in planning:

1. **Provide your youth group with a choice of possible locations.** Let them brainstorm their own ideas or you can suggest possibilities from which they can make a selection. Your minister can obtain information about your denominational offices and mission locations. Youth workers in neighboring churches will also have ideas.

2. **Recognize that a trip of any significant length or distance will necessitate a lot of fund-raising activity.** Most church youth trips are financed by a combination of:

- money raised by the youth group,

- individual fees paid by youth group members,

- scholarships to pay the fees for youth who need financial assistance.

The chapter "Raising Money for Your Youth Group and Other Needy Causes" is filled with ideas which can help you.

It is important for most of the money to be raised by the group working together on projects. This helps build group identity, and it also keeps the out-of-pocket expense for individual young people from being too high. I am opposed to youth groups spending time and energy to raise money for their own basic programming, but a special trip is a very appropriate purpose for fund raising.

It's also important to have scholarships available through your church budget, other church organizations, or private individuals. No matter how affluent your church's young people may appear, there will always be youth who cannot go on the trip without financial assistance. Adult advisors need to be very sensitive to this and offer financial assistance to those who may need it. Such offers should always be discretely made so other group members are not aware the assistance has been given to a particular person.

3. **Most trips need to be planned between six and twelve months in advance.** Clear dates carefully with the young people in your group to avoid as many conflicts as possible with summer jobs, summer school, and other activities. Most churches find that the two weeks immediately after school ends in early summer or immediately before school begins in early fall are the best times for group travel. Many young people can arrange to start summer employment immediately after an early summer trip or to end summer employment immediately before an early fall trip. Those time periods are not as likely to conflict with summer school or family vacations. The more in advance you set the date for your trip, the easier it will be for families and young people to reserve those dates. You will inevitably have a few young people who cannot go because of conflicts, other priorities, or parental reluctance; but you want to minimize this as much as possible.

If you are visiting a church agency or mission site, you can't consider your dates firm until accepted by the organization(s) you plan to visit. Some mission sites in the United States receive dozens of visits each summer and require reservations far in advance.

4. **Build a tentative budget for the trip as quickly as possible.** This lets you set clear goals for fund raising and enables you to communicate to families what expenses will

be involved. A rule of thumb practiced by many churches is for 50 percent of the trip's cost to be raised by the group and for 50 percent to be paid by individual young people. Here's the budget a group in the Midwest developed for a trip to Washington, D.C., involving seventeen young people and five adult advisors:

2000 miles round trip at $ .15 per mile = $300.00 per car.
    Cost for four cars: $1,200.00

Four nights in a motel in a Washington suburb: $50 per room per night = $250.00 for five rooms.
    Cost for four nights: $1,000.00

Two nights in local churches while in route. Donation of $50 to each church in appreciation.
    Cost for two nights: $100.00

Meals for seven days. Estimated to be $9 a person a day = $198.00 a day for 22 people.
    Cost for seven days: $1,386.00

Admissions and fees (no admission is charged to most Washington D.C. national institutions). The group budgeted for the cost of one movie while there and a few minor admission charges.
    Admissions: $220.00

    TOTAL $3,906.00

Although the adults who were driving were all willing to absorb the total car expense, it was agreed that doing so would set an awkward precedent for future trips. The fifteen cents a mile was a compromise figure—more than enough to pay for out-of-pocket gasoline and oil expenses but not enough to fully reimburse for vehicle depreciation. The adults did want to pay their portion of total trip expenses in the same way the young people did, and that was accepted.

The group determined that each participant would pay a fee of $80.00 and also pay for all personal snacks and purchases. Eighty dollars for each of 22 people generated $1,760.00, leaving $2,146.00 for the group to raise. The church budget and the church women's organization quietly provided full scholarships for three young people and a partial scholarship for a fourth.

5. **Have an informational meeting as early as possible for young people and their parents.** Parents always feel better about such events when they've been informed far in advance of the purposes of the trip, the dates, and the cost involved. An early meeting with them alleviates anxiety and gains support.

6. **While rented vans, rented buses, and air travel are all possibilities, most church youth groups continue to travel by automobile.** Church-owned buses are often not very comfortable for long trips, and rented buses are very expensive. Air travel is usually prohibitive in cost. Rented vans can be an option depending on the arrangements available in your community. Personally owned automobiles and/or vans will usually be the means of transportation. A large van gives considerably lower gas mileage than an automobile, so you should offer a higher compensation to anyone providing a van.

Suggest that drivers consider increasing their vehicle liability insurance. The cost of an additional million dollars of liability protection is generally very low, sometimes only $25–$30 for the whole year. Also find out what insurance coverage your church's blanket policy has for such an event.

7. **Many options are available for overnight accommodations.** These include camping, sleeping in local churches along the way or at your destination, and motels or hotels. Don't be bashful about asking motels and hotels for reduced rates and for permission to put several people in the same room (subject, of course to fire regulations and safety concerns). The group traveling to Washington D.C., got rooms in a beautiful Alexandria, Virginia, motel for $50 a room per night instead of the usual rate of $82 per night. Each room had two double-beds, and two rooms had roll-a-ways. An adult advisor slept in each room. Young people generally won't object to taking turns sleeping in sleeping bags on the floor if necessary.

Many churches are very glad to let a youth group sleep in the church for one or two nights. The common absence of shower facilities keeps this from being an option that can be used for every night of a trip, but there are some churches with shower facilities.

Camping can be great fun with a youth group. This approach doesn't always save as much in cost as anticipated because so much equipment is required, making it difficult to have as many people in each vehicle. And the time required to camp means less distance can be covered in a day. Camp because you want to enjoy the camping experience—not to save money.

8. **I recommend that all meals be paid for by the group budget rather than individual young people.** If young people pay for their own meal, many will be tempted to eat very little in order to have more money for shopping. That's not healthy. Before entering a restaurant, give young people a price range they should attempt to stay within when ordering. Fast-food restaurants similar to McDonald's are relatively inexpensive for breakfast and lunch; you can explore more varied options for the evening meal.

9. **Arrange times to talk together about the experiences the young people are having**— whether at a mission site, visiting the capital, or backpacking in the Rocky Mountains. Sharing together and looking at experiences from a Christian perspective help the trip be far more meaningful.

10. **Have devotions together to close each day.** Adults can give some of the leadership but young people should be involved as well. Use an area church, a hotel meeting room, a motel room, a campfire, or whatever setting is available. Daily devotions keep everyone aware of the Christian context of the experience.

11. **You want to have an emergency medical permission slip for each young person** (see the sample under "Purpose, Theme, and Planning" earlier in this chapter). You should also have with you a list of any allergies or other medical conditions of the youth with whom you are traveling.

12. **Develop a list of what young people should bring with them and share guidelines on the amount of luggage they should bring.** Failure to provide clear guidelines will result in more luggage than can possibly be accommodated in the vehicles. If the trip is a fairly lengthy one, you may need to arrange an evening in a laundromat along the way.

13. **You want to have each day's events carefully planned, but it's important to remember that the unexpected can always happen.** Then you need to make adjustments as gracefully as possible. I've been on trips when:

249

● a young person became very ill and had to be flown home.

● a major automobile repair meant part of the group had to arrive at the destination a day late. (The members in that car wanted the others to go ahead to meet our commitment on a work project.)

● everyone pooled their extra money so we could attend an unexpected rock concert.

● our host at a mission site became ill, and our group had to assume extra responsibilities.

A calm attitude and a willingness to roll with the unexpected is just as important as careful planning if your trip is to be enjoyable.

14. **And you do want the trip to be enjoyable for young people and adults.** Few experiences can be as rewarding for your young people or yourself.

RESOURCES

During the years since the first edition of the *Youth Workers Handbook* was published, there has been enormous growth in the number of resources available for youth work and Christian education. Many of the materials available are of extremely high quality.

A complete listing of resources would go beyond the scope of this book. What we have attempted to do is list the best resources of which we are aware in each category. Since many resources come from the same suppliers, we have listed company and organization addresses separately at the end of this section. Media addresses are listed in the "Media" category.

The materials listed in each category represent the best resources of which we are aware. The fact that a particular book, magazine, or other resource is not included here does not imply anything negative about that resource. We may not have been aware of the resource, or space limitations may have made its inclusion impossible.

For basic Christian education materials, be certain to rely primarily on the resources produced by your own denomination. Those reflect your particular traditions and beliefs. Note the denominational addresses section.

The very best resources are people: other youth workers with whom you can share ideas and experiences. Be alert for training events sponsored by your denomination or offered on an ecumenical basis. Consider forming your own support group with other youth teachers and workers in your church or other churches in your community. Other adult support will help you give your best to the young people about whom you care so much. Most important, develop your own spiritual life, for we can all succeed only as God's grace flows through us.

GENERAL YOUTH WORK RESOURCES

Adventures with Youth. From Christian Leadership Systems. Bimonthly publication with resources and ideas—Bible study, games, etc.

The Basic Encyclopedia for Youth Ministry, by Dennis Benson and William Wolfe (Group, 1981). An excellent youth resource that covers youth ministry from A to Z (from aaugh! to zits). Information on sexuality, food for youth groups, retreats, and much more.

Becoming Peacemakers, by Diane Stanton-Rich (Brethren Press, 1987). Excellent factual background on current threats to world peace and on strategies for changes. Many practical ideas for helping youth groups with peace issues. Attractively illustrated including cartoons.

Christian Education as Evangelism, by Steve Clapp *(faithQuest*, 1981, 1983). How to reach more people through the church's educational program. Filled with creative teaching methods and approaches to evangelism.

Church Teachers. Magazine published five times a year by the National Teacher Education Program. Primarily for local volunteer church teachers.

Common Focus. From the Center for Early Adolescence. Newsletter released five times a year with excellent research information about early adolescents (ten- to fifteen-year olds).

The Complete Youth Ministries Handbook, edited by David Stone (Abingdon, 1980). Dave and a creative group of people got together to write a complete handbook and then discovered that one was not enough to do the job! Contains a number of suggestions. This will probably be of most help to those working in fairly large churches. Available from Youth Ministries Consultation Service.

Catching the Rainbow, edited by David Stone (Abingdon, 1981). This is the second volume of *The Complete Youth Ministries Handbook.* This volume is even better than the first. Dave has done a great job bringing together a wide range of people with skill in youth work. Available from Youth Ministries Consultation Service.

Determining Needs in Your Youth Ministry, by Peter Benson and Dorothy Williams (Group, 1987). A survey kit to help youth leaders determine the needs of young people.

Effective Adolescent Religious Education. Video from St. Mary's (1985). Excellent background on parish youth work, designed for use in workshop settings. Expensive but very high quality. Primarily for Catholic parishes.

The Exuberant Years, by Ginny Ward Holderness (John Knox, 1976). Even though a little dated, absolutely the best book available for working with junior highs in the church. Sections on structuring meetings, methods that work, mini-courses, special events, and more.

Five Cries of Parents, by Merton and Irene Strommen (Harper and Row, 1985). What parents go through during their children's adolescence. Based on a major survey and filled with helpful insights to teens and their parents.

Five Cries of Youth, by Merton Strommen (Harper and Row, 1988). A revised version of Strommen's classic study on the values and self-image of young people. You should read this.

Group Magazine. From Group Publishing. Monthly. Practical ideas for youth workers. Excellent.

Group Members Only. From Group Publishing. Written for teens. Probably the best interdenominational youth periodical available. Free leader guide with bulk subscriptions.

Group Jr High Ministry. From Group Publishing. Bimonthly for junior high youth workers. Includes activity suggestions.

Growing a Junior High Ministry, by David Shaheen (Group, 1986). Solid material about junior highs, successful meetings, attendance building, etc.

Hard Times Catalog for Youth Ministry, by Marilyn and Dennis Benson (Group, 1982). Marilyn and Dennis have put together outstanding meeting ideas—all can be done at no cost or very little cost. One of the best resources available.

High School Ministry, by Mike Yaconelli and Jim Burns (Youth Specialties, 1986). Good background on the social, emotional, and spiritual life of teens. Programming suggestions.

Ideas, edited by Wayne Rice and Mike Yaconelli (Youth Specialties, copyright dates begin in 1968 and continue to the present). Over forty volumes, with additional volumes published each year. Games, skits, Bible studies, attendance builders, discussion starters, and more. All tested ideas contributed by youth workers. Extremely helpful in doing planning with youth. You should have several of these volumes.

Ideas for Social Action, by Anthony Campolo (Youth Specialties, 1983). Excellent strategies for involving youth in outreach to others. Many specific suggestions.

Involving Youth in Youth Ministry, by Thom and Joani Schultz (Group, 1987). How to get youth directly involved in responsibility for their own programs and ministry.

Junior High Ministry, by Wayne Rice (Youth Specialties). A good basic book on work with junior highs written by an experienced, creative, youth worker.

Keys to Building Youth Ministry, by Glenn E. Ludwig (Abingdon, 1988). One of the finest resources on the market—goes beyond gimmicks to show how to involve the entire church in youth ministry.

On the Wings of a Butterfly, by Shirley Heckman (Brethren Press, 1981). An overall philosophy and approach to Christian education centered on helping people grow in the faith. An extremely helpful guide in examining your total Christian education program.

PRRC Emerging Trends. From Princeton Religious Research Center. These are the Gallup Poll folks, and no one does better research. Not just about youth; always current and helpful in understanding religion in the United States.

253

The Quicksilver Years, by Peter Benson, Dorothy Williams, and Arthur Johnson (Harper and Row, 1987). Results of a major survey of fifth through ninth graders and their parents. Very helpful in understanding junior high youth.

Readings in Youth Ministry, Vol. 1, edited by John Roberto (National Federation for Catholic Youth Ministry, 1986). Articles from various authors. Written especially for Catholics but helpful to Protestants as well.

Source. From Search Institute. A quarterly newsletter about youth work. Each issue focuses on a particular topic. Search is an excellent research organization. Free.

Volunteers! The Comprehensive Guide to Voluntary Service in the U.S. and Abroad (Intercultural Press, 1988). A comprehensive listing of denominational, private, and public volunteer service agencies.

Young Catholics, by Fee, Greeley, McCready, and Sullivan (Sadlier, 1981). This book is a careful research study which has a lot to say about how young people view the church.

Youth and the Future of the Church, by Michael Warren (Harper and Row, 1986). Shows the crucial role youth can play in the future of the church and in the church of today.

The Youth Group Meeting Guide, by Rich Bimler and others (Group, 1984). How to plan and conduct effective meetings. Actual meeting outlines. Bimler is an experienced, capable youth leader and a good communicator.

Youth Ministry Encyclopedia, by Lyman Coleman (Serendipity, 1985). Packed with Bible studies, communication exercises, and group-building activities. No one knows more about the group-building process than Lyman Coleman. Lots of good material here.

The Youth Ministry Resource, edited by Eugene Roehlkepartain (Group, 1988). Lots of helpful, current background on many aspects of teenage life. Significant help understanding today's teens; cites many studies. Tremendous list of all kinds of resources. Also helpful information for professional youth workers. A "must have" book.

Youth Ministry Resource Network. From Center for Youth Ministry Development. Quarterly newsletter and several papers each year on youth ministry. Roman Catholic orientation. High quality.

Youthworker. Quarterly journal from Youth Specialties. Practical, high quality. Especially good for clergy and professional youth workers but also helpful to volunteers.

Youthworker Update. Monthly newsletter from Youth Specialties. Lots of information on resources.

BIBLE STUDY AND DEVOTIONAL LIFE

The Bible and the Devotional Life, by Steve Clapp (*faithQuest,* 1987). The book takes youth on a six-week journey through Scripture which includes daily devotions and weekly meetings. Each week focuses on a major division of Scripture.

The Bible and Major Issues, by Steve Clapp (*faithQuest,* 1986, 1990). Topical Bible studies for junior and senior high youth. Discussion questions, factual information on contemporary problems (drugs, sex, gossip, vocational choice, physical appearance, and much more), background on the Scriptures, simulation games, mini-dramas, and other creative activities.

The Bible Game Collection, by Don Kreiss and Steve Clapp (*faithQuest,* 1987). Bible studies, quizzes, contests, relays, scavenger hunts, mini-dramas, and other games—all based on the Scripture. Comes with a gameboard for "The Bible Game" described in the book.

C-4 Devotional Journal, edited by Steve Clapp (*faithQuest,* 1981, et al.). Material for over a month of personal devotions plus activities for class, group, or retreat use. This journal has been especially popular with Roman Catholics and Protestants for use in retreat settings with junior and senior high youth. Now in its 12th printing.

C-4 Retreat Guide (*faithQuest,* 1981). Designed for use with the *C-4 Devotional Journal.*

Dennis Benson's Creative Bible Studies: Matthew through Acts, by Dennis Benson (Group, 1985). Material for hundreds of sessions on the Gospels and Acts. Tells you how to prepare sessions and gives you needed background. Excellent.

Dennis Benson's Creative Bible Studies: Romans through Revelation, by Dennis Benson (Group, 1988). Similar to the above. Excellent.

Serendipity New Testament for Youth, by Lyman Coleman, Denny Rydberg, Richard Peace, and Gary Christopherson (Serendipity, 1986). Has the text of the New International Version of the New Testament with questions and reflections in the margin of each page.

Spiritual Growth in the Church, by Steve Clapp, Lisa Sensel, Rodney Herrick, and Don Kreiss (*faithQuest,* 1986). Strategies for nurturing children, youth, and adults in Bible study, prayer, and the devotional life.

Spiritual Growth Journal (faithQuest, 1986). An attractive, moving set of meditations, Scripture readings, and journal-writing exercises designed for youth and adults. (This book is incorporated in *Spiritual Growth in the Church* but is available separately.)

Spiritual Growth in Youth Ministry, by David Stone (Group, 1985). Programs for youth workers and group members. Outstanding. Can rejuvenate youth leaders and youth groups.

Youth Ministry Encyclopedia, by Lyman Coleman (Serendipity, 1985). In addition to many group-building activities, this resource has 48 outstanding Bible studies.

RECREATION

The Bible Game Collection by Don Kreiss and Steve Clapp *(faithQuest,* 1987). All kinds of games based on the Bible. Includes not only paper-and-pencil games but also outdoor recreation! Comes with a gameboard and permission to photocopy.

Creative Games I, II, and III, edited by Wayne Rice, John Roberto, and Mike Yaconelli (St. Mary's, 1982). Crowdbreakers, relays, team games, special events, and more. Many of these were originally published in the *Ideas* books.

Games, compiled by Mary Hohenstein (Bethany, 1980). Lots of outdoor games and group-building games.

Good Clean Fun, by Tom Finely (Youth Specialties, 1986). Games with a Biblical foundation on topics like dating, faith, etc.

Ideas, edited by Wayne Rice and Mike Yaconelli (Youth Specialties, various copyright dates). Over forty volumes with more published each year. A superb recreational resource.

Quick Crowdbreakers and Games for Youth Groups (Group, 1981). Over 200 games. Good, clear instructions.

MUSIC, WORSHIP, DRAMA AND CLOWN MINISTRY

Clown Ministry, by Floyd Shaffer and Penne Sewall (Group, 1984). Floyd Shaffer is the best clown ministry resource person in the country. Tells how to use clown ministry in your youth group. Makeup, costumes, mime, staging, etc.

The Clown as Minister, I, II, by Janet Litherland (Contemporary Drama, 1980, 1981). Clown skits for church use. Practical, creative.

Come Join the Circle Songbook (Brethren Press, 1988). A booklet containing 44 songs. Though produced for outdoor ministries, it can be used in other settings.

Creative Projects and Worship Experiences, edited by Wayne Rice, John Roberto, and Mike Yaconelli (St. Mary's, 1981). All kinds of worship ideas.

Creative Worship in Youth Ministry, by Dennis Benson (Group, 1985). All kinds of worship designs and ideas.

The Greatest Skits on Earth, Vols. I, II, III, by Wayne Rice and Mike Yaconelli (Youth Specialties, 1986, 1987). Great skits for group use. Titles like "Sumu Wrestlers" and "Submarine Ride."

The Popcorn Connection, by Joe T. Miller (Contemporary Drama, 1985). Skits dealing with faith in God, nuclear war, intolerance, and more.

Send in His Clowns, by Stephen Perrone and James Spata (Contemporary Drama, 1985). Tells how to train clown ministers.

Worship Resources for Youth, by Jerry O. Cook (*faithQuest,* 1983). Worship experiences for youth group meetings, weekend retreats, camps, and special youth worship services. The youth meeting suggestions are so creative you can plan an entire meeting around them. Includes permission to photocopy.

SELF-ESTEEM AND SEXUALITY

How Can I Tell If I'm Really in Love? Videocassette (VHS or Beta) from Ed-U Press. Justine Bateman, Jason Bateman, Ted Danson, psychologist Sol Gordon, and a group of teens. All about love, sex, relationships, commitment, and marriage. This is a great video, and youth groups respond very positively to it.

Loving Relationships, by Robert L. Shelton (Brethren Press, 1987). Not a direct resource for youth but an excellent guide for those who work with them. A sensitive yet straightforward approach to understanding what loving means in the total framework of life.

Parenting, by Sol Gordon and Mina Wollin (Ed-U Press, 1987). To prepare young people for mature parenting roles. Whom to marry, contraception, pregnancy, and more.

Strong Kids, Safe Kids. Videocassette (VHS or Beta) from Ed-U Press. Henry Winkler and Sol Gordon on preventing child abuse. While the primary focus is on children and parents, teens respond well to this video; and it raises important issues for them.

Teenage Sexuality: Local Church and Christian Home Program Guide, by Steve Clapp (*faithQuest*, 1985). Results of survey on the sexual values and practices of church active teens. Information here that is available from no other source. Lots of practical program ideas and permission to photocopy are included.

When Living Hurts, by Sol Gordon (Available from *faithQuest*). Helps teens deal with the pain, depression, and frustration that are an inevitable part of life. The book confronts the problem of teen suicide and shows young people how to reach out to others. A marvelous book that really speaks to teens.

When Living Hurts Guide (available from *faithQuest*). Helps youth leaders, ministers, parents, teachers, and others work effectively with youth who are experiencing hard times. Includes plans for four to eight class or group sessions. Designed for use with *When Living Hurts.*

Yes, No, or Maybe So, by David Lynn (Youth Specialties 1986). A card deck to generate discussion on sexuality. Comes with a leader guide.

Yes You Can!, edited by Dorothy Williams (Search Institute, 1987). A sex education guide urging abstinence.

MEDIA

Roger Ebert's Home Movie Companion, by Roger Ebert (Universal Press Syndicate; new edition each year). Reviews over 800 films which are available on video. Good insight into the message of the films. Many interviews with motion picture stars. An excellent guide.

Order film/video catalogs from:
Concordia/Family Films, 3558 South Jefferson, St. Louis, MO 63118.

LIFE Productions, 200 Galleria Parkway, Atlanta, GA 30339.

Mass Media Ministries, 2116 North Charles St., Baltimore, MD 21218.

Palisades Institute/Religious Home Video, 153 Waverly Place, New York, NY 10014.

Paulist Productions, P.O. Box 1057, Pacific Palisades, CA 90272.

Word, Box 1790, Waco, TX 76796.

World Wide Pictures, Billy Graham Film Ministry, 1201 Hennepin Avenue, Minneapolis, MN 55403.

DENOMINATIONAL ADDRESSES

Basic Christian education materials should come from denominational agencies. The materials that we recommend are not meant to replace resources from your own denomination. The following listing is certainly not an exhaustive one (and hardly could be with over 300 denominations in existence).

If you are not familiar with the youth materials from your denomination, write for information. Also, Protestants of almost every theological persuasion should have no hesitancy in taking advantage of some of the excellent Roman Catholic materials.

African Methodist Episcopal Zion Church, 128 E. 58th St., Chicago, IL 37203.

American Baptist Churches in the U.S.A., Box 851, Valley Forge, PA 19482.

The Anglican Church of Canada, 600 Jarvis St., Toronto, Ontario, Canada.

Assemblies of God, Youth Division, 1445 Boonville Ave., Springfield, MO 65802.

Baptist Department of Christian Education, 1233 Central St., Evanston, IL 60201.

Church of the Brethren, 1451 Dundee Ave., Elgin, IL 60120.

Church of God, Board of Christian Education, P.O. Box 2458, Anderson, IN 46011.

Church of the Nazarene, Youth Ministries, 6401 The Paseo, Kansas City, MO 64131.

Disciples of Christ, Department of Christian Education, P.O. Box 1986, Indianapolis, IN 46206.

The Episcopal Church, Office of Religious Education, 815 Second Ave., New York, NY 10017.

The Evangelical Covenant Church, Christian Education Department, 5101 N. Francisco Ave., Chicago, IL 60625.

Evangelical Lutheran Church in America, 8765 W. Higgins Rd., Chicago, IL 60631.

Free Methodist Church, Christian Education Department, 901 College Ave., Winona Lake, IN 46590.

Friends United Meeting, 101 Quaker Hill Dr., Richmond, IN 47374.

General Church of the New Jerusalem, Box 278, Bryn Athyn, PA 19009.

General Conference Mennonite Church, Box 347, Newton, KS 67114.

Graded Press, 201 Eighth Ave., S., Nashville, TN 37202. (Curriculum division of the United Methodist Church.)

Greek Orthodox Church, 27-09 Crescent St., Long Island, NY 11102.

The Lutheran Church–Missouri Synod, Board of Youth Ministry, 1333 S. Kirkwood Rd., St. Louis, MO 63122.

Mennonite Church, Box 1245, Elkhart, IN 46515.

National Federation for Catholic Youth Ministry, 8900-A Harewood Rd., NE, Washington, DC 20017.

Paulist Press, 545 Island Rd., Ramsey, NJ 07446. (Roman Catholic. Many materials.)

Presbyterian Church in America, 1852 Century Place, Suite 101, Atlanta, GA 30345.

Presbyterian Church, U.S.A., 100 Witherspoon St., Louisville, KY 40202-1396.

The Reformed Church in America, 42 N. Broadway, Tarrytown, NY 10591.

Salvation Army, 799 Bloomfield Ave., Verona, NJ 07044.

Southern Baptist Convention, 127 Ninth Ave., N., Nashville, TN 37234.

United Church in Canada, 85 St. Clair Ave., E., Toronto M4T1M8, Canada.

Unitarian Universalist Association, 25 Beacon St., Boston, MA 02108.

United Church of Christ, 700 Prospect Ave., Cleveland, OH 44115.

United Methodist Church, Board of Discipleship, Box 840, Nashville, TN 37202.

ADDRESSES

Abingdon Press, 201 Eighth Ave., S., Nashville, TN 37202. Books and other materials.

Augsburg Publishing House, Box 1209, Minneapolis MN 55440. Books and other materials.

Baker Book House, 6030 East Fulton St., Ada, MI 49301. Books and other resources.

Baker's Plays, 100 Chauncy St., Boston, MA 02111. Tremendous assortment of plays for religious and secular use.

Bethany House Publishers, 6820 Auto Club Road, Minneapolis, MN 55438. Books and other resources.

Brethren Press, 1451 Dundee Avenue, Elgin, IL 60120.

Center for Early Adolescence, University of North Carolina, Suite 223, Carr Mill Mall, Carrboro, NC 27510. *Common Focus* and other materials and information from this excellent center.

Center for Youth Ministry Development, Box 699, Naugatuck, CT 06770. Basically a Roman Catholic organization. Very fine materials; will provide training and consulting services.

Christian Leadership Systems, 8342 North 7th Street, Phoenix, AZ 85020. *Adventures with Youth* publication and many other resources.

Contemporary Drama, 885 Elkton Drive, Colorado Springs, CO 80907. High quality drama and media resources.

Ed-U Press, 7174 Mott Road, Fayetteville, NY 13066. Excellent self-esteem and sexuality materials.

faithQuest, 1451 Dundee Avenue, Elgin, IL 60120. Publishers of *Youth Workers Handbook* and other high quality resources.

Group Publishing, Box 481, Loveland, CO 80539. Numerous books, magazines (including *Group),* and many events for teens and leaders. Interdenominational in nature. You will want to subscribe to *Group* Magazine.

Intercultural Press, P.O. Box 788, Kremouth, ME 04096.

John Knox Press, 341 Ponce de Leon Ave., NE, Atlanta, GA 30365. Books and other resources.

National Federation for Catholic Youth Ministry, 3025 Fourth St., NE, Washington, DC 20017. High quality resources. Protestants should sample some of these fine materials.

National Teacher Education Program, 2504 North Roxboro St., Durham, NC 27704. *Church Teachers* magazine and other resources.

Princeton Religious Research Center, Box 310, 53 Bank St., Princeton, NJ 08542. *PRRC Emerging Trends* and other top quality research information.

St. Mary's Press, Terrace Heights, Winona, MN 55987. High quality resources.

Search Institute, 122 West Franklin, Suite 525, Minneapolis, MN 55404. *Source* and other resources. An excellent research organization.

Serendipity, Box 1012, Littleton, CO 80160. Excellent materials.

Student Venture, Campus Crusade for Christ, 17150 Via Del Camp, Suite 200, San Diego, CA 92127. Publications, resources, and events.

Visual Parables, First Presbyterian Church, 49 South Portage St., Westfield, NY 14787. Resources from talented Ed McNulty. When his schedule permits, Ed is an excellent workshop leader on media concerns.

Youth for Christ, Box 419, Wheaton, IL 60189. Many materials and programs.

Youth Ministry Consultation Service, 500 Common St., Shreveport, LA 71101. Dave Stone's organization provides outstanding seminars and materials. Any event he conducts is sure to be excellent.

Youth Specialties, 1224 Greenfield Drive, El Cajon, CA 92021. *Youthworker* and *Youthworker Journal* plus many other resources and events. Their National Youth Workers Convention is generally the best youth worker event in the country. You will want to own at least a few volumes of *Ideas*.

NOTES

264